# STABILITY,
## SECURITY,
# AND
# CONTINUITY

September 1945—President Truman appoints Burton to the Supreme
Court and congratulates him on that appointment.

# STABILITY, SECURITY, AND CONTINUITY

*Mr. Justice Burton and Decision-Making in the Supreme Court 1945-1958*

## MARY FRANCES BERRY

*Contributions in Legal Studies, Number 1*

GREENWOOD PRESS

WESTPORT, CONNECTICUT • LONDON, ENGLAND

**Library of Congress Cataloging in Publication Data**

Berry, Mary Frances.
    Stability, security, and continuity.

    (Contributions in legal studies; no. 1 ISSN 0147-1074)
    Bibliography: p.
    Includes index.
    1. United States. Supreme Court—History—20th century. 2. Burton, Harold
Hitz, 1888-1964. 3. Judicial process—United States. I. Title. II. Series: Contributions
in legal studies; no. 1.
    KF8742.B47        347'.73'2634 [B]        77-84772
    ISBN 0-8371-9798-8

Library of Congress Catalog Card Number: 77-84772
ISBN: 0-8371-9798-8
ISSN: 0147-1074

First published in 1978

Greenwood Press, Inc.
51 Riverside Avenue, Westport, Connecticut 06880

Printed in the United States of America

10 9 8 7 6 5 4 3 2 1

# Contents

# Preface

The overwhelming majority of Supreme Court justices have been white Anglo-Saxon Protestants, born in urban or small town environments to fathers with high-status occupations and a sense of responsibility and political involvement. They have been graduates of prestigious colleges and law schools and were partisan political activists before appointment to the Supreme Court. Harold Hitz Burton fit the pattern perfectly. Born in Jamaica Plain, Massachusetts, in an upper-middle-class family headed by a father who was then dean at Massachusetts Institute of Technology, he migrated to Ohio after graduation from Bowdoin College and Harvard Law School, and there he practiced corporate law for many years before entering politics. Burton was active in civic and patriotic affairs and became a dedicated Unitarian, a Protestant religion he regarded as respectable with sufficient flexibility not to interfere with his personal habits of mind. An ardent Republican, he was elected to the Ohio House of Representatives, as mayor of Cleveland, and then to the United States Senate in 1940. After serving five years in the Senate, where he was a "crony" of Harry S Truman, Burton was appointed by Truman to the Supreme Court, on which he served until illness compelled his retirement in 1958.

This study of Harold H. Burton is an attempt to describe the internal decision-making process in the Supreme Court from his vantage point. Burton, an average justice, was not a bright, witty intellectual like a Frankfurter or a Black; but great personalities and outstanding justices have always been on the fringes of the Court. He was a quiet, unassuming, competent justice. His career is an example of the Court, not just in the rare instances when a case of monumental significance was decided, such as the school desegregation cases, or when some particularly flamboyant or outstanding justice devised some innovation in the law, but as a day-to-day institution in the American system of government.

Burton made his large collection of private papers available for public scrutiny because he believed it would facilitate understanding of the judicial process. This account of the decision-making process during his tenure on the Court is based on his papers, the papers of other appropriate persons, oral interviews, Supreme Court records, and other scattered materials. This study should add to our historical understanding of the role of the Court as a political institution and of the activities of Burton and its other justices.

# STABILITY,
## SECURITY,
# AND
# CONTINUITY

# 1
## The Pre-Court Years

H A R O L D Hitz Burton has been described by most commentators on the Supreme Court as one of the majority of middling men who have served throughout the Court's history. In background and experience, he was a typical justice, just as he had been a typical senator before his Supreme Court appointment. In 1958, when he retired from the Court at age seventy, the general consensus among commentators was that he had been a conscientious, patient, tolerant, hard-working justice whose opinions possessed great clarity and persuasiveness. Burton succeeded, consciously, in his attempt to impress others as a moral man and judge. His biography, said Felix Frankfurter, ought to be called "The Triumph of Character."[1]

Some insight into Burton's behavior as a Supreme Court justice can be gained by considering his background and pre-court experiences. Burton was born into a solid upper-middle-class family on June 22, 1888, in Jamaica Plain, Massachusetts. His father, Alfred Edgar Burton, was a professor of civil engineering at Massachusetts Institute of Technology when Burton was born and later became dean of the faculty, a position he held for twenty years. Burton's mother, Gertrude Hitz Burton, who was chronically ill for many years, died in Switzerland when Burton was seven. Until her death, Burton and his older brother, Felix, attended school in Leysin, where Gertrude often visited with relatives. As a result of these years spent in Switzerland, Burton became fluent in French and developed an interest in his Swiss origins which he maintained throughout his life. The deep involvement of Gertrude's grandfather John Hitz in civic activities and public service also influenced the life of young Burton. Hitz was named the first

Swiss consul general to the United States in 1853 and continued a career of voluntary public service.[2]

After they returned from Switzerland, Burton and his brother were sent by their father to Allen Boarding School in West Newton, Massachusetts. They both attended Newton High School and then Bowdoin College, as their father had done before them. At Bowdoin, Burton roomed with Owen Brewster, a lifelong friend, who was also later elected to the Senate. Burton distinguished himself at Bowdoin by graduating summa cum laude and Phi Beta Kappa in 1909. A great sports enthusiast, Burton played quarterback on the varsity football team and was a pole-vaulter on the track team. He was also a member of Delta Kappa Epsilon fraternity. During these years, he became engaged to Selma Florence Smith, whom he had known since childhood. When Burton entered Harvard Law School in 1909, he again roomed with Owen Brewster and continued his engagement to Selma. During this time, Burton and Selma made plans to settle in Cleveland, Ohio, where, with the aid of Selma's uncle, Rollin A. Wilbur, who was a lawyer, Burton could begin practicing law.

Burton's choice to live in Cleveland was also influenced by the publicity Cleveland had recently received as a result of the municipal reforms initiated by Mayor Tom L. Johnson and his city solicitor, Newton D. Baker. Almost immediately after Burton graduated from law school in June 1912, he and Selma were married at her home in West Newton, Massachusetts, by a Unitarian minister. They then moved to Cleveland, where Burton joined Wilbur in the corporate law firm of Gage, Wilbur, and Wachner.[3]

When Wilbur moved to Salt Lake City in 1914 to become general counsel to the Utah Power and Light Company, the Burtons decided to go with him. In December 1915, Burton became head of the legal department of the Idaho Power Company in Boise, Idaho, a position which he held until World War I began. With the outbreak of the war, Burton entered the army officer-training program and was commissioned a first lieutenant and later a captain. He served in France from June 1918, participating in the St. Mihiel offensive in September, in the Meuse-Argonne, and later in Belgium as operations officer in his regiment, the 361st Infantry. As a result of his service, he was awarded the Belgian Croix de Guerre and the

United States Army Meritorious Service Citation. In addition, when the Order of the Purple Heart was established in 1932, he received its medal.[4]

After the war, the Burtons decided to return to Cleveland. Here, the Burton family, which began with Barbara and William, born before the war, grew to include Deborah, born in 1920, and Robert, in 1921. During the next ten years, Burton was in private practice, first with the firm of Day, Day, and Wilkin until 1925, and then with the firm of Cull, Burton, and Laughlin. Burton gradually established a solid reputation as an able lawyer. In an effort to build his law practice and establish a base for entering politics, he was active in veterans' affairs and served as commander of the Cuyahoga County Council of the American Legion. He also taught a corporation law course at the Western Reserve University Law School from 1923 through 1925, was commander of the Cleveland Grays, a local military-social organization, in 1921 and 1922, and in 1927 was elected to the East Cleveland Board of Education, on which he served until 1929.

Burton's character and reputation were well enough known by this time to attract the attention of the local citizens' committee which worked with the Republican organization in an effort to encourage and support young men in campaigning for the state legislature. The committee invited him to run in the 1928 election for the Ohio House of Representatives. In the primary election, he ran a close second among the sixteen Republicans nominated for the House of Representatives, and he led the legislative ticket in Cuyahoga County, where all the Republicans were elected in the general election. While he was running for the Ohio House seat, a campaign developed to have Burton appointed to a United States district judgeship. A vacancy had been created by the death of one of the district judges; and since Calvin Coolidge was in the White House, it was logical to assume that a Republican would receive the appointment. After Newton Baker, a leading local Democrat, suggested Burton's name for the position, Burton wrote numerous letters to friends asking for advice on how to campaign for the nomination. He asked his onetime college and law school roommate, Owen Brewster, who was then governor of Maine, not only to give advice but also to write seemingly unsolicited letters to appropriate people in Washington underscoring Burton's qualifications. Although later Burton minimized his own efforts to obtain the judgeship, he eagerly pursued the appointment and was excited at the prospect of attaining it at the early age of forty. Burton did not receive the appointment; it went instead to Samuel West, a local corporation lawyer who was at the top of a list of five names submitted to the president by the Cleveland Bar Association. Burton's name was not among the five. A last gasp effort failed to enlist the aid of Ohio's U.S. Senate nominee, Theodore Burton (not a relative of Harold Burton), who did not want to get involved. The Ohio Bar, he concluded, preferred older men. Burton made a point thereafter of never openly pursuing a public office, always emphatically disavowing any interest in a particular position until it was offered.[5]

Relatively unscathed by the failed campaign for judicial appointment, Burton took his seat in the Ohio legislature in January 1929. There he established a reputation as an intelligent, well-liked, and industrious legislator. When the legislature adjourned on October 15, 1929, Burton was appointed director of law for the city of Cleveland, at the suggestion of Newton Baker. He served from 1929 to 1932 as chief legal officer for the city government, which was then in a period of transition. About three months after his appointment, the city council ousted the city manager; and for the two weeks until Daniel Morgan was chosen, Burton was acting city manager. When the voters of Cleveland abandoned their city manager government and adopted a mayoralty form, in November 1931, Burton also served as interim mayor for three months until the election of a mayor in February 1932.

The election of a Democrat as mayor temporarily pushed Burton out of politics. In 1932 he accepted an invitation from John A. Hadden, who had been speaker pro tem while Burton served in the legislature, to join the firm of Andrews, Hadden, and Burton. He specialized in municipal law, sometimes representing communities on utility and bond issues, and was associate counsel for the city of Cleveland in its gas rate litigation. However, Burton remained primarily interested in politics. While in the House he had sponsored a resolution providing for the consolidation of the functions of the municipal governments within the individual counties in the state. From this resolution, an amendment to the Ohio Constitution was adopted in 1933 which provided for county referenda on the issue of whether to elect a commission to prepare a possible new charter form of government. After this referendum was approved by Cleveland voters in 1934, Burton, one of forty persons who ran for the commission, was elected chairman and prepared a charter to be submitted in the November 1935 election.

Although Democratic Ray T. Miller, former county prosecutor, had been elected in February 1932 for the short term as mayor, a Republican, Harry L. Davis, was elected in the regular 1933 election. Davis was generally castigated for inefficiency during his term, as he had embarrassed some members of the party with his use of a blatant spoils system. When Miller became mayor, the superintendent of the city hospital was coerced into hiring many Democrats. After Davis was elected, he continued the practice by forcing the removal of 470 employees to make way for his supporters. Burton's reputation for integrity, his record of public service, and his demonstrated vote-getting ability led Republicans, Independents, and even some Democrats to support him for the mayoralty in the 1934 election. Burton was recognized as "an ambitious politician who knew how to project himself on the public scene while mayor."[6]

In what appeared to be antiincumbent sweep, Burton, with the support of the three city newspapers, won the mayoralty by forty thousand votes. Earl Hart, his friend from when they both held office in the American Legion, began his career as Burton's campaign manager in this election. Burton was still chairman and Hart secretary of the Cleveland Chamber of Commerce; but Burton resigned upon being elected mayor with the words, "I am looking out from the house of have to the house of want and I find my associates uninterested in the house of want." However, Burton had the support of the businessmen in the party, as well as that of a leading Republican, Daniel Morgan, who campaigned for him among blacks, and the labor organizations. Despite the fact that he was a Republican whose party lost almost every contest for county, legislative, and state offices, Burton was reelected mayor in the nonpartisan elections of 1937 and 1939. As mayor, he did not follow the traditional Republican line: he astutely made nonpar-

September 1937—Burton campaigning for his second term as Mayor of Cleveland.

tisan use of patronage to reorganize city government in a city where the mayoralty election was on a nonpartisan ballot. He did, however, have some difficulties with the city council which, although predominantly Republican, consisted of inflexible old-liners.[7]

The electorate generally regarded Burton as a clean-living, moral family man of the people, who had a listed phone number, and who worked long hours as law director and mayor. They called him the "Boy Scout Mayor." He so carefully approached his job that in preparation for throwing out the baseball on opening day of the baseball season, he even practiced with Earl Hart on some out-of-the-way sandlot. Burton's public life, as is often the case, had a deleterious effect on his family life. He had little time to spend with his family, which unnerved his two younger children. Burton rarely saw his children for any sustained period of time, and they would sometimes have to make office appointments to visit him. Also, Selma, who gradually blossomed into an extrovert and an active campaigner and helpmate for her husband in his public career, had less time for the children.[8]

As mayor, Burton emphasized governmental economy and pay-as-you-go financing. He reduced the overall debt of the city by about $15.6 million, no mean feat during the Depression. In addition, he named as safety director Eliot Ness, who succeeded in lowering the crime rate in the city. Along with the strikes, bread lines, and marches on city hall, which plagued Burton during his terms in office, the city began the development of the Memorial Shoreway and the construction of the municipal light plant. He and Traction Commissioner Edward J. Schweid attacked the problem of a low-cost transportation system for Cleveland, and eventually their work resulted in a plan for municipal ownership of the city transit facilities.

Relief and the economic problems of the Depression plagued his administration. Burton was not opposed to relief; yet he believed that able-bodied men should perform some public work for their payments and that safeguards should be taken to insure that no chiselers were on the rolls. He set an example of austerity by taking a pay cut required for other city employees even though he was not obligated to do so under the charter. As the relief crisis grew more severe, Burton pleaded that the size and special economic problems of cities made necessary closer city-federal relationships that could bypass state government. His difficulties with Governor Martin A. Davey and his successor, John Bricker, on this issue probably led him to become an advocate of direct federal-municipal relationships.

In the spring of 1938, while Democratic Governor Davey was in office, a welfare crisis began in Cleveland after WPA rolls were cut. The state government took no action; and in 1939, after Republican Burton was reelected, the state government appropriated a minimum amount for relief, leaving Cleveland some $1 million short with about seventy-five thousand people on the rolls. When Burton informed Governor John Bricker that there was a crisis situation in Cleveland and requested additional state aid, Bricker accused him of exaggerating the city's needs and took no action. The conflict gained national attention. The state finally gave some relief, and Burton solved the immediate crisis by borrowing on future revenues. However, the scars were deep and bitter between Burton and Bricker. The existing antagonism between downstate Republicans and the Clevelanders intensified, although it was papered over in public in the interest of party unity. Bricker and Burton heartily disavowed any disagreement whenever asked; however, Burton privately asserted that statehouse politicians allowed politics to interfere with their best judgment of the actual needs of the people.

Although he had his difficulties with the regular Republican organization, Burton's wide-margin victories (over thirty-four thousand votes in the 1935, 1937, and 1939 mayoralty elections in Cleveland) led him and his supporters to consider a campaign for a seat in the United States Senate in 1940. Downstaters, even if they disliked Burton, were likely to vote Republican; and his strength and popularity in a Democratic stronghold such as the Cleveland area could be expected to have a salutary effect on the entire Republican ticket. His supporters took soundings throughout the state and reported favorable sentiments. On January 29, 1940, Burton publicly announced his candidacy for the May 14 primary. In order to obtain enough nominating petitions to list his name on the ballot, Burton's campaign committee paid Republicans throughout the state ten cents for each name they collected. The petitions in, Burton prepared to take on his major opponent, Republican Dudley White, a colorless small town newspaperman turned bland congressman. White had strong support downstate and within the Republican machine, but Burton had demonstrated that he was a formidable vote-getter for Republicans in a period of Democratic ascendency.[9]

Burton's campaign for the party nomination centered on two issues: (1) that, if nominated, the Republican party could expect his aid in the election of all Republican candidates and his strong support of John Bricker, and (2) that in the Senate he would represent the needs of the entire state, not just those of Cleveland. Burton found support in the black community, the Cleveland nationality groups, the newspapers, and the industrial counties in northern and eastern Ohio. His opposition came mainly from the state party organization under Chairman Edward D. Schorr. Continuing the pattern of behavior he had followed when he opposed Daniel Morgan's campaign for governor in 1934, Schorr accused Burton of "willfully" misrepresenting the situation in Cleveland. Schorr preferred a party regular and was suspicious of Burton for his role in the relief crisis with Bricker. Burton filed a protest with the Republican state central committee. The whole issue was publicized as a struggle between Burton, who wanted to be "the people's Senator," and Schorr, who wanted to be the party boss. Burton won the nomination easily.

After the nomination, the party closed ranks; and the regulars gave Burton their firm support. During the campaign, Burton attacked the New Deal economic policy and advocated more self-reliance, fewer governmental social programs, and less bureaucracy. He also hammered away at FDR's court-packing debacle and the perils of a presidential third term. On international affairs, he at first emphasized his opposition to American entry into the European war; but as the crisis intensified, he became less an isolationist and began speaking about the need to repel totalitarian aggression. Even though Roosevelt carried Ohio in defeating Wendell Wilkie, Burton won the Senate seat by a substantial margin of 145,000 votes over John McSweeney. He and his wife moved to Washington and settled in at the Dodge Hotel near Capitol Hill.

Selma was soon caught up in the social whirl of Washington and established an image of wearing flamboyant hats and two earrings on one ear. Because they were Unitarians, the Burtons joined All Souls Church in Washington, the congregation of many leading political families. Burton's expressed religious views emphasized the importance of deep-seated moral convictions as a basis for daily decisions in business and in government on the domestic and international fronts.[10]

Upon taking his seat in January 1941, Burton immediately attacked his senatorial work. His office staff of six people included his old friend Earl Hart, who served as secretary. Burton worked long hours, as he had done in Cleveland, and rarely took a day off. He answered all correspondence and inquiries by constituents concerning such routine matters as licenses to export goods, approval of visas, and support of private resolutions. He established a congenial relationship with his fellow Ohioan, Senator Robert Taft, although they parted company on some votes; and he served on the judiciary, commerce, civil service, immigration, and District of Columbia committees. The major issues during Burton's tenure in the Senate were the war effort, labor policy, farm policy, peacemaking, and the formation of a postwar international organization. The executive branch usually exercised almost complete power in all these areas, but Congress did assert its authority in labor relations by overriding a presidential veto of the so-called Smith-Connally Act of 1943. Farm policy presented a challenge to Congress on the question of how such issues as parity price of farm crops, the content of the parity formula, the sale of surplus commodities, and the use of consumer subsidies should be decided. With Roosevelt's blessings, Congress liquidated much of the New Deal during the war.[11]

Burton—under the banners of Win the War, Stop the Waste, Preserve the Constitution, and Develop a Vigorous International Policy—stood in a moderate voting position in the Senate. Occasionally, as was the case with his vote in favor of removing the oleomargarine tax, he was the only Republican to vote with the Democrats on important issues. As Burton explained his position, "I voted yes because there is a shortage of butter during the war; the tax is a prohibitory tax and probably unreasonable from the point of view of the consumer." The war legislation which Burton helped to sponsor was primarily bipartisan. The same independence of mind which characterized his Ohio career was still predominant, and his penchant for tedious work probably led to his selection as secretary of the Senate Republicans.[12]

Burton probably should be labeled a middle-of-the-roader with a conservative slant. Roland Young, in his study of congressional politics during World War II, characterizes Burton as a moderate party supporter and Taft as a strong party supporter. On labor relation issues, Burton's position could be described as promanagement. He regarded himself as a member of the conservative "economic bloc," and his attitude toward public spending accurately reflected the frugality exhibited in his private life. For example, his opposition to the nomination of Henry Wallace for secretary of commerce in March 1945 was based largely on his belief that Wallace thought that the objectives of government could be reached through "prodigal government spending, governmental deficits and governmental borrowing." However, Burton's frugality did not stand in the way of his support, along with Senator Lister Hill, of the Hill-Burton Hospital Act. The bill, introduced after a professional study of hospital needs throughout the country indicated that about fifteen million people had no hospital facilities available to them, provided $5 million to be used for a survey of existing facilities and $100 million for federal construction funds. Local funds were to be used to maintain the facilities. The Hill-Burton Act was the basis for most hospital construction in communities throughout the nation in the 1950s and 1960s. In addition, Burton claimed that he had maintained a strong internationalist position throughout the war and had been opposed to isolation since World War I. He supported Lend Lease, the Dumbarton Oaks Proposals, the Moscow agreements, the United Nations, the idea of American postwar involvement in international affairs, and a peacetime draft to provide an adequate military force to keep the peace.[13]

Burton regarded his service on the Truman special committee to investigate the national defense program as his most significant role in the Senate. In addition, his close contact with Truman on the committee influenced Truman's later decision to appoint him to the

Supreme Court. Truman began the formation of the investigative committee during the military buildup prior to the bombing of Pearl Harbor. He believed that the military had an inadequate wartime defense program under which manufacturers were reaping inordinate profits. In February 1941, he proposed his special committee to a listless Senate, which approved a seven-man committee with Truman as chairman and an initial appropriation of only fifteen thousand dollars. Burton was appointed to the committee on March 16, 1942, when he joined the original members—Tom Connally of Texas, Carl Hatch of New Mexico, James Mead of New York, Mon Wallgren of Washington, Joseph Ball of Minnesota, and Owen Brewster of Maine. Burton's appointment probably came as a result of his friendship with Brewster and his reputation among his colleagues for long hours and hard work. During the next three years, the committee gained a great deal of publicity and respect as a result of its disclosures and recommendations. To avoid antagonizing the executive branch, the committee limited its investigation to business related to the war effort and the performance of the bureaucracy. Many crooked contractors and influence peddlers were spotlighted, and reforms in government contract procedures were suggested. Sometimes by mere exposure, the committee broke bottlenecks in the production of armaments and other war materials. By the summer of 1944, it had issued forty-four studies and reports and according to Truman, had saved the government $15 billion.[14]

In addition to his work on the Truman committee, Burton believed that his work on the Ball-Burton-Hill-Hatch Resolution ($B_2H_2$), which provided for an international organization after the war, was a significant senatorial contribution. He regarded $B_2H_2$ as one way of enabling the Senate to have some input on the question of an international organization before a treaty was signed. He explained that his interest in international affairs stemmed in part from his Swiss ancestry and his work in Swiss immigrant affairs, but his efforts were also designed to establish his name and reputation in the Senate.[15]

$B_2H_2$ originated at an informal meeting held on March 4, 1943, to which Truman invited Vice-President Henry Wallace and Senators Lister Hill, Carl Hatch, Joseph Ball, and Burton. Truman asked that they begin work on a resolution, drafted by Ball, which dealt with postwar planning for an international peace organization. On March 6, the four sponsors—Hill, Hatch, Ball, and Burton—met and revised the resolution. A week later during a meeting at the White House, President Roosevelt emphasized the importance of having the resolution pass by at least the two-thirds vote which would be required to ratify a treaty. He wanted to bypass a struggle with the isolationists in the Senate which could easily materialize if the resolution stood only on the vote of a simple majority. The resolution was introduced into the Senate on March 16 by Ball. Thereafter, Burton and the other sponsors campaigned for it vigorously in a summer bipartisan speaking campaign and in discussion on the Senate floor. They were opposed by the Foreign Relations Committee under the chairmanship of Connally. A power struggle ensued as the committee members drafted a substitute resolution which, they maintained, would gain more support on the floor. More realistically, the members probably wanted a resolution on the international question of postwar planning to originate from the Foreign Relations Committee.[16]

When the attempt to obtain approval of the $B_2H_2$ resolution failed in the Foreign Relations Committee, Burton and the other sponsors channeled their efforts toward strengthening the substitute resolution which Connally had introduced in the committee. The major difference between the more specific $B_2H_2$ and the vaguely worded Connally Resolution was the absence in the Connally Resolution of $B_2H_2$'s insistence that a United Nations military force be maintained to suppress military aggression in the postwar world. The sponsors of $B_2H_2$ were largely unsuccessful in their attempts to clarify and strengthen the Connally Resolution. Meanwhile, Secretary of State Cordell Hull was in Moscow hammering out an agreement with the Russians on postwar international organization. The conclusion of this agreement by November 2 made the final passage of the Connally Resolution on November 5, by a vote of 85-5, somewhat anticlimatic. At the last minute, the Connally Resolution was rewritten to conform to much of the relevant language of the Moscow Agreement.[17] Therefore, despite Burton's concern, the Senate had little impact on the treaty itself; but the experience did set the stage for the successful ratifica-

March 1943—Coauthors (from left to right) Burton, Hatch, Ball, and Hill of the $B_2H_2$ Senate Resolution, which later with the Connally Agreement became the basis for the postwar formation of the United Nations

*Photo by John Goski*

tion of the United Nations agreement. During the debate over $B_2H_2$ and thereafter, Burton supported the idea of amending the Constitution to require a simple majority of either the Senate or both houses to ratify a treaty. He believed that the two-thirds rule provided for "a dictatorship of the minority over our treaty-making powers. It is directly contrary to the principle of majority rule on which America is founded." In addition, Burton believed that the change to a simple majority was necessary because, with the ratification of the United Nations Charter, closer foreign relations would demand an easier route to decision-making action in the Congress.[18]

Throughout the negotiations leading toward the United Nations treaty and its ratification on July 27, 1945, Burton remained a strong supporter. However, he was disturbed by the controversy over the issue of voting rights in the Security Council. He believed it did not matter that unanimity of the big powers would be necessary before undertaking military action; what was important, he optimistically asserted, was the possibility of deterring aggression through the formation of the General Assembly, the International Court of Justice, and the various United Nations agencies. With the advent of the atomic bomb, Burton feared that if the formation of the international organization failed, the stage would be set for World War III. In addition, during this period Burton tried to parlay his support of $B_2H_2$ and his involvement in legislation dealing with international affairs into an appointment to the Senate Foreign Relations Committee. In November 1944, he asked for a slot on the committee. However, as a freshman senator, he was too junior for this important assignment.[19]

During the war, Burton shared the prevalent hostility toward the Japanese and Germans. His two sons served in the military; and his elder son, William, was wounded in the Pacific. However, when the chairman of the Ohio Development and Publicity Commission wrote that he thought Germany should be reduced and maintained as an agricultural state after war, Burton answered that he did not believe this would be possible, and even if it were, "the German genius for industry cannot be stopped and from the point of view of the benefits to the world at large it should not be stopped." He also held the common view that the internment of Japanese-

American citizens was an administrative matter which deserved the confidence and support of Congress. Another issue of significant concern to Burton and other members of the Senate during the war was labor relations. As labor unions insisted on maintaining the economic growth which resulted from the war effort, strikes and production difficulties grew. Early in the war, Burton became concerned about the extent of the power of the unions over their own members. He believed that the closed shop racketeering, check-off on dues, and other methods of building up union strength were open to serious misuse.[20]

Although public pressure for legislation to regulate or prohibit labor strikes continued spasmodically during the war, Congress was reluctant to consider such bills. However, in the late spring of 1943, reaction to the United Mine Workers strikes led Congress to enact the War Labor Disputes Act, which was known as the Smith-Connally Act. The measure required that before a union could strike in a war plant, a strike notice, which was to be followed by a thirty-day cooling-off period, must be issued. On the thirtieth day, the National Labor Relations Board (NLRB) was required to conduct a strike vote. In addition, the bill empowered the president to seize any plant under strike and to penalize a union by fine or imprisonment once a plant was in the government's possession. Additionally, union political contributions to federal elections were outlawed. The act had been proposed at an earlier time and contained specific language that did not relate to the actual situation; workers certainly were not being driven into wartime strikes by unpatriotic and autocratic leaders. President Roosevelt vetoed the bill, believing that its provision for a strike vote might actually instigate a strike. The Congress passed the bill over his veto by a margin of 65-25 in the Senate, with 60 percent of the Democrats and 76 percent of the Republicans voting in favor of it. Burton voted with the Republican majority to overrule.[21]

After its passage, it became obvious to Congress that the act actually had a deleterious effect on the potential for strikes. Instead of looking upon a strike vote as a plebiscite on the wisdom of a strike during the war, workers regarded it as a device to exert pressure upon employers. A great deal of feverish legislative activity ensued on such matters as strike limitations, violence, coercion, and restrictions on the closed shop. In June 1945, when the war was in its final phase, a comprehensive federal industrial relations bill ($B_2H_1$) was introduced by Senators Hatch, Ball, and Burton. Peacetime strikes aroused less opposition than did wartime stoppages, and they offered less opportunity to congressmen hostile to unions to present their proposals as patriotism personified. However, the unprecedented wave of 116,000 man-days of strike idleness in 1946, which tripled the previous record in 1945, and 4,985 strikes, aroused congressional tempers to the point that new legislation had a possibility of passage.[22]

Hatch, Ball, and Burton, without Hill of the original $B_2H_2$, decided to introduce their comprehensive labor bill to pave the way for labor-management peace in the postwar period. Even though the bill never became law, it served to crystallize Senate opinion on the issue, just as $B_2H_2$ had done in 1943; and it paved the way for the passage of the Taft-Hartley Act. Burton considered it one of his major contributions. In addition, the publicity from both $B_2H_2$ and $B_2H_1$ helped Burton to consolidate his reputation during his first term in the Senate. Introduced on June 20, 1945, the bill had been largely drafted by Donald Richberg, who had earlier authored the Railway Labor Act and coauthored the Norris-LaGuardia Act. The bill would have replaced the National Labor Relations Board and other conciliation services with a five-man federal labor relations board and would have compelled arbitration of all grievance cases and all other cases in which a strike "would result in severe hardship to the public." It also proposed revising the Wagner Act to allow a closed shop only if 75 percent of the workers elected to join the union and 60 percent of the workers ratified the content of the agreement with the management.[23]

Labor unions reacted to the bill immediately, vehemently, and with great hostility. John L. Lewis of the United Mine Workers called it a "cleverly designed ripper bill which would . . . regiment American workers." Phillip Murray of the Congress of Industrial Organizations called it "the most bald-faced attempt to destroy labor unions." In addition, some of Burton's constituents in Ohio were very unhappy. On June 29, 1945, the *Toledo Union Leader* commented editorially that since Burton had been considered fair on labor issues, his name as cosponsor might "tend to lull many of our workers to sleep on the dangers of the bill." When Truman suggested Burton for the Supreme Court shortly thereafter, the *Cleveland Union Leader* reported that the Cleveland Industrial Council had written the president to oppose the appointment on the grounds that "any person who is so gullible as to be taken in by the sham, fraud and pretense of such legislation as that proposed in the Burton-Ball-Hatch bill does not possess the kind of clear, analytical, unbiased mind which is the prerequisite of any aspirant to the judgeship of the highest tribunal in the land."[24]

However, a Gallup poll taken at the time reported that 50 percent of the public desired increased restriction of union activity and that two-thirds wanted changes which were antiunion to some degree. On July 19, 1945, the *Washington Post* editorialized on the need for some such measure and voiced the opinion that the labor attack on $B_2H_1$ was exaggerated. Responding to criticism from some of his constituents, Burton asserted that the bill was introduced in the public interest and that it would provide a basis for further discussion in the proposed united peace conference of management and labor, which could possibly iron out the differences and produce a suitable bill. Privately, $B_2H_1$ had the support of President Truman, who told Burton that they were "on the right track . . . that is a good bill—don't let them talk you out of it." However, when questioned about the bill at a press conference on October 18, 1945, the president hedged, responding, "I am not familiar enough with the provisions of the Hatch-Ball-Burton bill because it was introduced just a short time before I left the Senate, and I can't answer the question." Actually, the bill, which generated a labor-management conference and the movement toward the Taft-Hartley Act (but was in itself too strong a medicine and died in committee), had been introduced after Truman left the Senate. As Burton hoped, $B_2H_1$ had served a useful purpose in channeling sentiment toward further regulation of labor.[25]

On race relations questions, throughout his public career, Burton behaved like a moderate, but politically astute, Republican. In his campaigns in Cleveland, he received black support partly because of his advocacy of relief measures. Furthermore, he was known as a strong supporter of Wings Over Jordan, a black choir which was organized in the Gethsemane Baptist Church in Cleveland by the

Reverend Glenn T. Settle in 1935. Its fame steadily grew from a local radio show to a CBS nationwide program and, in 1945, to a tour of Europe. Burton helped it to become incorporated and to arrange broadcasts over CBS; and in 1943, he became one of the choir's trustees. He also supported Settle in his efforts to gain federal support for participation in the war bond drive, made frequent contributions, and gave speeches during the choir's radio programs. Burton often described Wings Over Jordan as a major enterprise "to assist in better understanding between the Negro and the white races."[26]

Additionally, Burton supported the anti-poll tax amendment and legislation which would have created a permanent Fair Employment Practices Commission (FEPC). He believed the poll tax arbitrarily interfered with the right to vote and that the FEPC would be needed to minimize racial problems during the reconversion period after the war. Also, when Burton made a small contribution in response to a letter from officials of Tuskegee Institute, he stated, "I have been familiar with the work of Tuskegee for many years and have the highest regard for the contribution which you are making to the development of your students and to our country." However, Burton's civil rights activities present a mixed record. He corresponded warmly with Mary McLeod Bethune, a well-known black educator and politician, and Walter White, Secretary of the NAACP; but when he received a petition against the Detroit Race Riot of 1943, he refused to sign it. Although he was a member of the Cleveland branch of the NAACP, Walter White could not persuade him to support the National Youth Administration and the Civilian Conservation Corps. Burton's political philosophy of local control and paring of expenditures made it impossible for him to support those particular measures.[27]

Burton had minimal contact with the Supreme Court during his tenure in the Senate. Although active as a member of the Committee on the Judiciary, he was more involved in foreign policy and labor matters. However, in late June 1941, when Attorney General Robert H. Jackson's nomination to the associate justiceship vacated by Harlan Stone came before the Judiciary Committee, he did express a point of view. In heated testimony in opposition to the appointment, Senator Millard E. Tydings of Maryland claimed

Jackson was unfit for the Court because he refused to prosecute columnist Drew Pearson for criminal libel when Pearson falsely broadcast in 1939 that Tydings had used Works Progress Administration (WPA) workers to build a road and yacht basin on his private property. Jackson had refused because, as a matter of prosecutorial discretion, he believed this was not a criminal matter and that Tydings should have brought a civil libel suit if he sued at all. Burton strongly supported Jackson's nomination against Tydings's attack; and in response, Burton said, "Tydings took a few cracks at me." Jackson was unanimously confirmed by the committee.[28]

As the 1944 presidential election campaign approached, considerable discussion arose as to Burton's potential as a dark horse candidate for president. As early as March 1943, Ohio newspapers were discussing Burton's chances. Burton himself scotched such rumors as "just a product of somebody's imagination." However, privately interested and flattered by the comments on his candidacy for the nomination, Burton noted in his diary in November that he conferred with Senator Charles L. McNary of Oregon, who "felt I might be a man to be considered for the Republican nomination for President in 1944." In August 1943, Burton even worked out a potential cabinet: Earl Warren as vice-president, Wendell Wilkie as secretary of state, Senator Robert Taft as secretary of the treasury, Herbert Hoover as secretary of commerce, and General Douglas MacArthur as secretary of war.[29]

In early 1944, the Burton boomlet continued to be a matter of discussion; a Drew Pearson column in February mentioned him as a possible dark horse candidate. Burton said that the Pearson article was 75 percent correct on its facts about his career, although he felt that Pearson gave the wrong impression of the controversy he had had with Governor Bricker over relief in Cleveland. The article reopened the old wounds between Burton and Bricker. Because Bricker was upset about the Pearson column, Burton wrote to ask that he ignore that portion of Pearson's comments and assure him of continued support. Even though Bricker was satisfied with Burton's comments, he called to ask Burton to send the same message to Pearson, which Burton did.[30]

Burton was encouraged in his hopes for the nomination by the apparent split in the Republican party among several candidates, including Wilkie, Stassen, Dewey, and Bricker. It seemed likely that the convention might become deadlocked and choose a dark horse such as Burton for the nomination. Some contributions to a possible Burton campaign were received as well as verbal commitments. Secretary of the Interior Harold Ickes told Burton in February that he was his Republican choice for the nomination; and in June 1944, shortly before the Republican convention, Democratic Senator Arthur Walsh of New Jersey confided to Burton that he could see his way clear to support him in the presidential campaign. When the convention opened, Wilkie was out of the running after losing the Wisconsin primary; and a fight between Bricker and Dewey seemed imminent. However, Burton's hopes died on June 25, for he recorded in his diary that despite the fight, "there is a steady drift of delegates towards Dewey."[31]

Although Burton was not catapulted to the presidency in 1944, he was soon elevated to the Supreme Court bench. There is practically nothing in Burton's papers which would give the impression that he actually campaigned for or believed he would be nominated to the Supreme Court. In fact, he continued preparations for his Senate reelection campaign in 1946. His experience with the 1928 attempt to obtain a federal court appointment led him to keep a very low profile. As late as February 1945, Hart was conferring with supporters in Ohio about Bricker and the Republican machine's posture in the up-and-coming campaign. In July, Burton answered inquiries on his Court nomination from several constituents by stating that he had received no indication that he was being considered to fill the vacancy created by the resignation of Justice Owen Roberts. Furthermore, he encouraged those who wrote to him to aid in obtaining the position for other Ohio politicians. When Daniel Morgan, who was then on the Cleveland Court of Appeals, was suggested, Burton responded that he thought the president might appoint a Republican from the midwest and "that the President wishes to strengthen the court in the confidence of the nation and for this reason,[he] may undertake to promote some member of a lower court to the Supreme Court." During the same month, Burton simply noted in his diary that he called Joseph B. Keenan, chief of the army's international prosecuting section, and another friend "for advice as to the Supreme Court vacancy"; and on July 24, he noted another conference with Keenan on the same subject. In the course of a conference, Thomas H. Jones, president of the Cleveland Bar Association, told Burton that he thought the executive committee of the association might endorse either Burton or a United States district court judge from Ohio for the Supreme Court vacancy.[32]

Newspaper reports that Burton was being considered for the Court resulted in an increased number of inquiries on the subject from constituents. Early in June, Earl Hart asserted that if the nomination were offered to Burton, he would, of course, accept it; but Burton continued to deny the possibility. In a letter written to Phillip Carter on July 25, Burton stated that there was no reason to think the president would "direct lightning" his way. However, while making a speech in Ohio in early August, Burton conferred with Governor Frank Lausche, a Democrat, who "urged me to consider favorably an offer of appointment to the U.S. Supreme Court and offered to help." To Lausche's statement, Burton responded that if an appointment were offered, he would consider it carefully and would be inclined to accept. On August 10, Earl Hart wrote Fred Cornell, a friend of Burton's, that "we know Harold is definitely being considered and that if it is offered he will take it." But few Ohioans were enthusiastic because they thought Burton was "too big a man to spend the rest of his life on the Court."[33]

It was fairly evident that President Truman would appoint a Republican to fill the vacancy. Franklin Roosevelt had appointed only Democrats to the Court, with the exception of Stone's elevation to the chief justiceship. Of the approximately two hundred appointments to vacancies on the lower court, Roosevelt had appointed only four Republicans. Although Truman lingered over the possibility of Robert Patterson, Patterson was needed as secretary of war and, furthermore, did not want the Court appointment. Truman then looked to the Senate. Of the Senate Republicans, Warren Austin of Vermont, a possibility, was already sixty-seven years of age. In addition, his replacement in Vermont would most likely be a Republican. Burton, a Republican from a state with a Democratic governor who could appoint a Democrat to run in 1946 as an incumbent in the Senate race, had a law background and was the right age, fifty-seven. Additionally, he had been with Truman on the defense investigating committee and on the $B_2H_2$, which Truman had instigated; and he was known as a congenial personality, a hard worker with an unbiased mind, who was often privately consulted by Truman about his difficulties with the Senate.[34]

Finally, amid all the rumors, Truman called Burton to the White House on September 17 to tell him of his decision. When Burton demurred by questioning his ability to fill the vacancy, Truman assured him that he was capable and advised him to "decide cases not make law," as the Court often did. Truman announced the appointment the next day. Within twenty-four hours of the appointment, Burton, the last member of the Senate or the House to be appointed to the Supreme Court, was confirmed. The Judiciary Committee met in an early morning session on September 19, took no testimony, and sent the nomination to the floor, where the question of Burton's nomination was introduced in the middle of a debate on an unemployment compensation bill. No actual vote was taken. When Senator Lucas, the president pro tempore, asked for objections, there were none; and Burton was approved unanimously. The whole process went so quickly that those who wished to speak in his favor, including Senators Taft and Brewster, spoke after confirmation.[35]

Ohio Republican party sentiment on his nomination was mixed; some members saw Burton's exit as preparing the way for Bricker's election to the Senate in 1946 en route to another presidential bid, while others were relieved by his appointment because Burton had never voted a strong Republican ticket. Burton received the normal letters of congratulation from members of the Court, other public officials, and constituents. Most of the editorial comment on the appointment emphasized his integrity, independence, hard-working habits, fair-mindedness, and middle-of-the-road position. Some referred to him as one of the best-loved members of the Senate.[36]

The Supreme Court greeted the announcement of Burton's appointment warmly. Hugo Black said that he could probably assist Burton in adjusting to the change from life in the Senate to the Court since he had made a similar transition. Harlan F. Stone regarded Burton's appointment as a sign that even the Supreme

Court might return to normalcy after the war and stated that "the new Justice is a very agreeable person, . . . and I believe [he] will be a good man. In that case he will be a great comfort to me." However, liberal commentators and Court watchers were less pleased with the appointment. Fred Rodell, law professor at Yale, wrote an open letter to Burton in October and pointed out that there were hundreds who had prior claim to the seat Burton had obtained because he was a Truman friend, a Republican, and by some standards, a liberal. Said Rodell, Burton was no Cardozo, Holmes, or Stone; in fact "you will be made much of, for a purpose, by Justice Frankfurter, whose penchant lies along lines of personal as opposed to purely intellectual persuasion and he will not fail to play on the fact that you are a graduate of the Harvard Law School."[37]

Despite this outcropping of discontent, in October 1945, with President Truman looking on in an unprecedented visit by a president to the Supreme Court, Harold Hitz Burton became an associate justice. He brought with him methodical habits, a strong streak of idealism, a persuasive but self-effacing personality which overcame the effect of his tendency to stutter, a proper New England background, and experience in a corporate law practice, as a chief executive of a major city, and as a senator in one fast-paced term. He was a supporter of free enterprise, local control of local affairs, and the necessity for order in public affairs. He was a believer in a moral purpose in the universe, the importance of family ties and background, education, and a concern for one's fellow man. He had emerged from the right roots, had experienced the right things, and was in the right place at the right time. Only time would tell whether he would become Frankfurter's or someone else's pawn or would remain his own man on the Supreme Court.

# 2

# The First Term, 1945: The Influence of Chief Justice Stone

T W O months after V-J Day, the nation was in the midst of planning for demobilization, the reabsorption of servicemen into civilian life, and reconversion of industry in the wake of the economic prosperity of the war. Harry Truman, only recently thrust into the presidency, carefully deliberated the method and timing for the relaxation of wartime wage and price controls so as to avoid shocking the economy into a depression. He knew that if price controls were relaxed precipitously, food shortages, housing shortages, and black markets might result. Labor was up in arms against wage controls; automobile, railroad, and coal workers agitated for strikes. In foreign policy, new relationships with the Russians, tariff agreements, and the movement toward establishing the United Nations were all being hotly pursued. In the Senate, Burton stood in the midst of the political ferment; on the Court, he was withdrawn into a body which could only act on cases presented.

A short time after Burton left the Senate for the Supreme Court, he was asked about the transition and replied, "have you ever gone direct from a circus to a monastery?"[1] If the Court that Burton joined in 1945 was a monastery, it was a most active one. Indeed, it was a constellation of judicial stars. On the bench sat Hugo Black, William Douglas, Frank Murphy, and Wiley Rutledge, who were generally regarded as civil libertarians; Robert Jackson and Stanley Reed, who were generally regarded as anti-civil libertarians; and Felix Frankfurter, who had a libertarian reputation but often voted with Jackson and Reed in the interest of judicial self-restraint.

1945—Sketch by Jim Beerman, which appeared in the *Washington Evening Star*

Chief Justice Harlan Fiske Stone, who often sided with the libertarians, served the Court for only one year during Burton's tenure, for he died in 1946. Arriving from the Senate like Burton, Black established his leadership of the civil libertarians after first being criticized for lack of technical legal expertise. Frankfurter, the premier intellectual, the professor on the Court who was fond of lecturing his colleagues, led a judicial self-restraint bloc which had most often included Owen Roberts and Jackson. The most libertarian of the justices, Murphy was often isolated even from Black and Douglas. In the confines of the Court, a long-standing feud between Jackson and Black still boiled. Since 1943, the disagreement between Black and Jackson over the interpretation of New Deal legislation had flared into personal animosity. The most recent dispute had arisen when the Court upheld, in *Jewell Ridge* on May 7, 1945, the claims of the United Mine Workers to portal-to-portal pay in the bituminous coal industry. Jackson formally criticized Black, in a brief concurrence to the denial of a petition for rehearing, for not disqualifying himself, since his former law partner was the victorious counsel in the case. The Court also generally resented Black's use of pressure tactics in conferences to obtain agreement with his point of view. Furthermore, the justices had to adapt to four years of somewhat weak leadership under Stone after being dominated by Charles Evans Hughes, who retired in 1941. Hughes, who had held the Court in tight rein, had been concerned mainly with the idea of reaching "justice" in a given case. Stone, however, emphasized the necessity of balancing opposing values and had a more limited view of the Court's powers. In administering the Court's work, he also permitted more discussion and argument than had Hughes. The absence of Jackson at the Nuremburg trials in Europe also irritated Stone. Reed assumed some of Jackson's duties, but Stone was bothered by Jackson's unavailability and the specter of an evenly divided Court in a close case.[2]

Perhaps in the light of his generally conservative views, it would have been tempting for Burton to acquiesce to being "made much of, for a purpose," by Frankfurter that first year, as Rodell had predicted; but the tenacity of his attempt to maintain his open-mindedness was an offsetting factor. In fact, Burton was most impressed with Stone; and if there was any danger which he found necessary to avoid during the first year, it was the tendency of new members to be dominated by the chief justice. In addition, as had been the experience of most newly appointed justices, Burton felt somewhat unbalanced during most of the first year.[3]

He rapidly discovered that although the Court might be a monastery in terms of the veil of secrecy which covered its deliberations and the sense of isolation from the public, he was working harder than ever. Shortly after Burton's swearing in, Frankfurter began catering to him by supplying him with lists of books and articles to read. Burton read the materials diligently. In their conferences, the justices usually scribbled notes when the cases were discussed in order to have the various points of view on hand as they prepared opinions. Burton elaborated on the practice by not only keeping a complete set of notes on every case discussed in conference, but also on every oral argument. The new justice worked on Court matters from nine in the morning until nearly midnight. During the first two weeks of each term, the justices routinely heard cases from 12:00 to 4:30 P.M. On Saturdays from noon until late evening, they were in conference until decisions were reached; and if issues remained unresolved, they would confer in the mornings during the week. And each week there were approximately twenty-five writs of certiorari from parties asking that their cases be heard, and these demanded Justice Burton's attention. As a new member of the Court "who must catch up with the other members in the consideration of the line of cases and statutes before the Court," Burton would find it impossible for one or two years "to do much of anything outside of the Court work." He was also encouraged in his decision to decline all speaking engagements by Chief Justice Stone, who believed members of the Court should remain primarily involved in their official duties. Burton spent what spare time he had reading law books and briefing cases previously decided by the Court.[4]

Because he was very uncertain during his first year on the Court, Burton relied heavily on his clerk, W. Howard Mann, who had previously clerked for Rutledge on the Court of Appeals. For the most part, the opinions of that first year represented a joint effort. Mann wrote a series of detailed memos on individual points in the cases and explained them to Burton. They worked almost every night in his chambers until Burton began to feel a surer grasp of the law, in the process developing procedures that Burton used throughout his years on the Court. Burton's secretary, Tess Cheatham, ran his office with an iron hand. In the beginning, Burton wrote few dissents, in part because of his lack of certainty but more importantly because he believed that if any justice could not persuade at least one other justice to join him, he was probably wrong. He regarded dissents primarily as vain shows of erudition rather than the results of profoundly held convictions which might someday become the majority view. Writing came hard to Burton; he painfully mulled over every possible precedent, briefing the cases out of his own hand and then laboring over writing an opinion. Ever mindful of the practical use of opinions by lawyers, the press, and laymen, he always explicitly stated the facts and the decision in the first few sentences of the opinion.[5]

For his first Court decision, the chief justice assigned Burton to write the unanimous opinion in a Fair Labor Standards Act (FLSA) case, *Roland Electrical Co.* v. *Walling,* which was largely a matter of statutory construction turning on the intent of the legislature, "a subject in which I [he] had special training in the Senate." Extending the coverage of the New Deal act, which provided minimum wages for certain categories of workers, was a matter of deep concern to reformers. The members of the Court were assiduous in giving Burton help with this first opinion. Douglas suggested, along with some minor changes in emphasis, that the names of justices be omitted when referring to prior cases involving present members of the Court and that Burton leave out Black's name as the chief advocate of the act while serving in the Senate during its passage. Rutledge, taking particular concern for Burton and Mann that first year, made extensive comments on the draft.[6]

Frankfurter offered some helpful comments but was "deeply troubled," as was Rutledge, by Burton's statement of the relationship between congressional power and administrative authority in the area of fair labor standards. In delivering one of his lengthy explanations on the powers of the courts as opposed to the legislature, Frankfurter asserted that

it is a disregard of the respective functions of legislation and adjudication to suggest that where Congress does not express its will, the duty of definition should authoritatively be determined by the administration the same as though Congress had so expressed its will. . . . In short it is the duty of the courts to apply and enforce the result of the process of legislation. But it is not the duty of the courts to complete the process of legislation. Indeed, it is the duty of the courts to abstain from doing so. Not to be fastidious in such obstruction would indeed merit the occasional suggestion that this court is the third house of legislature.

Frankfurter further suggested that Burton not use such terms as *liberal* and *strict construction*, as he did in the draft, since "these adjectives mean all things to all men." He should instead convey the same idea by using "less dubious, less tarnished words."[7]

During that term, Burton wrote majority opinions in two other FLSA cases in which the issues were similar to those in the *Roland* case. In the first case, Burton found that employees at industrial plants operated by the producers of goods for use in interstate commerce were engaged in the production of goods for commerce as defined in the FLSA and so were covered by the overtime provisions of the act. In the second case, Burton wrote for the majority that mechanics maintaining equipment used in interstate commerce were covered by the FLSA, were employees of a service company employed by the carriers, and were not employees of the carriers for whom the Interstate Commerce Commission (ICC) had exclusive power to set maximum hours of service under the Motor Carrier Act of 1935. Douglas dissented, joined by Frankfurter and Rutledge, and held that being an employee of a service company which is employed by a carrier was sufficient to bring the worker within the exemption concerning employees regulated by the ICC. Douglas was persuaded that these employees should remain covered by ICC rules, which insisted on very stringent safety regulations for the vehicles involved. Rutledge also parted company with Burton since he feared, as did Douglas, the consequences for safety regulations, which to him were more important than the fair labor standards which seem to have gained precedence as a result of their influence on Burton's opinion.[8]

Burton, becoming steadily more assured as the year progressed, soon began commenting on the opinions of other justices. In a leading case on the right of the Federal Power Commission to regulate the building and use of waterpower facilities, he refused to agree with Frankfurter primarily because his clerk insisted on the validity of his views. In another case involving a district court's denial of a certificate of convenience and necessity to operate a carrier of motor vehicles in water transportation, after the Interstate Commerce Commission had permitted it, Burton eagerly read and commented on Douglas's opinion for a unanimous Court. Douglas, reversing the district court and upholding the ICC, took Burton's advice to use the term *vessel* to replace the term *boat* in certain parts of the opinion in order "to conform to the balance of the opinion and to the customs of the lakes."[9]

In a case involving the conviction of three Mormons for allegedly violating the federal kidnapping statute by taking a fifteen-year-old girl, who was plurally married, to Arizona from Utah to evade juvenile authorities, the Court showed its hostility toward efforts to use federal criminal statutes to interfere with Mormon religious practices. Burton agreed with Murphy's opinion for a unanimous Court, which found no violation of the statute because the girl had not been held for ransom and there was no evidence that she had been decoyed or inveigled away, as was specifically required for conviction under the statute. However, Burton suggested, unsuccessfully, that Murphy's opinion would be on "firmer ground" if it were based on a failure of the record to show any "holding" of the victim rather than on the assumption that she had not been decoyed. Burton also believed that Murphy need not refer to the IQ of the alleged victim. After Murphy refused to redraft the opinion to meet these objections, Burton concurred without opinion.[10]

Burton was exposed to a great variety of cases and controversies during his first term. When the Court considered a Nebraska Supreme Court order dismissing a writ of habeas corpus filed by a convicted murderer who claimed he had been denied his right to effective defense counsel, Burton first encountered the difficult problem of postconviction remedies for prisoners. The petitioner was given an opportunity for a trial to determine whether he had been given the right to an adequate defense. In his draft opinion reversing the decision below, Reed first included a lengthy discussion of the necessity for raising numerous objections and exceptions on the subject of appeal and then turned to the writ of habeas corpus.

Chief Justice Stone then concurred with the result in the draft but attacked Reed for muddying the issues with extraneous matter. Mann encouraged Burton to concur with Stone's opinion instead of Reed's because, he said, "I think it is wholly unwarranted to branch out into a discussion of 'appeal.' . . . J. Reed is going to hem in the great protective remedy of habeas corpus against constitutional violations of state procedure rules by precluding the remedy if [the] accused fails to appeal. Such a suggestion seems terrible to me." Reed's attitude should have been particulary objectionable in this case, since the route of appeal for release after conviction was indeed a sticky one for prisoners to take if they wished to be freed. Most of the controversy in such instances usually involved the procedure for appealing cases. Such issues as to which court the imprisoned must go and what writ should be filed —coram nobis, common law certiorari, or habeas corpus— would be considered over and over again. The case came up to Court after some fifteen or more proceedings in Nebraska courts and in all three levels of federal courts; and now even with the Supreme Court command that a hearing be given, the defendant might have taken an improper form of appeal. The lower court could simply send him off to file another kind of writ, from which more appeals could result. The objections of Burton and Stone led Reed to remove what they regarded as "extraneous material" before he wrote his final draft of the opinion, which finally gained the approval of a unanimous Court.[11]

When the ubiquitous Jehovah's Witnesses came before the Court during that term, Burton parted company with his clerk for the first time. The Court had increasingly been asked to decide cases involving conviction of Jehovah's Witnesses engaged in proselytizing. Two cases involving the distribution of literature by the Witnesses were reviewed, one in a privately owned company town, *Marsh* v. *Alabama*, and the other in a village constructed for workers in national defense activities on federally owned lands, *Tucker* v. *Texas*. In both cases, state trespass statutes made it an offense to remain, willfully, on the premises of another after being warned by the owner either not to enter or to leave. In conference in December, Stone announced that he was persuaded by Alabama's definition of the town in *Marsh* as private property "much like a man's store—people can go in for the purposes stated. [This] would not violate a constitutional restriction." Burton, who rarely jotted down his own views, also noted that he thought it was a "private enterprise." Black asserted that although he recognized that the state claimed the property was not public, it was public for all intents and purposes and should be treated like any other political subdivision. Agreeing with Black, Frankfurter said he regarded this as a political community operating as such and not a business enterprise. Reed commented that the case was unlike earlier cases in which the picketing was on company property: this was "not a street situation. [People] had a right . . . [to use] the public road." Although Douglas finally voted with Black, he noted his agreement with Frankfurter, while Murphy and Rutledge agreed with Black without additional comment. In the *Tucker* case, the only discussion took place among Frankfurter, Murphy, and Stone. Frankfurter stated that he was "troubled" about the case since if the Witnesses had just been ordinary peddlers or hawkers, the Constitution would not have protected them. He also wanted to make sure that "the people in the government project have the same freedom as people elsewhere," while Murphy favored the Witnesses because he thought that the Constitution "applied to all alike to preach religion." Stone replied perhaps so, "but not in his parlor."[12]

Burton's clerk, in complete disagreement with his justice in these two cases, asserted that when private corporations and federal corporations were set up by towns and villages, "they are bound by the legal significance of any other town or village as far as freedom of religion and the press are concerned." He felt the towns were not in any way "analogous to a private home or the corporation's business activity; certainly the company town is not anyone's castle." Mann thought that if the dissenters wanted to undermine the prior case law protecting the Witnesses in their exercise of the freedoms of religion and speech, he could not agree with them, for: "I dislike them with a vengeance; I think their whole business is an unholy racket. But just the same, the fundamental freedoms are too fundamental to run the risk of restricting the Witnesses' exercise of religion and speech. It is one of the great battles of the times to see that those freedoms are not restricted in any degree whatsoever."

Black wrote the majority opinion in favor of the Witnesses on the basis of the First Amendment guarantees of freedom of the press and religion in both cases. Frankfurter concurred, parting company with Black's strained analogy of a private corporation interfering with federal power to regulate commerce in the first case and his allusion to an act of Congress that might violate the First Amendment in the second case. Joined by Burton and Stone, Reed dissented in both cases. The dissenters asserted that while every man has a right to expression in an orderly fashion, he has no right to trespass on private property for that purpose. To them the towns involved were legally classified as private property. With his dissent in this case, Burton demonstrated clearly his willingness to disagree with anyone, including his clerk and Frankfurter, during that first difficult year.[13]

Left over from the 1944 term was an important but divisive federal-state case which involved the immunity of state-run enterprise from federal taxation. In conference on the case on December 8, Black took the position that the earlier cases ought to be overruled, that the Court ought to announce that this problem had been hanging fire for years, and that the tests used previously were invalid. After talking with Frankfurter, Mann advised Burton that even though Frankfurter's opinion (which had failed to gain a majority in the previous term) was logical and "will be the eventual or ultimate position on this problem," the Court should follow the more traditional method of arriving there case by case rather than to "lay it down broadside." A rather fiery exchange of views among members of the Court ensued. Frankfurter, who felt particularly pressured by his inability to gather support for his opinion, wrote a barrage of memos and notes clarifying certain aspects of it in the hope of persuading other justices to join him. Meanwhile, "in view of the confusion arising from the number of opinions in this case, and agreeable to the desires of some of the brethren," Stone calmly kept making changes in his hoped for concurrence.[14]

In late December, Frankfurter deleted a sentence in his opinion concerning exempting a state instrumentality from federal taxation in order to meet Stone's concern about "taxation of a statehouse or taxation of a state's revenues.'' He did so after the chief justice circulated a concurrence expressing his own views. At this point, Frankfurter commented that all he was trying to do was "to clear away rubbish" used in past decisions and to formulate a rational basis for present ones. In an unsubtle slap at his brethren, he continued, "for myself, I do not think that at this stage it is intellectually adequate merely to conclude that if a state liquor business is not immune, neither is a state's mineral water business." Frankfurter finally wrote a Court opinion in which Rutledge joined, while Stone, Reed, Burton, and Murphy concurred. Although all agreed that the state's sales of mineral water were subject to federal taxation and that such an enterprise was not an essential governmental function, Stone and his supporters believed that there may be some nonessential activities in which a state might engage which should be immune from federal taxation. They preferred a rule which made "the nature and extent of the activity by whomsoever performed" the relevant consideration. Dissenting, with the concurrence of Black, Douglas asserted that the earlier cases pertaining to this issue were wrong and that whenever a state decided an activity was an essential governmental function, the function should not be subject to federal taxation. When the opinion was finally approved, Burton, who was interested in the Inter-American Bar Association and had been reminded by one of its officers that the Court might refer to Latin American law in its opinions whenever possible, persuaded Frankfurter to include two such citations in his opinion.[15]

When two cases involving freedom of the press, but which appeared to concern only the coverage of the Fair Labor Standards Act, were decided that term, Burton displayed his growing self-confidence. In the first case, since he was writing in three other FLSA cases, Burton felt himself somewhat more knowledgeable. In conference, he expressed his views quite freely. Furthermore, his clerk's advice that he should go along with Douglas's opinion instead of writing himself, even if some employees were not "in" or "necessary to" production, came after he had already decided that they were in production. In the second case, which was decided the same day, Burton went along with the majority despite his clerk's severe criticism that the Rutledge opinion discussed an irrelevant case as a "blooming flower" in order to bring in an "offensive" discussion of search and seizure and self-incrimination, instead of being limited to the question of whether newspapers were covered by the act. Burton took note of his clerk's opinion but explained that he preferred the majority position.[16]

In another case more directly concerned with civil liberties, *Duncan* v. *Kahanamoku*, the Court decided, in a Black opinion, that since martial law cannot be used to give the armed forces the power to supplant civilian laws and trials, military trials held in Hawaii were illegal when the civilian courts were open. When the case was discussed in conference, Frankfurter agreed with Reed that detention by the military was legal but that civilian trials should have been held after martial law was ended. He indicated he would reverse in both cases. After the discussions, Frankfurter changed his mind and decided to join in a Burton dissent. He liberally provided Burton with bits of rhetoric to insert in his opinion; Burton included most of the advice but rewrote the words to fit his own ideas and vocabulary. Frankfurter suggested that "expansive rhetoric about the dreadful 'brass hats' after they have safeguarded our liberty, stirs such a responsive chord in people that you may agree with me in thinking it worthwhile to engage in a little puncturing rhetoric," the real question here is "what were the requirements of the Constitution and the law which controlled the conduct of the Commander-in-Chief and the other military authorities during the period here in question in Hawaii." Restating the point later, Frankfurter suggested that one ought to ask "is it conceivable that an injunction would have been issued or, if issued, would have been sustained by this Court if application had been made contemporaneously with the conduct of the military which we now retrospectively say was lawless?" However, Burton had already made the same points in a different way.[17]

In his dissent, with the concurrence of Frankfurter, Burton emphasized that the majority were using hindsight; no one could say that conditions at the time were not such that executive discretion under the war powers should not have required military trials. The test, Burton asserted, is to ask ourselves whether or not on those dates, with the war against Japan in full swing, this Court would have, or should have, granted a writ of habeas corpus, an injunction or a writ of prohibition to release the petitioners or otherwise to oust the provost court of its claimed jurisdiction. This court might well have found itself embarrassed had it ordered such relief and then had attempted to enforce its order in the theater of military operations, at a time when the area was under martial law and the writ of habeas corpus was still suspended, all in accordance with the orders of the President of the United States.[18]

Although commentators gave Burton little credit for drafting the dissent, Burton was proud of his opinion in the case. He wrote to President Truman that

it occurs to me that you, as an old front line soldier, may be interested in my enclosed dissent in the Hawaii martial law cases. . . . [I]n emphasizing the zones of discretion which the Constitution allows to the executive and legislative branches of the Government as well as the judiciary you will recognize that this point of view is drawn from my experience in France as an infantry officer, my experience as an executive officer as mayor of Cleveland, my experience in the Senate as a legislative officer, as well as in the practice of law, and for the past few months, on the Bench.

Truman, in thanking Burton for the opinions, commented, "I think your approach to the situation is much more in line with what is necessary, than is the majority opinion, although I am no lawyer as you know."[19]

In two cases involving appeals by General Tonoyaka Yamashita, the "tiger of Malaya," and General Masahura Homma, commander of the Bataan Death March, both of whom had been sentenced to hanging by a military commission for war crimes, the Court faced another civil liberties issue arising out of World War II. Justice Stone obtained a majority opinion after considerable effort; but Murphy and Rutledge, in impassioned separate dissents, found the convictions invalid in that the petitioners should have had the same constitutional safeguards as citizens since surrender and an armistice had been declared, and military necessity did not abrogate procedural due process. Furthermore, they saw the real issue as whether it was a crime in the time of war to command soldiers who committed crimes. Believing as he did in judicial restraint, executive discretion, and legislative supremacy under the war powers, Burton went with the majority in the cases. Agreeing with Stone in his opinion, he saw the case narrowly as turning solely on the issue of whether the proceedings, involving war criminals as they did, conformed to constitutional requirements. However, his clerk, concerned that the majority opinion as written overly narrowed the scope of review on a habeas corpus petition, disagreed with him. The clerk believed it was important, for future cases, to note that habeas corpus was no longer as restricted as the view taken by the majority on the early cases they had cited.[20]

In a tax case, Burton's lone dissent from the majority view that embezzled money does not constitute taxable income to the embezzler, even though he has used it for his own purposes and the embezzlement may have given rise to a deductible loss for the owner, had to await later vindication. Burton dissented because he thought that the Internal Revenue Code, which specifically taxed income derived from any source whatever, should be strictly interpreted. Although he was a freshman and did not really believe in dissenting, he accepted Mann's advice that he should not hesitate to write some sort of opinion. After Mann had finished his clerkship and was teaching at Indiana University Law School, he wrote Burton that the law review staff was preparing a comment on the case and that he was the only one there who agreed with Burton's dissent. In 1961, the Court reversed itself and adopted Burton's position.[21]

Burton and Frankfurter continued to work well together. In a state taxation of interstate commerce case, Frankfurter instructed Burton on the difference between considering the validity of a state statute on a writ of certiorari and on an appeal, while invalidating the tax. In a criminal case involving kickbacks paid to labor union officials, Frankfurter gracefully dissented from Murphy's reversal of the conviction of the officials, using language which Burton had supplied. But Frankfurter, Reed, and Rutledge chided Burton when he wanted to emphasize that adultery had been committed in the case of a married white man who had sexual intercourse with an Indian girl who was over sixteen but under eighteen, on a reservation in Arizona, even though the conviction would be reversed. Reed was concerned that Burton was overemphasizing the guilt of the petitioner under the adultery statute, which was not at issue. Rutledge made the same point more strongly, stating that while he might agree with Burton, he did not think they "should convict him of that offense [adultery] before trial for it." After he removed the offending language, Rutledge wrote to say "I'm glad that you have relieved Williams of liability for adultery."[22]

When the Court was confronted with the possibility of having to overrule a number of earlier cases, including *Schwimmer* v. *U.S.*, on the issue of whether unwillingness to bear arms in the country's defense excluded an applicant from admission to citizenship, Frankfurter worked assiduously in an unsuccessful effort to woo Burton to the position he held with Reed and Stone and so gain an even 4-4 decision. Because Jackson was still absent, this would have resulted in an affirmance of the court below. In addition to talking to Burton about the case, Frankfurter wrote to him twice on March 20 to persuade him that the congressional intention in amending the naturalization law as announced in the earlier cases had been to confirm the Court's earlier decisions. Frankfurter argued that the chairmen of the House and Senate committees, who considered amending the act to dispute the Court's earlier decision, had decided not to do so. Furthermore, "he [Frankfurter] did not need Stanley Reed's [then solicitor general] knowledge that the *Schwimmer* problem was considered by a Cabinet Committee." Additionally, even though Stone had dissented in *Schwimmer*, he had opposed granting certiorari and was refusing to overrule the case in the interest of stare decisis. Frankfurter explained that he would like to depart from the *Schwimmer* doctrine but could find no grounds for doing so and therefore wanted to acquiesce in congressional supremacy.[23]

After the majority of Rutledge, Murphy, Black, Burton, and Douglas (in a Douglas opinion) overruled *Schwimmer*, Frankfurter enlisted Burton's aid in an attempt to change Douglas's opinion so that "pronouncements by the highest court in the land would not be disfigured by such specious rhetoric" as Douglas used. Frankfurter objected to Douglas's statement that "it is hard to believe that one need forsake his religious scruples to become a citizen but not to sit in the high councils of state." Furthermore, he pointed out that Douglas had erroneously cited a case to support the statement that it would "require very persuasive circumstances enveloping congressional silence to deter this Court from reexamining its own doctrines." He asked Burton to read the case and then judge for himself "whether the legislative circumstances following the *Schwimmer* case are remotely comparable to the circumstances narrated in the full paragraph from which the single sentence is quoted." Despite Frankfurter's efforts, the offending statements remained in Douglas's opinion.[24]

When the Court, on freedom of the press grounds, reversed the contempt convictions of a newspaper publisher and editor who had published two editorials and a cartoon criticizing certain actions of a Florida trial court as being too favorable to criminals and gambling establishments, Burton had difficulty in reaching a decision to support Reed's majority opinion. In conference, he announced that he thought the newspaper articles were not aiming at the court but at the system. Except for an earlier decision in the *Bridges* case, he thought the state of Florida had enough latitude to permit or punish such comments without violating the Fourteenth Amendment. In addition, he was impressed with Frankfurter's assertion in conference that free speech does not mean "[you] can club a court into line with a newspaper threat. You can't say to [a] judge 'You SOB—We will [be] judges at the next election.' A judge should be able to stop that." Nonetheless, when the opinions were in, Douglas, Murphy, Rutledge, Burton, and Black all voted to reverse without overruling the *Bridges* case. Burton read Frankfurter's concurrence but could not join it because it was "too discursive and personalized" in that "the legal discussion, such as it is, comes at the end."[25]

The Court, including Burton, was not yet ready to enter the political thicket of deciding whether representation based on the principle of "one man one vote" was constitutionally required. In the one case that raised the issue during that term, the Court, in a Frankfurter opinion, affirmed a district court judgment against the plaintiffs. Burton agreed in conference with Stone, Reed, and Rutledge that reapportionment was a political question. Any effort on the part of the Court to intervene, he asserted, would "create a chaotic condition."[26]

After Burton dissented from a Court opinion involving a controversy over when the working time of miners began and ended, he found the Congress enacting new legislation based on his opinion. In 1944, the Court had decided that subterranean travel to work, portal to portal, in iron mines constituted work time, which would entitle miners to retroactive payment for overtime. Also, in the *Jewell Ridge* case, the claims of the United Mine Workers to such pay in the bituminous coal industry were upheld. Murphy had written the opinion of the Court in both cases. This time, in a 5-2 decision with Murphy again writing the opinion for the Court, the majority extended travel as work time to surface industries, thus setting off a storm of threatened union suits for back pay. Douglas, Frankfurter, Reed, and Stone had initially voted to refuse certiorari, which would have left portal-to-portal pay inapplicable to surface industries, while Burton, Rutledge, Murphy, and Black voted to grant certiorari. As the final opinions were announced, everyone except Frankfurter and Burton went with Murphy. Burton was persuaded by the fact that the time spent in preparation for work was insubstantial, and record keeping would be difficult because only the employees themselves would know what they did after punching in. In his dissent, he emphasized that in the FLSA Congress meant the work week to be from "whistle to whistle." His dissent received very little publicity; yet Congress took note of the controversy and his views.[27]

For his first race relations opinion, Burton received a great deal of publicity and mail; but much of it was unfavorable. He dissented alone when, in *Morgan* v. *Virginia*, Reed wrote for the majority that a statute providing for segregation of black and white passengers in interstate commerce was an unconstitutional burden on interstate commerce. Burton believed that no undue burden had been shown and stated that the "basic weakness in the appellant's case is the lack of facts and findings essential to demonstrate the existence of such a serious and major burden upon the national interest in interstate commerce as to outweigh whatever state or local benefits are attributable to the statute and which would be lost by its invalidation." Furthermore, he did not see the need for a uniform rule on this issue since there were diverse conditions in different areas of the country. In an earlier typed draft of his opinion, Burton had stated, even more affirmatively, his belief in local control in race relations just as he believed in local control in almost every issue as a matter of policy. As long as no questions were raised under the Fourteenth Amendment and Fifteenth Amendment, "the legislative regulation of race relations has fallen naturally into the constitutional division of powers between the state and federal governments. It has been one of the greatest elements of strength and stability of the nation that in this and many other fields diversity of treatment has been made available to meet diversified needs."[28]

While he prepared his dissent, Burton was thwarted in his desire to include a note indicating that recently deceased Chief Justice Stone had agreed with his position in the case. Although Frankfurter and Douglas agreed that it would be appropriate to do so, Murphy was opposed. Frankfurter reminded Murphy of a justice's right to autonomy in writing dissenting opinions. However, when Murphy finally said that although he would not give his consent, Burton could include whatever he wanted as a matter of right, Burton conceded. Judging from the few citations in Burton's diary concerning Murphy, it appears that they were not friends. Furthermore, Burton was so influenced by Stone that his own attitude in the case was probably a reflection of Stone's views. In the end, Black and Rutledge concurred in the result of the majority. Also concurring, Frankfurter commented that although he approved of Burton's reasoning, he believed that stare decisis dictated the majority opinion.[29]

Much of the mail Burton received in the *Morgan* case criticized him as a fallen-from-grace liberal. The local NAACP, the Future Outlook League, and some Clevelanders reminded him of the strong support black voters had given him in his political campaigns. Supporters of his dissent pointed out that the majority opinion was further undermining states' rights and that the interstate commerce clause had already been "stretched almost to the breaking point." In response to the unfavorable letters, Burton commented that he was merely addressing himself to the limited issue before the Court; and he sent notes of appreciation to the favorable commentators. Howard Mann, who was still at Indiana School of Law, wrote that he had heard some very good comments on the Burton dissent. One lawyer, in whom Mann had great confidence, thought it was "one of the best jobs done in the court last year, if not the best." The lawyer thought it was impossible to disprove Burton's position, "but it was just one of those areas where he would refuse to follow precedent." In addition to the correspondence Burton received, there was a great deal of newspaper comment on the decision. The *Washington Post*, in an editorial on June 6, 1946, approved the decision in principle but lamented its reliance on the interstate commerce clause: "we have to remember that policy-making decisions of this sort might operate with equal force to invalidate state laws forbidding segregation . . . if a majority of the court were inclined to favor universal segregation of the races."[30]

During that first term, although Frankfurter presented two tables setting forth prior decisions on the issues and asked the justices to adopt British legal views on the subject, Burton voted with the majority to uphold the warrantless seizure of evidence in his first two search and seizure cases. Burton also delivered the Court opinion in his first antitrust case, *American Tobacco Co.* v. *United*, affirming the convictions of company officials for monopolizing in violation of the Sherman Act. In the *Tobacco* case he followed Rutledge's suggestion that he change the wording of his opinion from "we welcome the opportunity" to "we endorse" because "the wise-cracking reader will say we were just settling back waiting joyfully for the chance to do this under the welfare formula."[31]

In addition to Burton's majority opinion in the *Tobacco* case, he wrote four more majority opinions during the term, three in Fair Labor Standards Act cases and one on a statutory interpretation conflict between federal criminal law and state law. He also wrote five dissenting opinions and one concurrence, an extremely good output for a justice in his first year. Frank Murphy, for example, wrote only five opinions (all for the majority), no concurrences, and no dissents in his first term. Burton had not avoided the "freshman effect" often noted in new justices, but he had developed an unequivocal style. He displayed his penchant for openmindedness, a posture he became noted for throughout his years on the Court; yet he did not hesitate to disagree with Frankfurter, his clerk, or any other justice on the Court. Although flattered by it, he also withstood the courtship which Frankfurter always provided for those he hoped to develop into allies.[32]

The greatest shock to Burton during that first year was the death of Chief Justice Stone, who fell ill while on the bench on April 22, 1946. Since Burton believed in experience and continuity, he was concerned that "the next senior person is Justice Black who has been there only eight years." In conference thereafter, he "missed the strength, experience, and wisdom of Chief Justice Stone." He guessed wrongly that Jackson, Douglas, or Reed would be made chief justice and that either Secretary of Labor Louis Swellenbach, Secretary of War Robert Patterson, Judge Oren Phillips of the Tenth Circuit, or Judge John Parker of the Fourth Circuit would be made an associate justice. When, on June 6, President Truman ended speculation by naming Secretary of the Treasury Fred Vinson chief justice, Burton commented, "I believe he will make a strong Chief. He should be able to serve for at least six years."[33]

Burton had friendly relations with most members of the Court. He lunched often with Stone, Reed, and Rutledge and occasionally with Black and Frankfurter. He had little contact with Murphy and Douglas, although when Douglas was suggested as secretary of the interior to replace Harry Ickes, who had resigned, Burton commented, "I hope he stays on the Court." He maintained a warm relationship with President Truman, with whom he exchanged notes from time to time. At a birthday luncheon for Truman, at which all the justices except Murphy and Jackson were present, Truman took Burton aside to discuss his difficulties with the Senate. Burton advised him to work personally with individual senators who might come to support his views. Truman also spoke of his lack of power to do anything about John L. Lewis and the coal strike which was in progress.[34]

Although he was no longer engaged in politics, Burton continued his long-standing practice of answering every inquiry, no matter how insignificant, as soon as it was received. He was still very interested in the United Nations and foreign affairs. When he received a letter expressing distrust of the Russians and a fear of their expansion and use of the atomic bomb and questioning the role of the UN, Burton replied at length that "human conduct and ideals seem to me more likely to respond to conviction based on such leadership as that of Jesus than to the force of a bomb." He added that the value of the UN can be assessed quickly by asking "if we did not have it what would we have in place of it?"[35]

At the end of the 1945 term, Burton appeared to have gained strength and confidence in his abilities. He displayed a generally moderate to conservative voting stance on civil liberties issues and a strong states' rightist and judicial self-restraint posture when interpreting the will of Congress and the powers of the president. The only influence which seemed to have a real impact on him was that of Chief Justice Stone. Burton's opinions proved to be sound and thoughtful; and his style, though not vibrant, was concise. He exercised a strong voice, often an instrumental one, in the decision making of the Court. If anything, he could be labeled the "swing man" of the 1945 term. It remained to be seen how the transition from Stone to Vinson and the return of Jackson would influence his future role on the Court.

# 3

## Under the New Chief Justice

D U R I N G the next three Supreme Court terms, with Vinson as chief of a divided Court on which Burton remained the junior justice, the nation was settling into the postwar period. Reconversion was completed; prices leveled off; and then an economic deflation took place throughout the fall of 1948 and the spring and summer of 1949. Labor unions had begun to find business management more productive than striking; but with the tumbling of prices, unemployment began to rise significantly. An easing of race relations became increasingly apparent, appropriately signaled in the popular culture by the signing of Jackie Robinson by the Brooklyn Dodgers. Politically, the nation's dissatisfaction with the Democrats over prices, foreign policy tensions, strikes, and the use of the atomic bomb gave the Republicans control of Congress for the first time in the fall election of 1946, a control which they maintained throughout the next three years. The conservatives were still led by Burton's former colleague Robert Taft of Ohio, who advocated an end to the New Deal revolution in economics and foreign policy. When Truman presented a whole series of New Deal domestic measures to the Congress after his victory over Dewey in the 1948 election, the members did nothing about such issues as civil rights, education, and health insurance. From the Republican controlled Congress came such legislation as the Taft-Hartley Act, which weakened the power of unions, and a new income tax formula that reduced taxes on higher incomes, both of which demanded interpretation by the Supreme Court. In foreign policy, the Greek-Turkish crisis, the ramifications of the Truman Doctrine, the cold war against Soviet imperialism (with the resulting fear of subversion), and the Marshall Plan dominated public discussion.

Fred Moore Vinson, who was sworn in as chief justice on June 24, 1946, and led the postwar Court until his death on September 8, 1958, had served five years on the Court of Appeals, District of Columbia Circuit, then as director of Economic Stabilization and of War Mobilization and Reconversion, and later as secretary of the treasury. President Truman hoped that Vinson's appointment would bring harmony and respect to a badly divided court. Even though Stone had been a great judge, he proved to be a poor administrator of the Court's business and an ineffective mediator of opposing views. During the 1945 term, dissents had been filed in over half of the opinions announced by the Court. Before Vinson's appointment, rumors circulated that Black and Murphy had threatened to resign if Truman should honor Roosevelt's pledge to appoint Jackson chief justice. Jackson publicly exploded about the Black and Murphy opposition to his elevation; and while the Senate was considering Vinson's nomination, he sent a wire to the Senate Judiciary Committee alluding to Black's role in the *Jewell Ridge* case and criticizing certain judges for hearing cases in which they held personal interests. This affair served to worsen the divisions in a Court that was torn by some of the most bitter conflicts of its history. Some minority justices considered Douglas to be motivated by political ambitions and inattentive to his work on the Court. They regarded Murphy and Rutledge as being overly influenced by their liberal ideologies and Black as being an intellectual and powerful, yet willful, populist. Civil libertarian justices regarded Frankfurter as a "puffed up" professor who delivered lengthy lectures to the Court and the public before getting on with business. They complained that Jackson was tough-minded but overly fond of judicial nonintervention, as reflected in his observation that the Court's decisions in the 1930s were self-inflicted wounds. Furthermore, the antagonism growing out of his absence at the War Crimes Trials in Nuremburg, which some regarded as inappropriate, was still evident among the justices. They did, however, manage to maintain a certain degree of cordiality.[1]

The Court at this time lay in a passive mood in regard to the number of decisions and public interest in the cases before it. By 1946, several of the most historically provocative issues had been decided and liquidated. Commerce, taxing power, and states' rights issues had been laid to rest in favor of national power during the Roosevelt period. Additionally, the postwar period seemed to be another return to normalcy, with Congress passing little legislation that raised important constitutional issues. However, there remained the unfinished business of the Roosevelt Court, the question of the extent of civil liberties protection under the Constitution, the issue of subversion in the cold war period, and the problem of civil rights spotlighted by the new international role of the United States. In addition, the controversy over federal aid to private parochial schools came to plague the Court. These issues were greatly challenging to Burton as he gained experience and sharpened his legal perspective.[2]

Burton's yearning for continuity and experience in the very inexperienced Court led to wide-ranging, long conversations with retired Chief Justice Charles Evans Hughes at his home in Northwest Washington. During Burton's visit to Hughes on October 12, 1946, the use of certiorari as an appropriate device for limiting the courts became a topic of discussion. Hughes explained his strongly held view of the need to limit the number of cases heard by the Court, adding that some justices, toward the close of his time on the Court, wanted to grant certiorari whenever they disagreed with the decisions of the lower courts, even when the cases had no major significance. At that time, according to Hughes, Justice Benjamin Cardozo thought that instead of a vote of only four, a majority should be required for the granting of certiorari, while Justice Willis VanDevanter even objected to the fact that the Court had committed itself to the rule of four. Burton, who thought more cases should be granted a hearing, persuaded Hughes to at least agree that more liberality was needed in granting certiorari from a court such as the court of claims, which had no reviewing court by statute. After spending a Sunday working on an analysis of the Court's history, Burton expressed an even greater sense of insecurity about the inexperience of the Court, concluding "that this was the first time since the Court had been in existence that it has been without someone of thirteen or more years of experience on it. (Except of course during the first thirteen years of the Court.)" However, he thought that it was somewhat reassuring to regard the Court as a continuous body of eighty-five members since 1789.[3]

During the next three terms, Burton, as junior justice, received few opportunities to display his opinion-writing talents. In at least eight cases of the highest social and legal importance, he voted with the majority but was not assigned to write an opinion. Of the twenty-nine other cases which were regarded as less important but not routine, he wrote some of the majority opinions and had a great influence in the result of the others. Out of the remaining routine cases decided by the Court came Burton's other majority opinions and dissents. His votes had generally followed those of Chief Justice Stone during his freshman term and followed those of Vinson during the next three terms.[4]

Even though this was a passive period in the Court's history, excitement enough and continued tensions among members of the Court persisted; and the process of decision indicated the development of Burton's and the other justices' views on major issues of law. Much of the important work of the Court was increasingly devoted to civil liberties cases, and the freedom of religion cases offered some of the most difficult issues for decision. During the 1946 term, when the Court was deciding a case involving the continuing Justice Department efforts to end the Mormon practice of polygamy through criminal sanctions, the four libertarians—Douglas, Murphy, Rutledge, and Black—who had voted as a bloc to grant certiorari, could not obtain a majority for reversal. Burton and Vinson were with the majority, Rutledge concurred, Black and Jackson were for reversal, and Murphy wrote an indignant dissent. As they discussed the case in conference in 1945, Stone, Frankfurter, Reed, and Burton were in favor of affirming the convictions on the basis of an earlier ruling on the scope of the Mann Act. Attempts to turn the four who had voted to grant certiorari into a majority foundered on the justices' different interpretations of the earlier case. Even the civil libertarians could not agree. Black thought the convictions should be reversed and the earlier case overruled; Murphy agreed with Black; Rutledge thought the earlier case was wrongly decided; and Douglas stated that he would probably join in overruling the earlier case. Since the case had to be held over for reargument, Jackson had returned from Europe by the time a decision was reached. He was in agreement with Black that the convictions should be reversed but felt that the earlier case should be held to its facts and not extended. When Jackson refused to go along with reversing the earlier case, Douglas switched sides, for there was no one to join him in overruling it. In order to hold his vote, the chief assigned him the task of writing the opinion. If Jackson, Black, Douglas, Rutledge, and Murphy had comprised the majority, the earlier case would have been overruled and the polygamous defendants acquitted. The four libertarians had enough votes to grant certiorari, but they could not get a majority in the final voting.[5]

Burton played a significant role in the Court's decisions in four other cases involving religious freedom: *Ballard* v. *United States* and *Everson* v. *United States* in the 1946 term, and *Cox* v. *United States* and *McCollum* v. *Board of Education* in the 1947 term. In the *Ballard* case the defendants, members of the "I am" sect, had been indicted for using the mails in order to defraud unsuspecting believers of contributions, in the course of making false claims about their religion. The Court had already reversed and remanded the case to the Court of Appeals in 1944. The reversal in 1944 occurred because the Court of Appeals had ruled that the trial judge should instruct the jury not to decide on the truthfulness of the religious beliefs involved but to consider subjectively whether an honest belief in miracles required acquittal. A new trial was then held using the subjective test; and the defendants were convicted, thus beginning the appellate procedure again. In the meantime, the Supreme Court's personnel had changed without a change in voting pattern. Stone and Roberts were replaced in fact and in voting behavior by Vinson and Burton.[6]

In the second hearing, however, the majority followed the typical Supreme Court practice of avoiding constitutional issues, if possible, and reversed on the statutory ground that women had been systematically excluded from juries in California at the time of the original indictment and trial. Vinson, Burton, and Frankfurter dissented. In December, Frankfurter shared with Burton his view that "it is always a little arrogant to be confident of what the great dead would think about a situation, but I have not the slightest doubt that Holmes, Brandeis and Cardozo would say 'Amen' to your refutation of the claim that exclusion of the women . . . was fatal to the indictment and verdict." Frankfurter discarded his separate dissent and joined Burton after the majority refused to respond to his challenge that they should resolve the First Amendment issue. Burton was not opposed to the service of women on juries, but he thought that not requiring women to sit was truly nondiscriminatory since it meant that men and women were equally qualified and interchangeable. Besides, he was hostile to the defendants and would have voted against them on the religious freedom issue since he thought that the case involved ". . . a fake belief in religion which was a disservice to religion." Douglas, however, in the majority opinion asserted that "if the shoe were on the other foot, who would claim that a jury was truly representative of the community if all men were intentionally and systematically excluded from the panel?" Frankfurter, in encouraging Burton to file his own dissent, said that although he recognized that "superfluous opinions were superfluous," he was not one of those who had a "queasy feeling" about many opinions. It was "within the old tradition of the court" and practiced by judges of "great stature." Again and again, Holmes and Brandeis, and following them, Cardozo and Stone, although on the same side of a case, joined in one another's opinions on "separate grounds." He believed this added to "the strength of the court rather than to its weakness." Although Burton probably had no delusions of such greatness, he sent his opinion off to the printer.[7]

The Jehovah's Witnesses, the religious minority who had been most often before the Court in the 1940s, gained solid support from the civil libertarians in the Court in the 1947 term in the *Cox* selective service case. The Court had previously announced that habeas corpus was available not only after conviction for refusing to report under the World War II draft statute but also after induction. According to this doctrine, the Jehovah's Witnesses had to submit to induction before raising their claims to exemption on the basis of religion. In *Cox*, the Court, in reviewing the convictions of some Jehovah's Witnesses for being absent without leave from a civilian public service camp in violation of the Selective Service Act, rejected their claim that they were ministers and not conscientious objectors. Reed's majority opinion was joined by Vinson, Burton, and Jackson, who commented in conference that he considered the Witnesses a "nuisance" but that the issue was a plain question of statutory construction; and if construed strictly, they were guilty. Black and Douglas had voted to deny certiorari because they knew that Reed, Vinson, Jackson, Burton, and Frankfurter would affirm the convictions and extend a doctrine unfavorable to the Witnesses. Once certiorari was granted, they voted to reverse, along with Murphy. To Burton it was a case in which a claim to religious freedom had to be rejected in the interest of preserving congressional authority to raise manpower in time of war.[8]

During the 1947 term, Burton's most significant service, aside from writing his opinions, was his persuasive role in influencing the Court's opinions in *McCollum*, the religious freedom, released-time case. When the Court had decided during the 1946 term in *Everson v. United States* that it was constitutional for the state of New Jersey to pay for school bus transportation for parochial school children, Jackson, Burton, Frankfurter, and Rutledge had dissented from Black's opinion for the majority. Rutledge had predicted in the conference on *Everson* that "once [the] door is open no telling where it will end—texts, transportation, next will be lunches. . . . [W]e can't draw a line between a little and a lot—[it's just] like pregnancy."

In *McCollum*, the issue was whether Champaign, Illinois, school buildings could be used for religious education in conjunction with a system of compulsory school attendance. The Champaign school teachers distributed cards on which parents could designate the religious course, if any, they desired their children to attend. Classes were held in the school buildings once a week by religious instructors who were not paid by the state; but attendance in these classes was compulsory, in accordance with the parents' wishes. Those children whose parents preferred that they not have religious education participated in required secular education at the same time. The Court reached its decision only with great difficulty and controversy, displaying an indecisiveness which forecast Court approval of released time outside of school buildings. Such approval came during the 1951 term. When *McCollum* was first discussed, it was obvious that a majority favored invalidating the Illinois practice as an infringement of the First Amendment Establishment Clause, but for different reasons. Reed, the only one who voted to affirm in conference, stated his opinion that there were fewer advantages to the Illinois schools than in *Everson*. Frankfurter commented that he felt *Everson* did not stand in the way of reversal in this case but that it was insufficient merely to say that the state should remain neutral on this issue, as was done in *Everson*. He believed that here the Court had to face the fact that "the impulse of [the] movement" for aid to education came from Protestants and not from a Catholic minority, as in *Everson*. Jackson indicated he would reverse but wanted *Everson* overruled due to the conflict between the two cases. To Jackson, a reversal in this case without overruling *Everson* would "cut the protestants out of school at the [same] time [that] we are paying for Catholic school buses." Murphy passed, with Burton, Rutledge, Douglas, Vinson, and Black voting to reverse.[9]

Because he had written the *Everson* opinion, Black received the assignment to write for the majority in *McCollum*. After Black circulated a draft, it became clear that only Vinson and Douglas would support his opinion, in which he reaffirmed *Everson* and at the same time invalidated the Illinois practice of using school buildings for religious instruction. Frankfurter, Jackson, Burton, and Rutledge, who remained unhappy with *Everson*, still advocated overruling it. However, Jackson wanted to write a separate opinion discussing the jurisdictional isssue of whether the complainants had standing to sue. He wanted to narrow the decision procedurally in order to bar innumerable suits over church-state issues. Murphy insisted upon writing his own separate opinion concurring with Black.[10]

Burton, in rejecting the advice of his clerk, told him that the decision should be affirmed because "released time is OK where school buildings are not used, etc. To use the school building for it [released time] is a question of local policy and use of public property for rent or not, [for] an extra day or [for] extra space, is not the same constitutional question as is released time for instruction in church." After Burton had seen Black's opinion, he wrote to Black on January 4, 1948, that he would wait to commit himself until he had read any concurring opinions. In the draft of the letter to Black, Burton wrote the view that "I hope something can be put into the opinion of the Court that will make it clear that in passing upon the facts of this case no opinion is expressed upon the constitutionality of . . . released time . . . as is contained in the New York statutes." Black replied on January 6 that he would welcome any suggestions regarding the opinion he had written and that

having been assigned the job of writing for the Court, I shall do what I can to reconcile the views of those who agree that the case should be reversed. In this delicate field it would seem wise to have a Court opinion if possible, although some views expressed at the conference indicated that accomplishment of such an objective might be difficult. Of course, it cannot be done if the parochial school issue [*Everson*] is injected into the different issue here [ ]

On the same day, Frankfurter asked those who had dissented in *Everson* to meet for an exchange of views. After the meeting, Frankfurter proceeded to write his own concurrence with Black's views, which he circulated only to those "Anti-McCollum lads" who had opposed Black's suggested support of *Everson*. He indicated that he wanted the "Anti-McCollum lads" to be "as free as the freest bird" in making suggestions which would then enable him to speak for four. In accepting Burton's comments, Frankfurter told Burton that he was quite willing to adjust the opinion, for he was willing to be "as free from any pride of authorship as the great object we have calls for." However, Reed responded that Frankfurter's concurrence was so prohibitive that it cast doubt on the constitutionality of the New York released-time statute, in which the instruction took place outside the classroom.[12] Reed's observation was correct; Frankfurter was also opposed to tax-supported released-time programs outside of the schools.

Burton was as disturbed as Black by the prospect of there being four different opinions with no Court opinion in such an important and delicate case. He was more interested in resolving that problem than he was in Frankfurter's efforts to overrule the opinion in *Everson*. After reading the various opinions, Burton decided to work for at least a majority of seven, which would be a true opinion of the Court, by suggesting changes in Frankfurter's and Black's opinion. If seven could agree with the changes, Burton believed the remaining Jackson concurrence, with a separate opinion on the standing issue, and Reed's dissent would leave a much more favorable public image of the Court as an institution and of the law. Burton was mindful of the barrage of public criticism of the Court and the letters that had greeted his opposition to aid to parochial schools in *Everson*. On February 6, 1948, he suggested to Black that he omit from his opinion all specific discussion of *Everson*; and he asked Frankfurter to delete several references to the validity of the dissent in *Everson*. In addition to writing, Burton talked to Black and Rutledge, Jackson, and then Frankfurter several times in the next few days.[13]

Despite Burton's efforts, the road to reconciliation was a difficult one. Although he agreed to make the changes Burton suggested, Frankfurter sent a memorandum to the conference on February 11, 1948, which hampered Burton's efforts. Concern about the number of opinions in a case was never a value which Frankfurter held dear. His frequent dissents, concurrences, and separate opinions expressed his preference even for opinions written seriatim. Said Frankfurter in the memo:

In as much as contemporaneous candor often forestalls later misunderstanding, I deem it important to make explicit my position in regard to the *Everson* case. In deference to the views of others who believe that it is desirable to secure a Court opinion in *McCollum*, even though this is to be had by omitting all reference to the *Everson* decision, in the Court's opinion [in] *McCollum*, I am prepared to delete all references to *Everson* in my concurring opinion. But since time has only confirmed my conviction that the decision in *Everson* was wrong and mischief breeding, and since I attach great importance to the constitutional questions involved, I desire to make it a matter of record that I do not deem myself in the slightest foreclosed by that decision should the issue again come before us.

Black, in interpreting Frankfurter's memo to mean that he would not agree to any opinion in *McCollum* which made reference to Black's opinion in *Everson*, drafted his own memo to the conference stating:

I will not agree to any opinion in the McCollum case which does not make reference to the Everson case. Time has confirmed my conviction that the decision in the Everson case was right, and since I attach great importance to the constitutional questions involved, I desire to supplement the record made by Justice Frankfurter by stating this fact. Of course there is nothing unusual about one who entertains the belief that the views opposite to his are mischief breeding.[14]

At that point, Frankfurter explained to Burton that his memo, which brought forth Black's indignant reply, was sent to the conference because after he had agreed to remain silent about *Everson*, he had read Jackson's concurrence, which gave so much support to *Everson* that he could not remain silent. Frankfurter commented that he would abide by his agreement with Burton but believed he must circulate the memorandum to avoid "all future misunderstanding since I do not have in everyone the same confidence that I have in you." Whatever Frankfurter's reasons and despite his attempted flattery, Burton's efforts seemed to have been partially aborted. Black wrote to Burton and Rutledge that further consideration of Burton's plan now seemed "futile," for apparently only five members were willing to agree on any opinion which decided the case on the basis of *Everson*. Black was not willing "to repudiate them [his earlier views in *Everson*] expressly or by failure to refer to them." To Black, it was better to let the case go down, and "any who desire to continue the school bus fight in this case should do so in filed opinions." However, Rutledge told Burton that "I hope you'll not give up or lose hope about *Everson*. These tempers flash too fast. But often they cool after the flash." Rutledge felt there was still a chance to obtain a majority of seven; and if not, five would join in the opinion of the Court despite the controversy.[15]

As a final effort, Burton told Rutledge that he would ask Black and Frankfurter to omit sufficient language from their opinions to make it possible for him and Rutledge to join both without appearing inconsistent. Upon his request, Frankfurter agreed to delete "We venture to express the hope that this decision may check any encouragement that may have been drawn from the decision in *Everson* v. *Board of Education*." Black also consented to omit "In the *Everson* case the Court was of the opinion that New Jersey contributed no money to church schools, that it did not support them, and that, in fact, it did no more than provide a general program to help parents get their children, regardless of religion, safely and expeditiously to and from accredited schools.'' From the beginning Burton cautioned Black and Frankfurter to avoid jeopardizing the issue of released time outside of school buildings, or he would not join them. Both assured him that they had left the way open to approve the New York plan, although Reed believed that Frankfurter had not. Burton carefully examined both opinions in that regard and found them acceptable. Since he succeeded in marshaling five justices to join in Black's opinion, which at first would only have been joined by two with no Court opinion resulting, Burton's efforts were partially successful. After the opinions were settled, Rutledge extended his "congratulations on a fine job."[16]

In criminal cases, the Vinson Court majority, of which Burton was a member, usually refused to reverse convictions, while Murphy, Rutledge, Black, and Douglas usually dissented. In the *Adamson* case, Reed sustained the constitutionality of California's rule permitting a jury to draw inferences from a defendant's failure to testify rather than a claim that it violated the Fourteenth Amendment. This decision was in conformity with the Court's unwillingness to break new ground on the issues. In separate opinions, Black and Frankfurter engaged in a great debate over the appropriate judicial function in such cases. However, the civil liberties revival of the 1960s was yet in the future, and the Court majority still viewed negatively appeals to the Fourteenth Amendment due process clause by state criminal defendants.

Aside from *Adamson*, while denying certiorari in *Barnes* v. *New York,* the Court's majority, including Burton, demonstrated their continued attachment to a state's right to conduct its police functions without interference. A black petitioner was convicted of murdering a white woman in the course of a rape and was sentenced to life imprisonment on the basis of oral and written confessions which were made to police but repudiated at the trial. During the three days which passed between arrest and arraignment, the petitioner claimed that he was beaten, struck, and called names repeatedly and that he was not permitted to see friends or advisers. At the trial, the jury was instructed to disregard the confessions if they believed them to be extorted. Burton believed that although "factually there may be a deprivation of due process, . . . we can't get to it," since the case was decided on an adequate state procedural ground.[17]

When Rutledge, Murphy, Douglas, and Black voted as a bloc to grant certiorari in *Bute* v. *Illinois*, the Court's majority (in a Burton opinion) repelled another assault on their view of the extent of due process. The right to counsel, they asserted, was not a general constitutional prerequisite to a fair trial in a state criminal proceeding. After Burton wrote his first draft in the case and circulated it, Frankfurter asked "whether this was one of those instances where a deep division in the Court is not allayed but intensified by [conclusiveness] of treatment." Although he knew that Vinson had suggested Burton's "fulldress treatment of the case," he was concerned about exacerbating the feelings of Murphy, Rutledge, Black, and Douglas. After the dissenting opinion was circulated, however, Frankfurter changed his position and asked Burton to state "explicitly and perhaps more than once that the Bill of Rights laid down for federal courts [held] not merely general standards of fair dealing and justice but also some technical procedural requirements," and also that "it does not mean that it is the kind of right that the Constitution asked the states to afford. He wanted explicitness in view of what he regarded as "the irresponsible utterances in dissent."[18]

However, the Court did make exceptions in some criminal due process cases. In *Wade* v. *Mayo*, a habeas corpus case, Frankfurter joined the four *Bute* dissenters in Murphy's majority opinion, which upheld the principle that there was a right to counsel in a noncapital case of a defendant who by reason of age, ignorance, or mental capacity was incapable of representing himself adequately in even a simple case. Joined by Vinson, Jackson, and Burton, Reed dissented, primarily because the defendants failed to exhaust state remedies, including obtaining a writ of certiorari from the Supreme Court before gaining a writ of habeas corpus in federal district court. In conference, Frankfurter had agreed; but he was drawn toward the dissenters after deciding that the procedural distinction of exhaustion of state remedies was invalid. Another exception was made in the right to counsel case *Townsend* v. *Burke*. Over the opposition of the chief justice, Reed, Burton, and Jackson joined Frankfurter and the liberals to upset a conviction for burglary on due process grounds. In the absence of counsel, and while the sentence was being determined, the prosecution had submitted misinformation regarding the defendant's prior record. During the 1948 term, Burton dissented from exceptions made by a majority in a Reed opinion in *Uveges* v. *Pennsylvania* and in a Frankfurter opinion in *Turner* v. *Pennsylvania*, which reversed convictions obtained without benefit of counsel in state courts.[19]

In the 1947 term, Burton wrote the dissenting opinion in one coerced confession case, *Haley* v. *Ohio*, and the opinion for the majority in another, *Taylor* v. *Alabama*. In *Haley*, Douglas, in a majority opinion which was joined by Black, Murphy, and Rutledge, reversed the murder conviction of a fifteen-year-old boy who was questioned for five hours without benefit of counsel or friends. Douglas ruled a confession the youth had signed inadmissible on Fourteenth Amendment due process grounds in an opinion which Frankfurter joined. Vinson, Reed, and Jackson concurred in Burton's dissent, which relied heavily upon a deep faith in the abilities of trial judges, juries, and the police.[20]

On the petition for certiorari, Rutledge, Murphy, Black, and Frankfurter had voted to grant; and the remainder, including Douglas, who wrote the majority opinion, and Burton, who dissented, voted to deny. Burton's clerk had recommended that he vote to grant certiorari since even though there were "difficulties and dangers" when the Supreme Court tried to supervise criminal procedure in the states, "the 14th Amendment has, however, imposed that task upon the Court. It cannot be avoided—the only question is where the line of due process should be drawn." Burton responded that three and one half hours of police questioning was not unreasonable; and additionally, the Court "should not assume 'violence' or 'infringement' of rights on the part of the police." He also added that juries, being close to the fact situation, were in a better position to judge the validity of the confession.[21]

When in another coerced confession case, *Lee* v. *Mississippi*, Murphy reversed the conviction of a seventeen-year-old black defendant who had been convicted of assault with intent to "ravish a white female of previous chaste character," Burton first voted to affirm and then changed his mind when everyone else on the Court voted to reverse. In *Taylor* v. *Alabama*, Burton, writing comfortably for the majority, upheld the action of the Supreme Court of Alabama in denying permission for a petitioner in a capital rape case to file a petition for review by the trial court of its previously affirmed judgment of guilty. The Court found that this action did not deprive the petitioner of due process of law. Murphy dissented. While Burton seemed unpersuaded of coercion in the light of police testimony and the trial court's view of the facts, Murphy believed that the evidence was sufficient to at least require a new hearing to resolve the issue. He also pointed out the availability of habeas corpus to the prisoner. Black took no part in the case. On the petition for certiorari, Burton, Reed, Murphy, Douglas, and Rutledge had voted to grant; Black had passed; and the remainder had voted to deny. Again in the 1948 term, Burton characteristically joined Vinson and Jackson in Reed's dissent when, in *Upshaw* v. *United States*, the Court held that a confession obtained during a thirty-hour period of arrest could not be used in federal court whether or not it had been obtained by coercion. Reed expressed the minority view that the majority decision was an ill-advised interference with the "maintenance of law and order."[22]

*In re Oliver* found Burton relenting from his hostility to due process claims. In this case the Court, in a majority opinion written by Black, with Frankfurter and Jackson dissenting, reversed a contempt conviction which was decided under the Michigan one-man grand jury system. The entire proceeding took place in private with the public excluded and with the defendant having no opportunity to seek the aid of friends or counsel. In his opinion, Black condemned the practice of secret trials as contrary and obnoxious to American ideas of due process. Only Rutledge, Murphy, Douglas, and Black had voted to grant certiorari. Although they had voted to deny certiorari, Burton, Reed, and Vinson voted with the liberal majority in the final decision. They were persuaded that even the most limited view of fair procedure precluded secret trials.[23]

But in search and seizure cases during the 1946 term, the Court's majority refused to change its permissive posture. The Court sanctioned the complete ransacking of a man's house, a so-called incidental search, by police without a warrant during an arrest. The Vinson majority opinion was supported by Burton along with Black, Douglas, and Reed. In the 1947 term, the Court considered, in *Trupiano* v. *United States*, a case in which government agents without warrants arrested the operators of an illegal still and seized their still and equipment. Since the raid had long been in the planning stage and a government operative had been posing as a member of the criminal gang, there had been ample time in which to obtain search warrants. In Murphy's opinion, the Court approved the arrests because the crime was clearly a felony but rejected the legality of the seizure, even though the objects were in plain sight, because no warrant had been obtained. Vinson dissented, and was joined by Black, Reed, and Burton.

Burton's position drew strong objections from his first clerk, Howard Mann, who was teaching at the Indiana Law School. He wrote to Burton that the "majority position in the Harris case . . . and the minority's position in the recent case would very effectively delete altogether the Search and Seizure Amendment from the Constitution." He thought that making an illegal search legal, based on the officers' after-the-fact validation, would mean "that it was all right to make unconstitutional investigations of one's private affairs if the officers are successful in the search." Mann did not understand that to Burton his decision was a matter of supporting order and the police within a narrow interpretation of constitutional demands which permitted him to support almost any but the most outrageous police practices.[24]

In the 1948 term, Burton, as part of the majority, voted against the defendants in each of four cases involving search-and-seizure issues. In the most important case, *Wolf* v. *Colorado*, the Court, through Frankfurter and with Black concurring, decided that evidence illegally seized by a state could be admitted at trial, although under a federal court such evidence would be inadmissible. Some portions of the search-and-seizure prohibition applied to the state, but persons victimized by police must resort "to the remedies of private action and such protection as the internal discipline of the police under the eyes of an alert public opinion may afford." Dissenting were Douglas, Murphy, and Rutledge who, along with Black, had voted to grant certiorari. In conference, Black passed but stated he would favor expansion of the Fourteenth Amendment to prohibit this type of search and seizure. Frankfurter commented that he agreed with Black that search and seizure "go to the heart of liberty"; but based on the states' right to determine remedies as well as the similarity of English and New Zealand law on the matter, he would leave the remedy to the states.[25]

The other search-and-seizure cases proved easier to resolve. When, on the basis of a 1925 decision, the Court permitted the warrantless search of a person who was attempting to escape from government agents in an automobile, Jackson, joined by Frankfurter and Murphy, dissented. However, Burton concurred, pointing out that even if probable cause did not exist until after government agents had stopped the petitioner's car and had asked him to state the amount of liquor he held, this was probable cause enough. In another case, the Court deemed illegal a search in which the police, without a warrant, sneaked into a house through a window and seized the implements a defendant was using in connection with playing "numbers" because they had actually seen the items. Although the defendant had been under observation for two months, no reason was even suggested for the absence of a warrant. Joined by Vinson and Reed, Burton dissented from Douglas's opinion; they believed it was a case of seizure incident to a lawful arrest for a crime committed in the presence of the officers. Burton considered the hallway outside the convicted person's room, from which the police had, after knocking, gained further view of the illegal implements, part of a public rooming house rather than part of a private dwelling. Therefore, the police did not actually enter until they arrived at the defendant's room.[26]

Burton, adamant in his support of lower court criminal decisions, objected when the Court, in a Black opinion in *Krulewitch* v. *United States*, reversed the conviction of a man for inducing a woman, the complaining witness, to go from New York to Florida for the purpose of prostitution. The majority held that the evidence admitted concerning a statement about the prostitution, made by the co-conspirator to the complaining witness more than six weeks after the transportation was completed, was not harmless error. Burton felt so strongly that he dissented alone on the grounds that "the evidence supporting the jury's verdict was cumulative, repetitive and corroborated to such a point that I cannot believe that the verdict or the right of the parties could have been appreciably affected by such weight as the jury may have attached to this reported snatch of conversation between two people of such negligible dependability as was demonstrated here."[27]

A sensational exception to Burton's support of police authority in criminal cases found Frankfurter struggling unsuccessfully during the 1946 term to persuade Burton to vote with the majority. In the case of *Louisiana ex rel. Francis* v.*Resweber*, equipment in a Louisiana prison malfunctioned, and a new death warrant was issued. Burton claimed that reexecution would constitute a denial of due process based on the double jeopardy provision of the Fifth Amendment and the cruel and unusual punishment provision of the Eighth Amendment. Reed's majority opinion denying the petitioner's appeal was joined by Vinson, Black, and Jackson. Concurring, with a discursive lecture on due process and the Fourteenth Amendment, Frankfurter made it clear that he was "strongly drawn" to Burton's dissenting view but did not want to enforce his "private view rather than that consensus of society's opinion which, for purposes of due process, is the standard enjoined by the Constitution."[28]

Of course, Frankfurter's comment might be taken to mean that Murphy, Rutledge, and Douglas, who joined in Burton's dissent, were imposing their "private view" rather than exercising restraint, as had Frankfurter. Murphy and Rutledge had prepared dissents but discarded them in order to join Douglas in Burton's dissent as the unexpected "participant's protest." Burton was offended by the majority's idea that as many applications of electrical current as necessary could be made, and still there would be no cruel and unusual punishment. One more was enough for him. He preferred asking the Louisiana courts to reexamine the facts and to resolve the issue of whether their statute permitted repeated electrocutions rather than leaving the whole matter up to the discretion of prison administrative officials.[29]

While the *Willie Francis* case was under consideration, considerable jockeying took place between Frankfurter and Burton, with Frankfurter attempting to persuade Burton to accept his point of view. Interestingly enough, Burton had strongly opposed granting certiorari in the first instance, for at that time he believed that it was a matter under state control, while Frankfurter felt strongly that the case was too important not to hear. However, after reading Burton's dissent, Frankfurter told him, "I have to hold on to myself not to reach your result." To underscore his feelings on the matter, Frankfurter sent Burton a copy of a letter he had written to Monte Lemonn, a Louisiana attorney, which encouraged Lemonn to persuade leading members of the bar to press for a grant of clemency in the case. Frankfurter wrote to Lemonn, "this case has been so heavily on my conscience that I finally could not overcome the impulse to write to you." Frankfurter was revolted by capital punishment. He repeatedly referred to his "agonizing" over the issue in an almost maudlin, self-righteous tone. But he stated to Burton that "all this is purely a state question beyond our purview." In conference, Frankfurter commented that there was a "need to say something, reexecution was hardly a defensible thing to do." In his opinion, the governor of the state, having done his duty, could exercise executive clemency, a course of action which Frankfurter must have known was unlikely in Louisiana in the case of a black defendant.[30] Burton was proud of his opinion in this case. He had thought he could ensnare a majority by appealing to Frankfurter's conscience, but he failed. He believed as strongly as Frankfurter that he had not based his opinion on any feeling about capital punishment or the standards for executive clemency but on his views of the scope of the due process and cruel and unusual punishment provisions in the Constitution. At first, Burton's law clerk was greatly excited by the prospect of an opportunity for *his* often-criticized justice to write a stirring dissent in a worthwhile case. The dissent was solitary at first; but as it gathered the support of three, and finally became the majority view, Burton and his clerk worked arduously on the opinion so that the constitutional theory on which it was based would withstand the long test of time as a leading decision.[31]

Some grist for the mill of understanding Burton's role in decision making was evident in the resolution of the other civil liberties cases during the three terms under discussion. In the contempt case of *Craig* v. *Harney*, they decided that a Texas court could not punish a publisher and employees of a newspaper for contempt as a result of their critical, and indeed unfair, comments upon a judge's handling of a trial. The Court felt that the publisher did not pose a "serious and imminent threat to the administration of justice." Burton voted with the majority; Vinson joined in Frankfurter's dissent; and Jackson dissented separately. Burton and his clerk believed that Frankfurter had never really reconciled himself to their majority decision in the *Pennekamp* case during the previous term, a decision which dictated the result in *Craig*. Frankfurter did not even mention the earlier case in his draft dissent.[32]

In *United States* v. *CIO*, a unanimous Court decided that labor unions could use union newspapers to exhort their members to desired political activity. The conference time in the case was devoted largely to Frankfurter's criticism of the inadequate time for consideration based on the fact that Vinson had passed instead of speaking first, as was the chief justice's usual role. If the case raised issues that Vinson, as chief, was not ready to discuss, Frankfurter suggested that the case should be held over until a later time. However, the other members were ready and decided to vote anyway.[33]

The utility of assigning the drafting of an opinion to a waverer was demonstrated when the Court, in *Winters* v. *New York*, considered the conviction of a book dealer for having in his possession, with intent to sell, magazines principally made up of criminal news, in violation of a New York statute. The majority found the statute to be void because of its vagueness under the Fourteenth Amendment due process clause. The Court vacillated during three separate arguments on the case. After the first argument on March 27, 1946, which was before Stone's death, Burton, Frankfurter, Reed, and Stone indicated they would affirm; and Rutledge, Murphy, Douglas, and Black would reverse. With Jackson absent, the decision below would stand. Therefore, they decided to hold the case over for reargument. By that time, Vinson had replaced Stone; three of the original four in favor of reversal were joined by Reed; and Douglas passed. The case was set down for reargument again, with only Rutledge, Douglas, Reed, and Black opposing. After the last reargument, when Rutledge, Murphy, Douglas, Reed, and Black voted to reverse, Reed was assigned to draft the opinion in order to hold him firm. After it was drafted, Vinson joined the majority in a 6-3 decision.[34]

Burton and the Court decided, with only Rutledge, Douglas, and Murphy dissenting, that Michigan could constitutionally protect the morals of women by excusing them from serving as bartenders unless they were the wives or daughters of male bar owners.[35] They also decided, in *Terminello* v. *Chicago*, that a right wing, anti-Semitic speaker (an associate of Gerald L. K. Smith) could not be convicted for breach of the peace when outsiders created a disturbance in opposition to his speech. Douglas's majority opinion gave constitutional protection to the speaker even when his speech invited rabid opposition. The trial judge's instruction to the jury that conviction was permitted if the speech stirred people to anger had not been objected to by the petitioner's attorney, a fact which formed the basis of Vinson's dissent and that of Frankfurter, Burton, and Jackson, who also dissented on the merits. In conference, Frankfurter had carefully explained to Vinson that "to note as error something not excepted to below and dismiss would be extreme error." Douglas initially said that he was "inclined to affirm in the setting of the speech . . . that was close to shouting 'fire' in a theatre," but he changed his mind. In another free speech case, *Kovacs* v. *Cooper*, the Court held valid a Trenton, New Jersey, prohibition of sound trucks. In the 1947 term, the Court had decided that if sound trucks were to be licensed, the procedure must be done on a nondiscriminatory basis; but it left undecided the right of a city to complete prohibition. The opinions went flying off in all directions; but Burton and Vinson finally joined Reed's three-man majority decision that total prohibition was probably unconstitutional but that in this case, the defendant had been guilty of making particularly raucous noise.[36]

Burton expressed his views concerning obscenity to his clerk when the Court considered a New York court's conviction of the Doubleday Company for publishing an obscene book, *Memoirs of Herate*. He believed that "obscenity is itself a statement of a standard that disgusts and offends the standards of decency of the country and time." The book under consideration

not only deals merely with sexual acts—but also shamelessly with adultery, not merely sophisticated—but with complete apparent disregard of the violations of criminal law and the law of domestic relations against adultery. The family is the most important unit of our social structure. This book brazenly not only condones, but to a degree it glorifies it [adultery].

He believed that New York should enforce its laws "to discourage the destruction of the family . . . and there is nothing in the Constitution that says that we must prevent her in this way." The decision was affirmed per curiam by a divided Court, with Burton voting for affirmation.[37]

The bulk of the important cases concerning race relations during the first three Vinson terms were decided during the 1947 term. The political setting in which the cases were decided was one in which Truman's legislative program "To Secure These Rights" for blacks had caused a revolt in his own party and had been killed quietly in Congress by the bipartisan opposition. Congress had recently passed a displaced persons act which discriminated against Jewish and Catholic immigrants, and the outlawing of the Communist party was being seriously considered. From the hindsight of the Warren Court, the Vinson Court might appear to be somewhat conservative; but at the time, its decisions were decidedly favorable toward civil rights.[38]

The Vinson Court decided several racial discrimination cases in favor of blacks and Japanese. By the early 1940s, the Court had outlawed some of the most glaring discriminations against blacks—physical torture, systematic exclusion from juries, and capital punishment without counsel. In addition to the necessity for further expansion of doctrines in crime-related areas, petitioners before the Court now demanded progress in such non-crime related areas as housing and education. The Court, including Burton, prohibited judicial enforcement of restrictive covenants in housing, held per curiam that a black person had a right to an equal law school education in Oklahoma, and held that a Michigan civil rights statute providing for equal access could be applied to a business transporting passengers from Detroit to Canada without regard to the power of Congress to regulate foreign commerce. The Court also held per curiam that a North Carolina black defendant was convicted unconstitutionally because blacks had been systematically excluded from the jury, and it unanimously reversed a murder conviction of a black male in Mississippi on the same grounds. Burton voted for the black petitioners in these cases.

Little disagreement was evident among the justices in conference on these cases. In *Bronson*, the North Carolina jury case, Black argued strongly that these issues should not still be coming before the Court in the light of their previous decisions. Upset at the continued pattern of discrimination, he asserted that even though

"This rule was announced 80 years ago—[it is] just getting to the point where there is a chance of [it] being carried out." Responding to Reed's statement that this case was clear discrimination "against Negroes as such," Frankfurter said he would affirm the conviction because he was not able to find anything in the record which "enables Reed to say *because* they are Negroes." When Reed retorted that the "percentage" was enough, Frankfurter insisted it was not enough to show that discrimination was "because" they were blacks. He added that he believed that in North Carolina, unlike the Mississippi case, there was no pattern of purposeful exclusion of blacks or particularly hostile discrimination. Jackson stated that he agreed with Vinson; but he thought the case should have been left without granting certiorari, for he could not see how one could decide not to affirm "without conflict with what has been said" in previous court decisions. He, along with Burton, Rutledge, Murphy, Douglas, Reed, and Black, voted to affirm. As Black suggested, the case was decided per curiam to emphasize their belief that the issues had been well settled long before and did not need a supporting opinion. They believed that states had been put on enough notice that racial discrimination would not be permitted in jury selection.[39]

Burton expressed his own civil rights views in discussing the *Patton* case with his clerk, who wanted to affirm the conviction. According to his clerk, the evidence from the record showed that blacks did not pay the poll tax required to be eligible for jury duty "because they were not interested enough to do so." He knew that the evidence in the record was taken from southerners and was "practically worthless"; but, he observed, "I suppose there is some sense in saying that a person who does not take a very keen interest in voting does not have enough interest in the judicial system of the county to qualify as a good juror." However, Burton objected that he did not think it provided equal protection or due process "to adopt any system that excludes economic or racial class or a party on a basis other than ability to perform duties."[40]

After the decision was announced in *Shelly* v. *Kramer*, the restrictive covenant case, Burton received a number of critical letters opposing his support of the majority position on the grounds that the Court was interfering with the right of white people not to be forced to live among blacks. One woman commented that the only solution to the problem was that "the Negro . . . has a country of his own," while another letter suggested that blacks build separate communities. Another comment came from a woman who said that "from your lofty pinnacle of financial security, there are a few of the higher type minorities who would be able to encroach on your territory, but in my money bracket there are millions who would not be desirable neighbors either from the standpoint of living habits or IQ." Burton responded to all inquiries with a careful statement of the constitutional requirements in the case.[41]

In addition to the cases dealing with discrimination against black people, the Court considered cases involving discrimination against Japanese Americans. Burton dissented from the majority and voted against the Japanese Americans in *Oyama* v. *California*, in which the Court invalidated a California statute which forbade "aliens ineligible for citizenship [Japanese]" from acquiring agricultural lands in that state. Reed, Burton, and Jackson believed that the answer to the problem in California was "to change the California statutes or more likely, do for the Japanese precisely what was done for the Chinese, change the federal rule of eligibility by [an] Act of Congress." In *Takahashi* v. *California,* Black wrote for the majority, including Burton, that a California statute which forbade fishing by aliens ineligible for citizenship was invalid. Dissenting, Jackson, who was joined by Reed, asserted that "any state that has power over real property could exclude any and all citizens from owning it." Joined by Rutledge, Murphy wrote a stinging concurrence, as he had done in the *Oyama* case, which primarily discussed the history of California's discrimination against the Japanese. Burton voted with the majority because he believed that a state might restrict land holding but could not totally exclude persons from the opportunity to earn a livelihood.[42]

The Court considered a few significant economic cases during the first three Vinson terms and was called upon to help settle the issues arising out of a threatened nationwide coal strike in November 1946. When John L. Lewis and the United Mine Workers (UMW) violated a temporary restraining order not to strike and were fined $10,000 and $3,500,000, respectively, the Court granted certiorari, bypassing the District of Columbia Court of Appeals in order to hear the case. The largest issues in the case were jurisdictional. The LaGuardia Act forbade the issuance of injunctions by federal courts in any case growing out of any labor dispute. Additionally, it was a well-settled equity rule that an order issued in violation of law need not be obeyed and that a party could not be punished for ignoring it. The Court's majority used two different theories to uphold the government: the first, that the coal miners were government employees by virtue of the nominal governmental seizure of the plant, and the act had nothing to do with strikes by government employees; the second, that the district court at least had before it the question of jurisdiction, which would permit it to decide whether or not it had jurisdiction. Since that issue was arguable, the parties could be expected to obey the temporary restraining order until it was decided.

The chief benefit of the conference and numerous recirculations of the opinions in the case was the reduction of the fine to seven hundred thousand dollars. While the conference was discussing the issue of fines, Vinson suggested that the case ought to be remanded to the district court for reassessment because everyone except him and Jackson thought the assessments were too large. But on February 3, Frankfurter wrote to Vinson, with a "private information" copy to Burton, that this would be a "deplorable" path to follow since "the controversy would again be opened with all the 'hullabaloo' that it would entail inside and outside District Court." He suggested that there was no difficulty in "cleaning up" the case once and for all because it was an equity proceeding which permitted flexibility. In his opinion, the Court itself could modify the fines without tossing the case back to the district court because that judge "has no better standards to apply than we have. . . . We lifted this case out of the Circuit Court of Appeals because of the exigencies of time and of public interest." Furthermore, sending it back would take time; and if appeals occurred from a new disposition in the district court, that time would be further extended, thus dangerously approaching the March deadline. Burton agreed with Frankfurter and opposed Vinson's effort to gain a remand.[43]

The other labor-relation cases during these three terms were decided without much difficulty. Included were three FLSA cases in which Burton, in writing the majority opinions, showed his hostility toward extending the coverage of the act to additional workers. However, during the 1948 term, of the five cases of greatest importance, three concerned *labor*. Burton wrote one of the opinions, and each was restrictive of labor organization practices. The cases grew out of state opposition to union efforts to force employers to fire employees who were not union members. In *Lincoln Federal Labor Union* v. *Northwestern Metal Co.*, the Court easily held valid a state statute which forbade "yellow dog" contracts in which workers pledged not to join a union and the closed shop. Burton joined in the Court's unanimous opinion. But in *Giboney* v. *Empire Storage Ice Co.,* the Court decision was difficult to reach. At issue was the legality of an injunction against unionized peddlers who picketed an ice company as part of an organizing campaign to force ice companies to sell only to union peddlers. The union's argument, in support of what was in effect a closed shop, was based on free speech, equal protection, and Thirteenth Amendment grounds.[44]

In the conference discussion, Vinson at first passed, commenting that he condoned peaceful picketing for lawful purposes but not for illegal purposes. Ultimately, he voted to affirm, stating that he believed the injunction was too broad; but to agree to "all picketing would be too much." His decision was motivated by the belief that use of pressure to compel the employer to comply with union wishes could be enjoined. Since he also thought it was too broad and that picketing required the same protection as speech, Black wanted to reverse the injunction. Reed agreed with Black. However, Frankfurter expressed a lack of understanding of Black's position because he could see no analogy between publishing and picketing. To him, the injunction was not too broad: the unions "can't bring this coercive pressure to bear—[we] don't have to wait to punish—[we] can enjoin." He announced that he would affirm on the basis of earlier case law. Douglas agreed with Black that picketing is a form of expression: "coercion does not spell the difference—every book is designed to (influence) coerece." But since he felt the question was not really coercion, he would tentatively reverse, along with Murphy and Rutledge, who were also uncertain. Voting to affirm, Jackson was persuaded that the unions were undermining the enforcement of a state statute. At this point,

Black interjected that he could not agree with Frankfurter that earlier cases applied here, to which Frankfurter responded by suggesting an earlier case that was against Black's position. Expressing his decision to affirm, Burton added that he felt the picketing was a restriction of trade in violation of state law and that such coercion could be enjoined. Black responded that he did not want their conclusion to be based on coercion because he did not believe that coercion had taken place. After their positions were fully aired, the justices unanimously decided to uphold the injunction.[45]

In another labor case, *National Labor Relations Board* v. *Crompton Highland Mills, Inc.*, Burton's opinion for a unanimous Court found that an employer had violated the National Labor Relations Act when, without consulting the union, he put into effect a substantially greater wage increase applicable to most of the employees represented in union negotiations that had broken down.[46] Burton rejected a suggestion by Jackson, who joined the opinion that the appendixes containing the board order should not be printed "in view of the persistent complaint of the bar that it is required to buy so much printed matter." Murphy liked the first part of Burton's opinion, but he had "misgivings" about the second part. He thought that the board affirmative order that notices be posted "would seem an essential way to inform employees that the management has been found guilty of the unfair practice." Burton considered both suggestions but let the opinion go down as it stood.[47]

A number of important antitrust cases were decided during these three terms. Many members of the Court demonstrated that they still had populist tendencies toward encouraging small business and discouraging large corporations, despite the fact that it was a time when business concentration was ever increasing. However, those opposed to this concentration still seemed to think in terms of finding offenders guilty even though the convictions might have minimal or no antitrust effect. Burton's position in antitrust cases was based, generally, on his background as a corporation lawyer and his conservative Republican philosophy. He found no reason to fear or morally judge economic concentration; and his support of the enforcement of antitrust acts was directed at encouraging, rather than discouraging, big business.

During the 1946 term, Burton's most important opinion was in a major antitrust case, *United States* v. *National Lead*, in which the primary issue concerned the contents of the lower court's decree. In 1920, National Lead had entered into a cartel with a foreign corporation in order to pool patents, divide the world market, and abstain from competition in titanium pigments used in the manufacture of paints, rubber, glass, paper, and many other products. The DuPont Company, also a defendant in the case, had entered the field by 1933 and had become a somewhat qualified member of the cartel. By 1943, through the extensive use of patents which were practically immunized from challenge by the agreement, the American defendants, National Lead and DuPont, had gained control of well over 90 percent of the basic types of titanium trade in the field, which included two other concerns.[48]

The principal issue before the Supreme Court was a provision of the decree requiring the defendants to license the use of their patents with a reasonable royalty to whoever desired them. However, the government and National Lead sought royalty-free licenses instead. The Court, in Burton's opinion, approved the decree written by the district judge as being within his sound discretion. Douglas dissented in part, while Murphy and Rutledge argued that royalty continuance gave the offenders a practical advantage in their long conspiracy and that the price situation was such that the allowance of any royalty would give the licenser (who, of course, would be free of payments) an undue advantage over possible competitors. Black and Jackson disqualified themselves because of personal financial interests in the outcome of the case.

Burton believed that the Court was severely limited by the failure of the government to offer factual proof supporting the idea that royalty-free licensing would really have the desired antitrust economic effect. Instead, the government spent all of its energy proving the guilt of the defendants, even though judgment of guilt in a modern antitrust case had little effect on a defendant as long as it involved no loss in revenue. In any case, the effect of royalty-free licensing would have benefited National Lead, because National Lead still needed DuPont patents, while DuPont had moved technologically beyond using National Lead patents. National Lead was, of course, the party that started the cartel and was therefore in no position to claim innocence. The main antitrust effect of the decision, which could not have been easily avoided, was to give DuPont even more market power and to injure National Lead. Douglas dissented; but even in his discussion of divestiture as a possible remedy, he did not indicate that it should have been used in this case. Rather, he limited his holding to royalty-free licensing.

Burton and one of his clerks had great difficulty wading through all the briefs in the case but had little difficulty obtaining a majority in support of the decree. However, once the opinion had been handed down and was being prepared for publication, two minor problems occurred. The acting solicitor general objected to Burton's statement in the slip opinion that: "existing precedents of divestiture provide examples of the restoration of a pre-existing separate status to companies or properties which have been unlawfully combined rather than to the fission of units which never have been separated." He thought that this was a more restrictive rule respecting divestiture and that it would "materially affect" pending antitrust cases since it might lead district courts to believe that "where there has been unlawful combination, it can only be broken up into the units from which it was formed." He suggested that Burton change the offending passage to read: "existing precedents of divestiture provide examples of relief of this nature where the defendants have unlawfully combined or acquired companies or properties which had previously been independent."[49]

After reading the solicitor general's letter, Burton noted that the statement was borrowed from an expression used by the trial judge. He thought that counsel for the opposing parties would not concur in the modification and that his own inclination was to either let it stand or omit the sentence and accompanying citations altogether. However, he asked his clerk to look into the authorities and to comment. After his clerk had researched the points and authorities, Burton recommended that the language be deleted, "not because it misstates what the existing cases seem to indicate the law is; nor because the authorities used to support it are miscited—but because it is a gratuitous statement, not necessary to the decision; and the problem as I have tried to indicate above is difficult of solution." He added that by leaving it out, since it was unnecessary anyway, they might save the Court "some future trouble in trying to explain the language or construe it in a manner to get harmony out of the decision." Burton then suggested to the Court that he be permitted to omit the language in order to allay the solicitor general's fears, and the conference gladly agreed.[50]

During the 1947 term Burton wrote, in an antitrust case, what he regarded as his most important opinion since joining the Court. *United States* v. *U.S. Gypsum Co.* and *United States* v. *Line Material* both involved patent licensing agreements connected with price fixing which, it was charged, resulted in unreasonable restraint of trade. Both defendants' convictions were upheld; but in *Gypsum*, a unanimous Court found a violation because the license was a mere subterfuge for price fixing which otherwise would have amounted to an unreasonable restraint in violation of the Sherman Act. In *Line Material*, when Black, Douglas, Murphy, and Rutledge concurred in Reed's majority opinion, Burton dissented. While it was written as a dissent on behalf of three justices, he believed it "amounted to much more, . . . because there were but eight Justices sitting in the case and it gave us an evenly divided Court on the underlying issues."[51]

While the opinions were being prepared in the two cases, Frankfurter, Reed, and Burton engaged in long consultations on fashioning the Reed opinion and the Burton dissent. Frankfurter and Burton discussed at length the difference between the terms *monopoly* and *patent monopoly*, and Frankfurter suggested to Burton articles and books on the subject. After Frankfurter had spent much time on Reed's opinion, he made some suggestions to Reed. One was that Reed delete the discussion of the district judge's opinion, for Frankfurter thought that the district judge

will be lucky if the Court does not animadvert upon what I regard as one of the most incompetent and wasteful uses of judicial time of which I have knowlege. Four and a half years were consumed by this litigation (I do not know how much of it continuous) and apparently two years were required to concoct about as indefensible an opinion as has come before the Court since I have been here.

Additionally, he criticized Reed for characterizing an important earlier case in a manner which "I think Harold [Burton] demonstrates is not correct." Apparently, Reed accepted these suggestions. Frankfurter, having had his input, was then satisfied with both opinions and told Burton that his opinion was written with "thoroughness" and "care" and that "not the least important service you have rendered by this massive piece of work—massive in labor—is to spell out clearly and effectively our patent law policy, and the constitutional duty to enforce it."[52]

Also during that term, Burton joined a unanimous Court in outlawing the practices of the five major movie firms of not only fixing prices but, with their control of most of the first-run theaters, forcing theaters to take all of a group of pictures or none at all. And he voted with the majority in a Reed opinion that the acquisition of Consolidated Steel Corporation by United States Steel was merely an expansion into a West Coast market and was not a violation of the Sherman Act. Douglas, Murphy, Black, and Rutledge opposed the acquisition on the grounds of "bigness" and market power. In *Mandeville Island Farms* v. *American Crystal Sugar Co.*, he decided with the majority that the Sherman Act covered restraints of trade between California sugar beet growers and California refiners.[53]

In *F.T.C.* v. *Morton Salt Co.*, Burton joined the majority in upholding the Federal Trade Commission in limiting more sharply the practice of giving quantity discounts with large purchases of salt. However, in *F.T.C.* v. *Cement Institute*, he prepared a solitary dissent to Black's opinion that the basing point system, which the cement industry worked out through its institute and which resulted in identical price quotations by "competitors" throughout the country, was illegal. The Court held this was an unfair method of competition prohibited by the Federal Trade Commission Act. Burton was persuaded by the lower court's findings of fact: that there was a long-established and widespread practice by cement manufacturers of bona fide competition by absorption of freight costs and that Congress had declined to interfere with the practice, although it had been asked to do so. Burton firmly dissented to a decision which he believed would have an unwarranted detrimental effect on the cement business. [54]

In the two major antitrust cases decided during the 1948 term, *Standard Oil* v. *United States* and *United States* v. *National City Lines, Inc.*, Burton voted for the corporations. In *Standard Oil*, Frankfurter, for a Court majority, upheld an injunction enjoining the company from utilizing exclusive contracts with service stations in violation of the Clayton Act. As it stood, the decision had less impact than it might have had because it left the way open for companies to make retailers their agents or to actually buy retailers and thus monopolize even further. This loophole became the primary motivation in the dissent entered by Douglas. Burton and Vinson joined Jackson's separate dissent, which was based largely on the grounds that there was no proof that the contracts substantially lessened competition and also on the majority's refusal to regard requirement contracts as a per se violation of the statutes. However, they were prepared to vote in favor of the government if proof could be obtained that the contracts had anticompetitive effects. Burton consistently maintained that the economic effects of antitrust decisions should be controlling and that there should not be an effort to attack big business for its own sake.[55]

In the other antitrust case, *United States* v. *National City Lines,* Burton joined in a Vinson opinion that the doctrine of forum nonconveniens (inconvenient place of trial) was applicable in an antitrust suit by the government against a corporation. When, during the 1947 term, the Court had decided the issue the opposite way, Frankfurter and Burton had dissented from Rutledge's majority opinion. They believed that despite the Clayton Act's provisions that an antitrust action could be brought wherever the defendant transacts business, such defendants were not excluded from the benefits of a change of venue (place of trial). Almost immediately after the 1947 case was decided, Congress passed the revised judicial code, which permitted the transfer of "any civil action." In the 1948 case, Douglas dissented, joined by Black on the grounds that by strictly reading the new code, its provisions could be enforced without affording antitrust defendants a change of venue. The Court could give effect to the words *any civil* action on a restricted basis. The decision was important because it gave wealthy defendants the legal grounds to wear out plaintiffs by litigating over the matter of venue, thus unduly protracting the litigation. Burton did not believe that corporations should be deprived of the benefit of the statute just because a corporation might be more financially able than an individual.[56]

During the 1946 term, Burton also wrote the opinion for a unanimous Court in one of the ever-present Federal Employees Liability

Act cases, *Myer* v. *Reading Company*, in which a decision was upheld in favor of a railroad company employee who had been injured on the job. His other opinion was on the important issue of
the collection of benefits on out-of-state insurance policies. In
*Order of Commercial Travelers of America* v. *Wolfe*, he reversed a
judgment obtained in a South Dakota court by an Ohio citizen
against a fraternal benefit society that was incorporated in Ohio.
The judgment had been for death benefits under an insurance
policy as a result of the death of an insured member who was a citizen of South Dakota.[57]

In the 1947 term, Burton dissented, with the concurrence of
Douglas, when Black reversed and remanded a district court order
enjoining enforcement of a fraud order issued by the postmaster
general in *Donaldson, Postmaster General* v. *Read Magazine, Inc.*
The postmaster general had ordered that mail addressed to *Read
Magazine* be returned to senders marked "fraudulent" and that
postal money-order sums payable to the company be returned to
the purchasers, for he had found that their advertisement of a so-
called puzzle contest was part of a scheme to obtain money through
the mails by means of false representations in violation of the
federal fraud statute. Burton held that the two lower courts could
find sufficient evidence in the record to justify such drastic administrative action and that their judgment should have been upheld.[58]

In one of the most significant and involved cases of the term,
*Lichter* v. *United States* (a renegotiation case), Burton was assigned
the majority opinion. This case dealt with a usual economic problem of war, profits control. The unfinished business of profits during World War I, for example, dragged on for twenty years. After
World War II began, the Court announced in 1942 that when profits were not excessive, a contract did not have to be renegotiated.
Two months after that decision, while Burton was in the Senate,
Congress passed the First Renegotiation Act. The act was amended
in October 1942 and frequently thereafter. One provision specified
that whenever it appeared that profits were excessive, the government could recoup them by the means laid out in the statute. Burton had been a member of Truman's Committee to Investigate the
National Defense, which took testimony and prepared several

reports on excess profits during the war, and so was a logical choice to prepare the opinion. He cited some of the committee reports in his opinion, in which he upheld the validity of the statute. It was just the kind of highly technical case which elicited little discussion and to which a junior justice could devote a great deal of energy and time.[59]

During the 1946 and 1947 terms, the Court attempted to clarify the full faith and credit issue in the determination of valid divorces, a persistent problem in that branch of private law, Conflict of Laws. The Court tried to respond to Jackson's observation that "if there is one thing that the people are entitled to expect from their lawmakers, it is rules that will enable individuals to tell whether they are married, and if so, to whom." Before Burton and Vinson came to the Court, two propositions had been established by the Court: (1) divorce decrees based on the domicile of one party and constructive service on the other are entitled to full faith and credit in other states *except* that (2) other states may, in appropriate proceedings, ignore such divorces if they find that the claimed residence of the moving party was a fraud upon the court which granted it. In the 1947 term, the Court decided cases in which a third proposition was added: if, however, both parties leave the state of origin, go to the divorcing state, participate, and receive full procedural due process there, neither party can subsequently attack the validity of the divorce in another state. The third proposition was established in *Sherrer* v. *Sherrer*, in which a wife living in Massachusetts obtained a Florida divorce. Her husband appeared in the Florida courts; but he later attacked the Florida judgment in a Massachusetts court, which held the Florida divorce invalid. In a Vinson decision, the Supreme Court, including Burton, with Murphy joining Frankfurter's dissent, reversed on full faith and credit grounds.[60]

In two other divorce cases that term, Frankfurter and Jackson dissented from a liberalization of the rules which Burton supported. In *Estin* v. *Estin* and *Krueger* v. *Krueger*, a companion case, Douglas decided for the majority that a husband could not relinquish his support money debt, which was awarded in a New York separation decree, by going to Nevada, where he obtained a valid divorce because Nevada had no jurisdiction over his creditor wife, who was served constructively but did not appear. Frank-furter's difficulties with these cases stemmed from his use of an analysis based on the interests of the states involved concerning the hoary status of domicile and states' rights. He thought parties would perjure themselves and that the Court was interfering in the states' interest in the family relations of its citizens. Furthermore, the Court in *Sherrer* was offering "a way out only to that small portion of those unhappily married who are sufficiently wealthy to be able to afford a trip to Nevada or Florida, and a six-week or three-month stay there." He footnoted the comment as follows: "the easier it is made for those who through affluence are able to exercise disproportionately large influence on legislation, to obtain migratory divorces, the less likely it is that the divorce laws of their home states will be liberalized." However, Burton was in favor of liberalizing the divorce laws. Burton noted that invalidating a divorce only when the opposing party "not only appeared but fully litigated" was "a dangerous and uncertain line to draw. Would it not be better to give effect where the party appeared . . . and also as to others unless collusion is a sham?" In conference, the justices listened to a lengthy lecture by Frankfurter, who cited case after case, congressional reports, and statutes on the question, before the majority voted for the more liberal rule.[61]

Burton wrote two additional opinions during the 1947 term, both dissents. One case involved a patent infringement, and the other was a matter of statutory construction concerning the power of the Interstate Commerce Commission. In the first case, Burton endorsed an inventor's claims that he had discovered a new method of mixing bacterial cultures. In the second, he asserted that the ICC had exceeded its jurisdiction in ordering a railroad to make deliveries of interstate carload shipments of livestock, without discrimination, to a shipper on the shipper's private sidetrack, even though compliance with that order would require the railroad to use an intermediate segment of track. This portion of track was maintained and operated by the railroad; but it was owned by and leased from a competing shipper, whose lease to the railroad precluded the use of the segment for the purpose of making such deliveries to its competitors.[62]

The 1948 term included two tax cases of tremendous importance to those who had trusts or estates and as a part of the ever-present efforts of those who possessed wealth to avoid the effect of the federal estate tax while not actually giving away their property before death. In these cases, Burton dissented from majority opinions in favor of the government. The first case concerned whether the Internal Revenue Code required, for estate tax purposes, including the value of property transferred from the decedent's estate by trust before his death. The Court held, in a Black opinion, that since the transfer was intended to take effect in possession or enjoyment after the decedent's death and was, in fact, designed for tax evasion, the property was therefore taxable. In so doing, the Court overruled an earlier decision which held that the corpus (the principal amount) of a trust transfer need not be included in a settlor's estate, even though the settlor retained for himself a life income from the corpus. The Court disallowed the trust because it reserved a life income in the trust property and was intended to take effect in possession or enjoyment at the settlor's death. In the second estate tax case, the Court, again in a Black opinion, invalidated a trust because under Illinois law there was a possibility that the principal could revert to the decedent. In that case, he had not in fact alienated all of his legal interest, as required by the code. In each case, the possibility of a reverter arose by operation of law rather than from the terms of the trust. Frankfurter and Burton dissented in both cases because of their concern for stare decisis, the tenuousness of the possibility of a reverter, and the legislative history of the act. In his dissent in the first case, Burton, incidentally, clarified his support of stare decisis by commenting on the overruling of an earlier case: "value is added to the fully considered decisions of this Court by our own respect for them."[63]

Unlike his protaxpayer views in the estate tax cases, Burton wrote opinions favorable to the government in four other tax cases that term. In *Commissioner of Internal Revenue* v. *Jacobson*, he decided for the majority that when a taxpayer repurchased bonds he had issued at a discount, the difference between the face amount they were issued for and the amount he paid for them was taxable gain and not a gift. In doing so, he distinguished an earlier decision in which the receipt of financial advantages gratuitously was held to be a gift; but this view was not to the satisfaction of Rutledge, Reed, and Douglas, who dissented because they thought the decisions were in conflict. Burton's decision in the second tax case, *Commissioner of Internal Revenue* v. *Wodehouse,* also drew a dissent, this time from Frankfurter, who was joined by Murphy and Jackson. In *Wodehouse,* Burton held for the majority that lump sum payments from American serial and book rights to a nonresident alien, who did not work or have an office in the United States, were taxable as rentals or royalties for the use of or for the privilege of using the United States copyrights and other like property. After argument, counsel for Wodehouse called Burton's attention to a law review article which completely supported the counsel's position, to no avail. Burton also concurred with Vinson in *Commissioner of Internal Revenue* v. *Culbertson,* in which Vinson decided that the entire income of a partnership set up by a father with his four sons was taxable to the father. The sons had contributed nothing in capital or vital services to what appeared to be in effect a "sham" partnership. The case was reversed and remanded to the tax court for further proceedings. In his concurrence, Burton stated that the tax court could find facts which would explain contributions of capital and services that could possibly make the partnership valid.[64]

In the fourth tax case, Burton reversed, for a unanimous Court, a court of appeals decision that certain United States tax liens did not have priority over all other claimants against the estate of a bankrupt. In *Goggin Trustee in Bankruptcy* v. *Division of Labor Enforcement of California,* Burton decided that the federal tax lien was perfected before bankruptcy and accompanied at the time of filing by the bankrupt's personal property and was therefore entitled to priority. As Burton's clerk pointed out to him, this case was one in which "the facts are undisputed. . . . [T]he legal issue is very simple although there is a scarcity of reasons to bolster the final conclusion." Burton had no trouble satisfying the Court; but when Frankfurter criticized his persistent practice of putting conclusions in the first paragraph, especially in short opinions, Burton ignored him and kept to his usual practice. He believed that the bar would best be served by knowing clearly the holding in any case at the outset.[65]

Burton wrote opinions in four other economic cases in the 1948 term. In *California* v. *Zook*, he dissented from the majority opinion of Murphy, which upheld the validity of a California statute prohibiting the sale or arrangement of any transportation over the public highways if the transporting carrier had no permit from the ICC. Again, Frankfurter flattered Burton by telling him that he was dissenting separately only to "emphasize" his "agreement with" the conclusion of Burton's dissent, which was joined by Douglas and Jackson. Burton's dissent relied heavily upon legislative history to support his conclusion that the California statute was no longer valid because federal action had preempted the field, leaving no room for state regulation. He also pointed out that federal policy had been made exclusive and that there was no intent to share the field with the state. Burton clearly expressed the distinction between his support of congressional power in economic cases and his usual support of states' rights in civil liberties cases.[66]

When the case first came before the Court, Douglas and Burton were the only justices who voted to affirm in conference; and few comments were made. After Murphy's opinion was circulated, Frankfurter responded that he "could not possibly join Murphy's opinion," which he regarded as completely inaccurate in its analysis. After Burton drafted his dissent, Frankfurter said he was persuaded by the dissent, primarily because it appeared to be the lesser of two evils. Nonetheless, he thought Burton might be able to obtain a majority for his position; and so he suggested they rewrite the position to delete the counterarguments and doubts which are appropriate for a dissent but not for a Court opinion. Despite Frankfurter's hopes and his disdain for Murphy's opinion, Murphy gained the crucial vote of Reed; and his opinion went down. Reed had written to Frankfurter that he was leaning toward the Murphy opinion: "I see no reason why where there is no inconsistency between the state and federal acts both should not be effective. It would seem . . . that the real exclusion of state action by congressional action exists when two statutes are inconsistent."[67]

Burton held the crucial vote in another case which raised the issue of state efforts to generate revenue by taxing businesses which were partly involved in interstate commerce. In *Interstate Oil Pipe Line Co* v. *Stone*, Rutledge, joined by Black, Douglas, and Murphy, upheld the validity of a state tax levied against a pipeline company. This tax was measured by receipts from the transportation of oil from leased tanks to loading racks for interstate shipment in railroad tank cars. The tax was held not to violate the Commerce Clause of the Constitution. Rejecting an onslaught of argument, memos, and letters from Frankfurter and Reed, Burton concurred in the judgment, making a majority of five. Burton parted company with the dissenters—Frankfurter, Vinson, Minton, and Reed—on the issue of whether the commerce involved was intra- or interstate. The dissenters deemed it interstate commerce. Furthermore, unlike the majority, who thought the tax was non-discriminatory regardless of whether the commerce involved was intra- or interstate, the dissenters believed that once they had established to their satisfaction that the commerce was interstate, the tax was invalid.[68]

Burton wrote three additional majority opinions during the 1948 term. In *United States* v. *Penn Manufacturing Co.*, he reversed a court of claims judgment awarding damages to a manufacturer for the loss of anticipated profits under a contract for the manufacture of gun mounts for the navy during World War II. This contract was canceled a few days after it was awarded. The Court noted that the court of claims had made no affirmative finding that the manufacturer was ready and able to perform and that the claim seemed to be an attempt to raid the public treasury. In *Grand River Dam Authority* v. *Grand Hydro*, with Murphy, Black, Rutledge, and Douglas dissenting, Burton held that although an Oklahoma state authority had a Federal Power Commission license to proceed with a power project on a nonnavigable stream which affected navigable streams, the condemnation price of the land involved was governed by state rather than federal law, for the provisions of the license did not include federal eminent domain principles. The decision benefited a private landowner at the expense of state taxpayers who provided support for the power project. He also wrote the majority opinion in *United States* v. *Wittek*, which found the District of Columbia Emergency Rent Act inapplicable to government-owned housing. In this case, Burton used the experience and knowledge of the alley dwellings and other Washington housing districts that he had gained from his service on the Congressional Committee on the District of Columbia.[69]

During the first three terms of Vinson's tenure as chief and the last three terms with Murphy and Rutledge, Burton rapidly developed command of the judicial function. He remained part of a generally anti-civil libertarian bloc on the Court. He, Reed, and Vinson were most often in the majority. As befitted the junior justice, he most often voted with the chief, which meant that he still wrote few important opinions. Burton regarded his opinions in the *Line Material, National Lead,* and *Willie Francis* cases as his most significant. He asserted in March 1948 that it was "difficult to appraise the services of a member of this Court and particularly those of a junior member. The best appraisal probably is to be found in a consideration of his votes . . . although these are but straws in the wind."[70]

In the most significant non-unanimous cases during the 1946 term, the Court split, with Frankfurter and Jackson on one side and Black, Douglas, Murphy, and Rutledge on the other. But Vinson, Burton, and Reed were more successful in drawing the votes of Frankfurter and Jackson for their opinions. In the 1947 non-unanimous cases, Black, Douglas, Murphy, and Rutledge most often persuaded Frankfurter and Jackson to vote with them, which resulted in a slight leftward tilt which continued through the 1948 term.

Burton's views on major legal issues became increasingly clear. He favored governmental taxing authority except in trust and estate cases. He usually supported police activities in criminal cases but thought a reexecution was cruel and unusual punishment. He opposed expansive governmental authority in antitrust cases; but he did not hesitate to allow some business activities which on the surface violated the antitrust acts. He opposed tax support of parochial schools, including released time for instruction in school buildings; but he relented when released time was provided for instruction off the school premises. He supported governmental action in opposition to polygamy but did not believe that women had the right to sit on federal juries. He believed governmental authority to raise and support armies outweighed the religious claims of Jehovah's Witnesses. He supported protection for newspapers from contempt charges, but he was against freedom of speech protection when a speaker invited rabid opposition or when sound trucks made too raucous noises. He was firmly opposed to the dissemination of what he regarded as pornographic literature and even regarded the condonation of adultery in a book as a basis for an obscenity finding. Except for a dissent in his first race relations case, he supported constitutional protection for blacks in race discrimination cases but was less favorably disposed toward the Japanese. In labor cases, he opted for a restrictive view of the Fair Labor Standards Act and limited protection for picketing and strikes. He favored a liberal interpretation of the migratory divorce laws in order to permit divorce when the parties wanted it.

The Court on which Burton sat was still deeply divided. Although the first Vinson term proved to be more quiet than those under Stone, the difficulties continued. Relations were still cool among the justices; they rarely saw one another outside the Court but refrained from criticizing each other publicly. Burton had formed a good relationship with Vinson, who was regarded as a competent chief. During his first term, Vinson had written no dissents, had been fair in handing out assignments, and had become a capable spokesman for the majority. Burton also enjoyed long conversations with both Vinson and Frankfurter, and he and Frankfurter flattered each other endlessly.

Despite his conscientious approach to opinion writing and his zealous undertaking of the work of the Court, commentators on the Court still critized Burton. In a June 1947 *Washington Post* article, Drew Pearson sharply attacked Burton's active social life. Pearson commented that Burton seemed to think that "being on the Supreme Court is not for the purpose of handing down opinions but to enjoy a continous round of parties." If Burton had been more productive, according to Pearson, Black, Douglas, and others might not have to work so hard. The journalist added that Burton's two full years on the Court gave him "ample time to begin to earn [his] $20,000 a year." Upon reading the article, the members of the Court offered Burton immediate consolation. Justice Douglas wrote to Burton the same day, commenting "that

was a most unfair below the belt article by Pearson this morning.
. . . All those who know the court well know that work habits of
the judges differ. And one's contribution to the work of the court is
not measured as we know, by the number of opinions written." He
also pointed out that "Pringles's book on Taft quoted Taft as saying that Van Devanter was the most valued man on the court. But
he wrote few opinions each year, even though he had had years of
judicial experience." Frankfurter also wrote on the same day that
he had known every man who sat on the Court since 1906, and "it
is on that basis that I can say to you what I have said behind your
back, that this court never had a Justice who was harder working or
more conscientious." Although Burton said nothing substantial to
his clerk or family about the Pearson article, he was obviously
stung. In his diary, he noted that Vinson, Black, Reed, and Jackson
spoke to him personally with comments similar to those of Douglas
and Frankfurter; yet, "nothing was said to me by Justice Murphy
or Rutledge." Burton also pointed out that he had actually written
eight opinions, not six as Pearson said.[71]

Surprisingly, talk still circulated among others who seemed to
think better of Burton than Pearson, about Burton's possible candidacy for the presidency. He warded off all such talk by repeating
his disinterest and expressing his confusion as to why the
Republican party should turn to him: "it is better for all concerned
that members of this Court be not called upon to take part in outside activities or to resign from the Court to accept political responsibilities. The situation in the Republican party today by no means
equals that which led to the nomination of Justice Hughes in
1916." He believed that his opportunities for service on the Court
were infinite and that members should stay on as long as possible in
order to give the Court the stability and competence which could be
gained only by actual service. In fact, "never since that Nation was
eleven years old until now has it been without a Supreme Court on
which there was not at least one member with more than eleven
years of service on it."[72]

Burton was under no illusions about his capabilities. He noted in
his diary that he did not have a good memory; and so in order to
enhance his ability to make good speeches, he had learned accurately a few important and useful quotations. His favorite, which he
used in letters while in the Senate and thereafter, was Lincoln's

definition of democracy: "as I would not be a slave, so I would not be a master." As a senator, he also initiated the habit of memorizing such series of facts as the states, their capitals, and senators, and the countries of the Americas and their capitals. Upon joining the Court, he became very interested in researching and writing part of its history as an institution. He utilized "many spare otherwise idle moments such as on walks, in steambaths, under sunlight, while swimming, while riding in cabs, etc. . . reviewing the entire membership of the Supreme Court since its organization and their appointing presidents and their successors one to another."[73]

The most unsettling events of these three terms for Burton and the Court came when Justice Murphy died of a heart attack in July and when Justice Rutledge died in September 1949. Two staunch liberals were now gone from the Court, and their replacements were a matter of greatest public concern between terms. As a result of this concern, when replacements were announced, Burton and the Court became the object of strong public criticism. On August 8, 1949, the *New Republic*, bastion of liberalism, carried an article lamenting the appointment of Attorney General Tom C. Clark to fill the seat vacated by the death of Murphy. The article asserted that Clark had been appointed only because he was a loyal member of the cabinet, cheerful, and a good Democrat. As a consequence of Clark's appointment, the liberals would now be isolated; and conservatism would become even more entrenched. Moreover, Clark would have to excuse himself in a number of important cases which had been initiated while he was attorney general. President Truman, the article continued, had a "penchant for selecting inferior men for positions of the highest national trust," including Vinson and Burton. The writer found that the chief difficulty with both Vinson and Burton was their lack of experience; and with such incompetent justices, the only reason the Court was able to keep "its head out of water" was the fact that the Court's docket was "temporarily" reduced by "chance." The writer would probably have been surprised to discover that Burton agreed with him concerning the lack of experience on the Court and objected only to his failure to recognize that a reduced docket resulted from substantive legal and political matters and not from the presence of Vinson or Burton.

# 4
# Burton and the Vinson Court

B Y T H E fall of 1949, as Truman's Supreme Court set about its work, the country was experiencing a series of national shocks. The economic decline of the previous year had ended; prices and incomes were again on the rise. However, the power of communism seemed to many to be a greater menace than ever, even though the containment of communism in Europe and the Marshall Plan seemed to be working. In China, the Communist armies were advancing in the wake of the flight of Chiang Kai Shek's Nationalists to Formosa in January 1949. On September 23, 1949, it was announced that the Russians had exploded the first atomic bomb. The furor mounted week by week. The cases of top Communist leaders were in the trial courts. In August 1948, Whittaker Chambers had accused Alger Hiss of being a member of the Communist party before the House Un-American Activities Committee; and by January 1949, Hiss had been indicted for perjury, with Felix Frankfurter, one of the Court's own, testifying in his behalf. As the second trial wore on until his conviction on January 21, 1950, the question of whether communism had in fact infiltrated the American government was raised more and more often by the public. Anti-New Dealers, Republican conservatives, and Catholic discontents all joined forces in beginning a new anti-Communist crusade. By Lincoln's birthday in February 1950, Senator Joseph McCarthy of Wisconsin had established himself as one of the leaders of the crusade.

By the time the 1950 term opened, the United States was heavily engaged in battle in Korea under the mandate of the United Nations in order to prevent a North Korean Communist take-over of South Korea. Before the term ended, Korea was stalemated; and

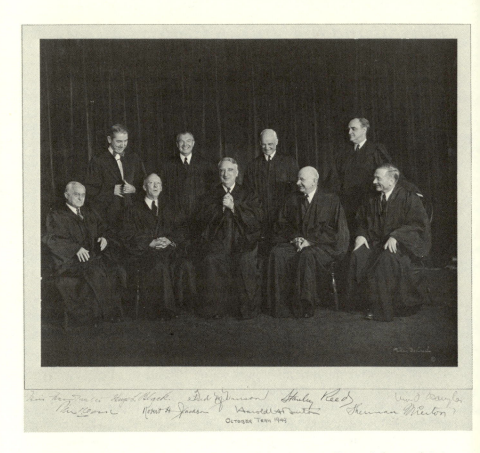

1949—The Vinson Court in a mirthful moment (from left to right): Frankfurter, Clark, Black, Jackson, Vinson, Burton, Reed, Minton, and Douglas

Harry Truman had fired General Douglas MacArthur for insisting on taking actions which Truman believed would bring on a full-scale war with China. The economy was surging upward again on the crest of the war. The Kefauver Special Committee to Investigate Organized Crime was crisscrossing the country; its televised examinations of the powerful Frank Costello attracted millions of viewers. In his expanding campaign against communism, Senator Joseph McCarthy heated up his attacks on the administration for permitting subversives to infiltrate the government. In defense, the Truman administration announced that millions of federal employees had been cleared under the Federal Loyalty and Security Program established in 1947 and that only a few hundred had been dismissed because of reasonable doubts about their loyalty. However, many apparently innocent people were hounded out of government positions; and the virulence penetrated universities, the arts, indeed every area of American life.

A year later, the controversy over General MacArthur's dismissal had subsided in the wake of committee hearings focusing on the consequences for American diplomatic relations with the Russians and Chinese of his unwillingness to follow orders in Korea. Many Americans had become bored with his platitudes and self-righteousness. The war in Korea, which exacted an ever-higher toll of American lives, staggered onward. And sensing the frustrations of people over the stalemate in Korea, the scandals uncovered by the Kefauver Committee, the Hiss trials, and the general malaise in the society, Senator McCarthy gathered more and more support as he heightened his attacks on the government leaders and intellectuals he chose to label as Communists. Burton's former colleague Robert A. Taft moved ever closer to becoming a solid Mc-Carthyite, as had a number of other members of the GOP, discontented Democrats, and Independents.

By the 1952 term, as the Truman era came to an end, Eisenhower's campaign against Adlai Stevenson moved swiftly ahead despite charges of a secret Nixon slush fund feathered with numerous campaign contributions from millionaires. The Supreme Court, during these turbulent four years of the Truman administration, presided over the liquidation of the civil libertarianism forged in the era of Hughes, Stone, Holmes, and

Brandeis; developed even more restrictive rules concerning the rights of criminal defendants; but paved the way for the Warren Court's assault on racial segregation.[1]

The 1949 term began with Sherman Minton and Tom C. Clark, both friends of President Truman, replacing Rutledge and Murphy. Some commentators predicted that the new Court would veer even more sharply to the right, denying claimed rights in civil liberties cases and favoring governmental power and authority in most instances. Clark had gained a reputation for conservatism based upon his role in assisting in removing the Japanese to internment camps during the war and the inactivity of the Civil Rights Division of the Justice Department while he was attorney general. However, Minton was viewed with less apprehension because of his friendship with Black, which began while they served together in the Senate. It was hoped this tie might influence him to follow Black's lead, but his apparent lack of interest in civil liberties in the past was regarded as a possible harbinger of evil.[2]

Historically, the Court had not served as an effective protector of rights during a period of repressive attitudes among the American public. Particularly sensitive because of its size and the possibility of long tenure for justices without personnel changes, the Court was often in tune with the predominant public attitudes; but when a change in public attitude occurred, it sometimes lagged behind. In the 1920s, anti-civil libertarian decisions (reflecting the public temper) were the rule, with Oliver Wendell Holmes and Louis Brandeis dissenting. When Charles Evans Hughes and Owen Roberts replaced William Howard Taft and Edward T. Sanford, the earlier trend was reversed in conjunction with the dying out of a national repressive temper. The Roosevelt justices with their pro-civil libertarian attitudes dominated the 1930s, generally carrying Stone along with them. But as time went on, their dominance was somewhat tempered by Frankfurter and Jackson. In the early years of the 1940s, the Court was still predominantly libertarian; but in the aftermath of World War II, the Court began to reflect the anti-Communist hysteria of the public and the two other branches of government. Prior to 1949, Jackson, Reed, Burton, and Vinson voted in opposition to civil libertarian claims; however, Black, Murphy, Douglas, and Rutledge could always join to grant certiorari and then attempt to obtain the support of Frankfurter in the final decision. But with the appointments of Clark and Minton, this bloc was broken up. Without Rutledge and Murphy, certiorari was denied in many cases in which Frankfurter would probably have voted against the claimed right. Additionally, Douglas was absent for most of the 1949 term as a result of a riding accident. Frankfurter ended up voting with Black in many of the cases that were granted, and as a result began to appear more libertarian. Reed, Burton, Vinson, Jackson, Minton, and Clark made up a new anti-civil libertarian majority; and the Court was temporarily in step with the repressive temper of the times.

In the 1949 through 1952 terms, the Court was usually unanimous in the race segregation cases and divided in the civil liberties cases, which were decided most often in opposition to the claimed right. Burton, often the most liberal member in the race cases, generally voted with the anti-civil libertarians in the civil liberties cases. The most important civil liberties case in the 1949 term was *American Communication Association* v. *Douds*, in which Burton and the Court, in sustaining the non-Communist affidavit provision of the Taft-Hartley Act, examined the "clear and present danger" test as a limitation on the First Amendment freedom of speech. During World War I, Holmes had enunciated his classic interpretation that speech must not be prohibited unless there was a clear and present danger of a substantive evil. Congress then had a right to prohibit such speech, as in a case dealing with the effect of a derogatory political speech on affairs of state. During the mid-1920s, the Court abandoned the Holmes test and adopted the so-called bad tendency test under which only slight evidence of the possibility of serious consequences of speech was necessary to cut away First Amendment protection. The Taft-Hartley provision required an oath as to personal conduct and beliefs as well as a specific reference to a belief in an organization which advocated the overthrow of the government.[3]

In conference, the Court had no great difficulties with the case. Burton, Vinson, and Reed were certain the statute was valid; Black felt that it was not; and Frankfurter treated the conference to a history of the "clear and present danger" test. He also insisted that since it was a labor statute and not a criminal one providing for punishment, the case could not be characterized as one in which individuals were being convicted for advocacy. In a Vinson opinion, with Jackson and Frankfurter concurring and Black dissenting, the Court upheld the validity of the act and indicated that the evidence needed to support the clear and present danger need not be overwhelming, thus, in effect, applying the "bad tendency" doctrine as the better rule. To the majority, when Congress passed the statute, it was legitimately protecting commerce from interruption by imposing this requirement on all unions, for substantial evidence of Communist participation in political strikes had been presented to Congress. All the opinions in the case accepted the notion that the Congress could enact stronger prohibitions against the Communist party than would ever be legitimate if applied to the Democratic or Republican parties.[4]

When the Court decided *Dennis* v. *United States* during the next term, a case that involved the convictions of twelve national Communist party leaders under the Smith Act for attempting to organize the Communist party to teach and advocate the overthrow of the government by force and violence, the "clear and present danger test" was again at issue. Overt acts other than teaching and advocacy were not alleged. Before argument began, Burton was certain he would vote to affirm the convictions in the case. On the bench memo, he noted that he would follow Justice Hand's opinion "on clear and present danger and . . . [not] overrule [the] Gitlow case." Congress "has acted and is within its constitutional right to protect this government." Whereas Burton, wanting to emphasize his open-mindedness, usually wrote "probably" affirm or reverse on his memos before argument or conference; in this case he wrote simply "affirm." In conference, Vinson, Reed, Burton, Frankfurter, and Minton, who was the only justice who had voted to deny certiorari, voted to affirm; Black wanted to reverse but at that time thought it should be done on the basis that there was no clear and present danger; Douglas passed because he had not finished reading the unusually long five-volume record; and Jackson also passed.[5]

Practically speaking, the decision affirming the convictions extended the doctrine announced in the *Douds* case and encouraged the Justice Department, congressional committees, and government agencies in the continuing anti-Communist crusade. There were five opinions from the eight participating justices—Vinson wrote the main opinion, which was joined by Reed, Burton, and Minton; Frankfurter and Jackson concurred; and Black and Douglas dissented. Frankfurter's opinion, typically, criticized governmental interference with freedom of expression and regretted the current repression but ended in approving it on the grounds of congressional power and judicial deference. Jackson's concurrence straightforwardly denounced the Communist conspiracy as an evil not falling within the bounds of the clear and present danger test, which was designated to deal with minor matters, such as a hotheaded speech on a street corner. However, Vinson said that although he was applying the clear and present danger test in this case, the test did not require a probability of success or an instantaneous imminence of revolution to sanction governmental control. In his dissent, Black was willing to make freedom of speech absolute, while Douglas stated that he was following the clear and present danger test as elaborated by Holmes and Louis Brandeis.[6]

That was not, however, the end of *Dennis*. Frankfurter became incensed at some of the publicity surrounding the case as well as the case of six defendants' attorneys who were held in contempt by the trial judge. In conference, while the case was being considered, Frankfurter explained that the Communist party had announced that if the decision in *Dennis* was not to its liking, there would be protest demonstrations throughout the nation. He added that the American Bar Association had approved a recommendation condemning the conduct of counsel for the defendants in the *Dennis* trial and calling for their disbarment. Frankfurter felt that these actions were interfering with the Court's duty of deciding cases before it and were "creating serious public sentiment in relation to adjudication not yet rendered." He wanted the Court, in announcing its decision, to "Issue an order to show cause why an attachment for contempt should not issue against the American Bar Association—who should know better—and the Communist Party." Despite his obvious concern, the other justices agreed not to follow his suggestion.[7]

Additionally, when the contempt conviction of the lawyers involved came up for review during the 1951 term, Burton at first voted with the majority to deny certiorari to review the contempt charges, with Black and Douglas dissenting. The attorneys filed a petition for a rehearing which would be devoted to only one question, whether the Federal Rules of Criminal Procedure required the judge to defer decision and punishment and to leave the judgment to another uninvolved judge after notice, hearing, and opportunity to defend. While the petition was being considered, Frankfurter lobbied to obtain a decision favorable to the attorneys. He told Burton that he thought a new situation had arisen by "virtue of the mass Communist prosecutions all over the United States." In an opinion by Jackson, five members of the Court, including Burton, agreed that the trial judge had the power to punish the contempt himself and that it was proper for him to defer decision until the end of the trial. Black dissented on the grounds that the judge should not have passed on the charges because the lawyers were entitled to a trial by jury. In a separate dissent, Frankfurter asserted that the judge should have invited the senior circuit judge to assign another judge to hear the charges. Douglas also dissented, concurring in both the Black and the Frankfurter opinions.[8]

Frankfurter had little doubt that the lower court decision would be affirmed. However, he believed that the judgment should not be allowed to stand without a hearing, and four justices had publicly announced that a hearing should be held. On the contrary, he said

if we do hear argument and the duties and obligations of the bar are defined with impressive dignity, and even sternness so far as I am concerned, while at the same time the obligation of the bar to give fearless defense even to the most outcast defendant is recognized as something to be lived up to by the bar and to be respected by courts, we will infuse into an atmosphere, which nobody can deny is much too fear-laden, an important element of sanity and moral health.

In a telephone conversation, Burton responded to Frankfurter that he had already told the chief justice earlier in the day that he expected to vote for reconsideration.[9]

During the 1950 term, in *Feiner* v. *New York*, the Court applied the test they had adopted to a pro-Communist speaker's conviction for provoking a breach of the peace by making a pro-Henry Wallace speech on a street corner in Syracuse, New York. On the facts, the speech was offensive to the audience; and at least one listener had threatened violence to the speaker. In the 1948 *Terminiello* case, Douglas, for the majority, had reversed the conviction of a speaker in Chicago for making a speech which stirred unrest. In conference, without mentioning the pro-Communist views of the speaker, Vinson asserted that the police were present to preserve order and that they did not have to wait until the situation exploded. Frankfurter held that the test was whether the police had reasonable grounds for doing what they did, while Douglas thought "the cops arrested the wrong man." Burton said that he believed the speaker had "egged to the limit."[10]

Burton's clerk wanted him to vote for reversal in *Feiner*. The clerk pointed out that no danger of an actual breach of the peace existed; only two persons complained to the police, and there was no suggestion that the speaker had obstructed traffic. To him, "the duty of the officers was to protect the speaker, if such protection became necessary rather than to arrest him." Burton, however, believed that the petitioner was being tried, "not the policeman, and the question is whether the petitioner went too far and the action of the policeman is not conclusive—as evidence—the judgments of the trial courts are important and we should not interfere."[11] The four dissenters in *Terminiello* were joined by Reed, who had voted with the majority and had also voted to deny certiorari in *Feiner*, and Clark in upholding the conviction in a Vinson opinion that did not mention *Terminiello*. Black, Douglas, and Minton dissented. When the Court decided in *Beauharnais* v. *Illinois*, an appeal from a conviction under a state group libel law for displaying a leaflet concerning the "rape, robbers, knives, guns and marihuana of the Negro," with an application form for a Chicago organization called the White Circle League, Burton at first thought that the statute should be found void for vagueness and also that a free speech "clear and present danger" question might be at issue. However, he changed his mind after reading Frankfurter's opinion for the majority, which he supported. Frankfurter, who with Minton and Vinson had voted to deny certiorari, upheld the law as a proper exercise of the state's power to ward off racial tensions. He asserted that no constitutional questions were at issue because free speech protections did not apply to libelous speech any more than they did to obscenity. Jackson, Reed, Douglas, and Black dissented to the decision, which was criticized as an interference with free speech that even the NAACP opposed.[12]

Three cases that came before the Court grew out of state legislative enactments requiring political oaths, in pursuit of those who might be tainted with un-Americanism. Burton joined unanimous opinions upholding one and rejecting another, and he dissented from a majority opinion upholding the third. In the 1949 *Gerende* v. *Board of Public Works* case, the Court unanimously upheld a Maryland statute which required that candidates for public office take an oath that they were neither engaged in attempting to overthrow the government nor acquainted with members of an organization having such a purpose. The requirement of present, knowing membership and the precise definition of subversion saved the statute from a ruling of unconstitutionality. The distinctions the Court made were clarified during the same term when a Los Angeles oath was challenged as a bill of attainder in *Garner* v. *Board of Public Works*. At issue was the legality of affidavits for municipal employees which required them to state whether they were or had been members of the Communist party and an oath which required that they swear that for five years past they had not advised, advocated, or taught the overthrow of government and had not been members of or affiliated with such an organization with such purposes in that time and would not be guilty of such conduct in the future.[13]

When Clark distinguished the earlier bill of attainder cases and upheld the oath as perfectly permissible legislation similar to "a statute elevating standards of qualification to practice medicine," Burton dissented, as did Frankfurter, Douglas, and Black. Frankfurter thought the oaths violated due process, while Burton thought it was as much a bill of attainder as those measures declared illegal in the earlier cases. He found that the oath was "restrospectively a perpetual bar" to employment, for "it leaves no room for a change of heart. It calls for more than a profession of present loyalty or promise of future attachment." Douglas and Black found both the oaths and the affidavits unconstitutional.[14]

At first Burton thought he could join Douglas's dissent if Douglas would change his opinion to affirm the convictions of two petitioners who signed the oath but refused to sign the affidavits. He told Douglas that "insofar as the affidavit elicits information relevant to present loyalty; I find it unobjectionable. . . . The requested disclosure of past Communist affiliation is not now before us." When Douglas refused to make the suggested change, Burton considered joining Frankfurter. However, he believed that Frankfurter went too far in supporting the affidavit. He decided to write his own dissent approving the requirement that employees give such information to employers but making it clear that employees could not be dismissed on the basis of the information supplied.[15]

The 1952 term's test oath case, *Wieman* v. *Updegraff*, involved the validity of an oath prescribed by an Oklahoma statute for all state officers and employees. This oath required the disavowal of membership in any group declared subversive by the attorney general of the United States during the preceding five years. The resulting case was handled easily by the Court . Justice Clark, for a unanimous Court, invalidated the statute on due process grounds, primarily because knowledge (scienter) of the unlawful purposes required by the decisions in *Gerende* and *Garner* was not a requirement in the statute. Burton concurred without opinion; however, he told the conference that the state "could prescribe limitations as to employment," but they "must be rational." He approved the termination of employees who were members of a subversive organization; but their termination, without judicial review, "looks like a bill of attainder."[16]

But the Court had a great deal of difficulty reaching a conclusion in *Joint Anti-Fascist Refugee Committee* v. *McGrath*, a case involving the constitutionality of the federal loyalty program instituted to screen out federal employees who were security risks, in which Burton wrote one of his most pro-libertarian opinions. In the conference, Minton, Reed, and Vinson, who were the only ones who had voted to deny certiorari, voted to reverse the decision below in order to uphold the attorney general's implementation of the program. Vinson and Minton believed that the Joint Anti-Fascist Committee had no standing to complain since it was not suffering direct injury. At first Reed agreed with Black that "no official has a right to stigmatize anyone without a right to be heard";

but he later concluded that mere membership in an organization would not, in reality, result in discharge from public employment and was simply one factor to be considered. Jackson commented that he could not find it "easy to say that these organizations have anything applied to them except epithets," while Burton asserted that "the government has the right to list subversive organizations" but could not be "capricious."[17]

The Court considered the case along with *Bailey* v. *Richardson*, in which a "nonsensitive" federal employee challenged her dismissal and in the process brought into question the conflict of the entire loyalty program with the due process and First Amendment provisions of the Constitution. The Court of Appeals for the District of Columbia upheld the validity of the program in a 2-1 decision. Frankfurter argued in a memo to the conference that the constitutionality of the attorney general's list was at issue in the *Bailey* case and should therefore not be avoided in the *Joint Anti-Fascist Refugee* case. However, Burton adhered to the view that the two issues were separate. Bailey had not challenged the list, only her removal based on the listing; and the review board which dismissed her had accepted the list as final and also had not challenged it.[18]

In the conference on *Bailey*, Vinson pointed out that there was "no vested right" to government employment; and the fact that the job involved was nonsensitive made no difference. In addition, the review board meetings were not really trials or hearings governed by due process rules. Reed was convinced of the wisdom of the process; to him, employees "must be loyal, not only to the people but to the government." Black commented that as far as he was concerned, the petitioner was "destroyed," for even though there was no inherent right to government employment, people could not be thrown out for political reasons; that was the "Law of Hitler or Nero." Frankfurter and Jackson were concerned because of the lack of procedural safeguards in the so-called hearing, which they asserted was worse than no hearing at all. Although Burton finally voted to affirm without comment, he indicated before oral argument that he would probably reverse on the ground that Miss Bailey's position was a "non-sensitive one."[19]

As the months wore on, Black became disturbed about the considerable time the Court was taking to arrive at decisions in the *Anti-Fascist* and *Bailey* cases. He told Burton on April 25 that "government employees are being tried and some discharged I suppose under Mandamus that a majority have voted [illegal]. It seems to me that we should insist on handing the cases down, even if judgment is rendered without opinions." Burton responded that he agreed that the cases should come down, but it was still necessary to wait a week or two for the other opinions.[20]

Finally, Burton found for the Court in his most libertarian opinion of the last three Vinson terms. His decision in *Joint Anti-Fascist*, which was joined by Douglas, restricted the power of the attorney general to put organizations on a subversive list. Burton held that the attorney general may make such listings; but when challenged, he must go to trial and offer proof to justify the listing. In addition, Burton declared that it was not necessary to reach the constitutionality of the attorney general's action because the president's Executive Order 9835 contained "no express or implied attempt to confer power on anyone to act arbitrarily or capriciously, even assuming constitutional power to do so." Frankfurter concurred because the due process right of a fair hearing had not been afforded; but he included a lengthy discussion on the existing issues of ripeness, justicability, and standing to sue in the case. Jackson concurred on the grounds of lack of due process; Black, on the grounds that the action violated the Fifth Amendment and was a bill of attainder; and Reed, with the concurrences of Vinson and Minton, dissented. Generally, the dissenters did not believe the organizations were seriously affected by the action: "there was no deprivation of any property or liberty of any listed organization." While they might find their prestige, reputation, or earning power diminished, that was a question for a damage action. In *Bailey*, with Clark not participating, the court of appeals decision upholding the validity of the program was affirmed by an equally divided Court; Burton, Vinson, Reed, and Minton voted to affirm "without opinion."[21]

For the remainder of Vinson's tenure, Burton did not write opinions in any other freedom of expression cases. However, he continued to exhibit a slightly anti-civil libertarian pattern in his votes. During the 1952 term, Vinson's last as chief, of the twenty civil liberties cases heard, the decision went against the claimed right in fifteen and in favor of the right in only five of the most insubstantial cases. Burton voted against the claimed right only a little over 50 percent of the time. He was part of the six-man majority which upheld New York's Feinberg Law, which excluded from teaching those affiliated with certain offensive organizations included on a list compiled by the State Board of Regents, in *Adler* v. *Board of Education*. Minton, in an opinion for six members of the Court, held that the statute did not interfere with freedom of speech or assembly; but Black and Douglas dissented on the grounds that the guilt of a teacher should turn solely on any overt acts within the school system. Also dissenting, Frankfurter asserted that the appeal should have been dismissed because the issues were still too abstract and speculative and because no real injury had been done to any person. In the conference, even the Vinson majority, including Burton, acknowledged that teachers might be terrorized. But they believed it was not an unconstitutional exercise of state power to regulate employment.[22]

The pattern of decision in other cases during the period under discussion remained largely unchanged. On the touchy subject of government aid to religious education, Burton's position and the Court decision upholding the New York released-time system for school children in *Zorach* v. *Clauson* could easily have been predicted. As was noted in Chapter 3, when the Court decided in *McCollum* v. *Board of Education* that an Illinois system which provided for released time on school property offended the constitutional principle of the separation of church and state, a great deal of needless public controversy ensued concerning aid to religion in the public schools. The justices already knew that by simply moving the instruction off school property, the Court would sanction its constitutionality. They had resolved the issue while discussing *McCollum*. Douglas, Burton, Vinson, and Reed had already committed themselves. All they needed was the vote of either Clark or Minton, the freshmen justices; they ensnared both. Douglas, for the 6-3 majority which included Burton, did not overrule *McCollum* but limited it to its facts. Dissenting in *Zorach*, Jackson commented that the distinction between the two cases was "trivial." Black, who wrote the *McCollum* decision, also dissented because he could see no difference between the cases. In each case, the power authority and machinery of the school system were used to direct students to religious training. Frankfurter dissented because there was no factual record in the case which could tell the Court whether the children were coerced into attendance at religious instruction, although the majority conceded that the use of coercion would be unconstitutional.

In conference, Vinson, noting the indication by some members during the preparation of *McCollum* that they would uphold the New York system, kept discussion to a minimum. He thought that the facts indicated that no state aid was being given to religion. However, Frankfurter objected to the idea that the public schools in New York were "being used by churches to get the pupils into classes." Burton voted to affirm without recorded comment; but on his bench memo, he noted that dismissing a child for religious education "was like excusing a child for medical treatment" and thus should be permitted. His clerk unsuccessfully attempted to convince him that released time was not the same as dismissed time, especially when, as in *Zorach*, the school was actively directing children to religious instruction.[23]

Frankfurter insisted on attempting to convince Burton that in *Zorach*, as in *McCollum* and *Everson*, the principle of separation of church and state was being violated. He sent Burton parts of a letter written to him by a schoolgirl on the unconstitutional effects of the released-time system which gave "concrete illustration . . . [that] the New York differences are legally and practically . . . wholly insignificant." In response, Burton stated that it was "an excellent argument against the merits of the plan" but that his main difficulty with the case was the issue of constitutionality. He felt that "religious instruction by Bible reading, etc. was a violation of the Constitution"; but he had trouble believing "that this released time system any more than many other approved recognitions of religion violates the Constitution—e.g. tax exemptions, oaths, prayers, chaplains, etc." To this, Frankfurter responded:

tax exemptions may be made for any reason the legislatures chose to give them, oaths are not here, and I don't believe that requiring a deistic oath which would treat those who do not want to give it differently would be sustained by you, and I should like you to consider why Madison thought that if the Congressmen wanted a chaplain, they, not the people, should pay for it. Chaplains for soldiers is [*sic*] different.

Unpersuaded, Burton still supported the New York plan.[24]

Closely related to the pattern of decision in freedom of expression cases was the Court's leaning in deportation cases. As part of the anti-Communist furor of the late 1940s and early 1950s, the Bureau of Immigration and Naturalization instituted denial of entry, denaturalization, and deportation proceedings against suspected subversive aliens. When these cases reached the Supreme Court, Burton was usually part of a majority which decided in favor of the government. He voted with the majority to uphold the denial of entry without a hearing to a German national married to an American soldier as prejudicial to the interests of the United States. In another alien case, he wrote the majority opinion upholding the deportation of a naturalized American citizen who was convicted of conspiracy to violate the Espionage Act of 1917 and subsequently had his citizenship canceled on the basis of fraud in its procurement. Believing that the statutory language reached even offenders who were naturalized at the time of their conviction, Burton sanctioned the deportation of any alien, whether naturalized or not, who was convicted of violation of the Espionage Act. Frankfurter dissented, joined by Black and Jackson, on the grounds that when a statute is ambiguous, "the construction which leads to hardship should be rejected." Even Burton's clerk disagreed with him, commenting that he was "very much impressed and troubled by the arguments" of the petitioners. He thought that, given the 1920 statutory language, Burton's opinion was justified but perhaps ought to emphasize that "the decision applies only to that Act and that no opinion is expressed on the issues of deportation for other reasons under other statutes." However, Burton did not want to limit the language of the opinion or the scope of the statute, and so did not heed his clerk's advice.[25]

Continuing to take a hard line in defense of congressional authority, Burton decided, for a six-man majority, that an

American citizen had conclusively expatriated herself when she expressly renounced her American citizenship and applied for Italian citizenship, married an Italian, and lived in Italy from 1941 to 1945 with her husband, who served in the Foreign Ministry. After returning to the United States, she asked to be declared an American citizen. The district court findings that the defendant had filed for Italian citizenship in order to have her marriage recognized in Italy, and that she had not intended to establish permanent residence abroad or to divest herself of her United States citizenship when she signed the instruments related to the renunciation, were embraced in a dissent by Frankfurter, which was joined by Black. Burton, in refusing to take the dual citizenship route as a means for resolving the problem, pointed out that "the United States has long recognized the general undesirability of dual allegiances." In formulating his position on alien rights, Burton maintained that the issues involved were matters of statutory interpretation; and if the decisions reached were harsh, Congress alone held the power to change the statutes.

In another case, Burton supported Jackson's majority opinion that the deportation of aliens who had briefly been members of the Communist party since entering the United States was valid and did not violate due process or the right of free speech. Burton was unpersuaded by Douglas's dissent, joined by Black, which asserted that the Constitution did not permit Congress to deport aliens "for what they once were." One of the aliens involved had come to the United States in 1920 at the age of sixteen, had been associated with Communist organizations from 1923 to 1929, but had been completely dissociated from such activities since that time. Furthermore, he had an American wife and child. Burton also rejected his clerk's suggestion that he vote for the alien, telling him that "deportation is not punishment and that the U.S. government's right to deport is substantially absolute."[26]

When the issue for decision was the detention of an alien without bail, Burton retreated somewhat from his position. For five members of the Court, Reed held that alien members of the Communist party who were detained pending final determination of their deportability could be held without bond under the discretion conferred upon the attorney general, even though their release on bond was refused solely on the grounds that they had been active in the Communist movement. Black dissented on the grounds that even if the statute was valid, the Eighth Amendment prohibition against excessive bail, the Fifth Amendment prohibition against deprivation of liberty without due process, and the First Amendment ban against abridgment of free speech were all violated. And Douglas again dissented on the grounds that expulsion of aliens for past actions or present expressions was unconstitutional. Burton concurred in Frankfurter's dissent, charging the attorney general with an abuse of his discretion; and he dissented separately in a short opinion, offering the Eighth Amendment's prohibition of cruel and unusual punishment as an additional ground for declaring illegal the attorney general's refusal to permit bail. He did not believe Congress had authorized the detention at issue.[27]

In the 1952 term, Burton utilized the statutory interpretation that he had developed in a majority opinion in *United States* v. *Grainger*, to uphold the indictment of wool purchasers for attempting to defraud the government, in another alien case, *Bridges* v. *United States*, which was argued immediately before the *Grainger* case and was decided at the same time. The case involved government efforts to deport Harry R. Bridges, a Pacific Coast Longshoreman's Union leader who immigrated to this country from Australia in 1920. In 1934, the San Francisco district director of Immigration and Naturalization instituted an investigation of Bridges's alien status to determine whether he was in any way connected with the Communist party; Bridges was cleared of any such connection. A subsequent investigation by the staff of the commissioner of Immigration and Naturalization reached the same conclusion. But in 1937, the Department of Labor conducted an investigation of his activities and, the following year, issued a warrant for his deportation. After a series of legal disputes, the deportation warrant was first canceled and then revived. When the attorney general ordered the deportation, Bridges petitioned for a writ of habeas corpus, which was denied by the federal district court and the court of appeals. However, it was upheld by the Supreme Court in 1945 when, in *Bridges* v. *Wixon*, the Court declared that the deportation order was illegal. Immediately after this decision, Bridges filed a preliminary petition for United States citizenship based on his testimony and that of two other persons that he was not a member of the Communist party. Later in the same year, he was admitted to citizenship after testifying again to the same effect. However, almost four years later, on the basis of this testimony, Bridges and his two witnesses were charged with willfully and knowingly making a false statement under oath in the naturalization proceedings. All three were charged with conspiracy to defraud the United States by impairing the administration of the naturalization laws. When the defendants pleaded that they could not be convicted because the three-year general statute of limitations had expired, the government responded that the Wartime Suspension of Limitations Act had extended the statute of limitation, thus validating the indictments. The defendants were found guilty. Burton, for three other members of the Court (Jackson and Clark did not participate), reversed the convictions on the ground that the Wartime Suspension Act did not apply. To Burton, the intent of Congress in passing the act was to protect the Treasury from the frauds which huge wartime procurement programs made possible and which were at issue in *Grainger*. Burton's opinion might be regarded as an inconsistent vote in favor of aliens when, in fact, it was purely a matter of interpreting the Wartime Suspension of Limitations Act consistently in two very different cases.[28]

Two aliens received very different treatment from Burton and the Court in the 1952 term. In *Shaughnessy* v. *United States ex rel. Mezei,* an alien who had lived in the United States for twenty-five years was detained at Ellis Island while attempting to return to this country after a temporary absence abroad to visit his dying mother in Rumania. He had left two years earlier without a reentry permit, had been denied entry into Rumania, and had encountered difficulty in securing permission to leave Hungary. He finally arrived in the United States with an immigration visa issued by the American consul in Budapest. Pursuant to an order by the attorney general, Mezei was excluded without a hearing, in accordance with the procedure provided in security cases. Other countries, following the United States precedent, also refused him admission. Faced with a permanent Ellis Island residence, Mezei filed an application for habeas corpus, which was granted by the district court when the government refused to disclose the evidence upon which it had based its finding that Mezei's entry would be prejudicial. Certiorari was narrowly granted in the case, for only Burton, Reed, Minton, and Vinson wanted to review the decision below.[29]

In conference, Vinson began with the observation that he found "it hard to understand why the United States must take him [Mezei]" and that the only reason why he was still on Ellis Island was that the country "can't get rid of him." Black retorted that the country had "already had him for 25 years." Reed commented that although it was really not a difficult case, for Mezei was never really admitted to the United States and so was an illegal alien, it was a rather "harsh" decision. Frankfurter argued strongly for the attorney general's discretion, but he asserted that the courts should have the power to give Mezei "some air." In agreement with Black, Douglas thought the length of time Mezei had been in the country vitiated any possibility of treating him as an alien. To Jackson, the real question in the case was "whether there can be an indefinite exclusion barring entry?" He doubted the possibility. Clark believed that the focus should be on the violation of Mezei's rights as an alien, rather than on the length of detention or its degree of reasonableness. Minton observed that the courts should not hear cases of this kind, which resulted in their "transferring discretion from the Attorney General to themselves." Burton voted to reverse without recording his comments in conference; but he noted that he would regard Mezei simply as an alien coming to the United States for the first time, since his first entry had been illegal. In a Clark opinion, which was supported by Burton, the Court upheld Mezei's exclusion, and rejected any suggestion that he be "assimilated to a status" other than that of an entering alien. Black joined by Douglas and Jackson joined by Frankfurter dissented in two separate opinions, both expressing the view that the continued imprisonment of Mezei without a hearing violated due process.[30]

In the other alien case, which involved one Kwong, Burton decided for the Court that an alien not physically present in the United States was categorized as a resident alien who could demand the right to a hearing before deportation. Kwong had been admitted to permanent residence in the United States before leaving the country as a seaman on an American vessel having scheduled stops at foreign ports. Although he had been cleared by the Coast Guard before leaving, he was excluded without a hearing when he attempted to reenter this country. Under prior interpretations of the immigration laws, Kwong would be treated as an entering alien subject to exclusion rather than to deportation procedures. To the members of the Court, the chief difference between *Mezei* and *Kwong* seemed to be that Kwong had been a legally admitted alien while Mezei was not. In *Mezei*, Clark distinguished Kwong on the basis that Mezei left for his visit to Rumania without authorization or reentry papers and broke his continued residence in the United States. Burton and the *Mezei* majority, by their willingness to uphold Kwong's claim, indicated that their votes were not always based on unrelenting hostility toward alien claims but rather on unwillingness to interfere with congressional power over immigration.[31]

In the area of constitutional criminal procedure, the Court heard very few cases during the last four Vinson terms. This trend was in keeping with the majority's deference to states' rights and police practices in criminal matters. Of the criminal procedure cases that were decided, four during the 1949 term were cases in which certiorari had been granted before the deaths of Murphy and Rutledge. However, one can exaggerate the philosophic positions of individual justices in criminal procedure cases. For example, while the controlling bloc, which included Frankfurter, voted to deny certiorari in most cases, Black frequently joined them, leaving Douglas to stand alone to grant.[32]

During the 1949 term, the Court's significant criminal procedure business involved overruling a libertarian search and seizure decision. The power to make a warrantless search of objects in plain sight when making a validly warranted arrest had been the rule before the 1946 term. Then, in *Harris* v. *United States*, the Court permitted the warrantless ransacking of a house incident to an arrest. In the 1947 *Trupiano* case, with Burton, Vinson, Black, and Reed dissenting, Murphy had modified the *Harris* rule by stating that the police were required to have a warrant if there was a reasonable opportunity to obtain one. In the 1949 term, in *United States* v. *Rabinowitz*, the Court considered the legality of the warrantless search of a desk safe and file cabinets in the one-room office of the defendant, who was validly arrested in the office on a charge of selling and having in his possession forged and altered government stamps.

In the conference, Vinson voted to reverse without comment. Black then announced that he still thought the Fourth Amendment applied to the states but that the rule excluding illegally obtained evidence from federal courts did not apply. Although he thought *Trupiano* was a departure in that it had injected a reasonable opportunity requirement and had "undercut the *Harris* case, . . . the court should stop flip flopping 'back and forth.'" To Reed, the case was "relatively simple and should be reversed on the basis of *Harris.*" Burton, predictably, agreed, commenting that *Trupiano* had been wrongly decided and that "search with a lawful arrest is good until changed by statute." When the Court, in a Minton opinion, upheld the search and overruled *Trupiano*, Frankfurter, Black, and Jackson pleaded for stare decisis and dissented. Frankfurter, Jackson, and Clark had voted to deny certiorari in the first place.[33]

Burton's hostility to interference with authority in search and seizure cases was again demonstrated that term in his dissent, which was joined by Reed, when Black held unconstitutional the conviction of a District of Columbia resident for not admitting into her home a health inspector who did not have a search warrant. In *District of Columbia* v. *Little,* Burton asserted that the petitioner's action was an effective interference with the performance of the inspector's duties. The inspections were of such "a reasonable, general, routine, accepted and important character, in the protection of the public health and safety, that they were being performed lawfully without such a search warrant as is required by the unreasonable search and seizures."[34]

The Court, as usual, expended a great deal of energy deciding criminal cases involving postconviction remedies. Characteristically, Burton and the majority wanted to restrict prisoner access to court procedures after trial and appeal. During the 1949 term, the Court overruled two majority decisions by Justice Murphy. In *Wade* v. *Mayo*, Murphy had held that while a convicted state prisoner must exhaust all state appellate remedies before applying to the federal district courts for release on a writ of habeas corpus, the exhaustion rule did not require him to pursue his "state remedies" to the point of petitioning for certiorari from the United States Supreme Court. The probability of a grant of certiorari was negligible anyway, given the large number of cases. During the 1949 term, in *Darr* v. *Buford*, the Court reconsidered the Murphy holding and the full meaning of a denial of certiorari.

In conference, Frankfurter, Black, and Jackson agreed that a denial meant nothing; therefore, the district court, upon considering a habeas corpus petition, should not insist upon application to the Supreme Court for the writ of certiorari. This position would thus uphold *Wade* v. *Mayo*. Reed thought that the district court should be required to ask whether there was any reason why the prisoner should be exempted from the rule that he must apply for a writ of certiorari; and if the prisoner had applied but had been denied, of what significance was this fact. The district court should take care not to interfere with state judicial proceedings. Once the votes were counted and Reed wrote the majority opinion incorporating his views, Burton had difficulty deciding whether to write a concurring opinion.[35]

Burton was just as interested in maintaining states' rights as Reed; but he wanted to make clear his belief that when the reasons for denial of certiorari were not stated, the denial should be disregarded by the district court. Reed made several changes in his opinion in order to obtain Burton's vote, but to no avail. On the other hand, Burton could not join Frankfurter's dissent, despite his clerk's advice that he do so, because he did not want to uphold *Wade* v. *Mayo*. Frankfurter also attempted to obtain Burton's support of his dissent but finally gave up, asking that at least Burton consent to "change 'implied to inferred' in the concurrence." Burton complied. Frankfurter was always irked by the frequent misuse of the terms by some of the justices. For example, he passed a note to Burton on the bench one day, after Reed read a decision, asking him to "please tell Stanley [Reed] the opinion implies and he infers."[36]

In *Darr* v. *Buford*, the Court had required the complete exhaustion of state remedies, including an application for a writ of certiorari to the Supreme Court, before a petition for habeas corpus could be filed in federal court; and a new federal statute made this requirement mandatory. This issue generated a divergence of opinion among the circuits concerning disposition of the numerous petitions filed by prisoners. The same issue was raised in the habeas corpus cases in the 1952 term, *Brown, Speller, Daniels* v. *Allen*, which involved three black males convicted of capital felonies in North Carolina. The men filed applications for habeas corpus in the federal district court, alleging that their convictions were illegal because of discrimination against blacks in the selection of jurors. In two of the cases, *Brown* and *Speller*, the constitutional issues had been raised and decided adversely by the state trial court, and the Supreme Court had denied certiorari. In the third case, *Daniels*, the state court dismissed the appeal for a late filing, and the Supreme Court again denied certiorari. In addition, the federal district court dismissed the petitions for habeas corpus, and the dismissals were affirmed by the court of appeals. In all the cases, the lower courts based their negative rulings on the denial of certiorari by the Supreme Court.

These cases caused the Court great difficulty and involved a considerable expenditure of time without changing the views of the justices or shedding much additional light on the issues. After the cases were argued in April 1952, Frankfurter announced that his clerks had begun researching the actual impact of the decision in *Darr* v. *Buford* on habeas corpus proceedings and state reviews of criminal convictions. According to Frankfurter, the project was "immense." Furthermore, judging from the size of the task and the necessity for deciding the case involving President Truman's seizure of the nation's steel mills, which "frustrated" completion of the research before the end of the 1951 term, he knew the case would have to be held over. Frankfurter was, however, "against setting the case down for reargument . . . [as that was] a transparent device . . . to enable it to be said that all matters before the court have been disposed of . . . a useless fiction for grown men and the Supreme Court to be indulging in.'' He suggested that the cases just be held over, stating that "of course nobody will be harmed if these cases are set down for reargument, (except counsel who will prepare to reargue them, and the petitioners) but I do not believe anybody would be helped, and I really don't see why we should be indulging in this playacting.'' Despite his suggestion, the cases were set down for reargument on October 13, 1952, and were decided in February 1953.[37]

After Frankfurter filed his report in October 1952, which concluded that "materials before the District Court very seldom furnish enough information about the Supreme Court proceedings to afford a guiding basis for interpretation of our denial of certiorari,'' the conference could not agree on a Court opinion which would satisfactorily deal with the cases at hand and give guidance on the procedure to be followed in later cases. Memos flew hard and fast between Frankfurter and Reed, the majority opinion writer in *Darr*, who had been assigned the Court opinion. Reed's draft opinion brought forth a memo to the conference from Frankfurter in which he outlined his disagreement. In an effort to resolve the conflict, Burton, ever the peacemaker, suggested that perhaps Frankfurter's views could appear as a per curiam or opinion of the Court, followed by Reed's dissent from it, and finally by a brief tabulation of the votes resulting in an affirmance of the instant cases.[38]

On New Year's Eve, in the interest of "putting an end to this blizzard of memoranda,'' Frankfurter again dissected Reed's opinion and made "a practical proposal,'' for he still disagreed with Reed's opinion because it gave no guidelines for the district judges. His proposal consisted, in part, of Burton's suggestion that the opinion on the nonsignificance of denial of certiorari appear as per curiam; but it would also include what Reed had to say on affirmance in the instant case, for Reed had a majority on that point. As many dissents as necessary could then follow. Frankfurter commented that although this would be an unusual form for the decisions, "we have an unusual situation.'' The final decision gave little additional guidance to the bench and bar. There was a Court opinion by Reed affirming the denial of habeas corpus; a majority opinion by Frankfurter; an adherence to their previous position announced in concurrence by Burton and Clark; an agreement with Frankfurter on nonsignificance by Black and Douglas; a concurrence in Reed's result on the jury discrimination issue by Black and Douglas; and a dissent by Black, Frankfurter, and Douglas from Reed's view that a district court's failure to apply the nonsignificance of certiorari rule was a harmless error.[39]

In another federal criminal case considered by the Court in the 1951 term, wiretapping was at issue, and Burton voted with the libertarians. In *OnLee* v. *United States*, Burton, with the concurrence of Frankfurter, who also dissented separately, dissented when Jackson's decision for the Court upheld a conviction which was based on testimony introduced by a federal agent, who from outside a Chinese laundryman's premises, listened to a conversation through a radio transmitter concealed for that purpose on another person who was speaking with the accused. The laundryman claimed that the wiretapping violated the constitutional prohibition against unreasonable searches and seizures, fair play, and the Federal Wiretapping Act. The Court had previously upheld wiretapping as a reasonable search and seizure in 1928 in *Olmstead* v. *United States* and in 1942 in *Goldman* v. *United States*. Burton, in his *OnLee* dissent, asserted that entering with a transmitter was the same as a surreptitious entry by the agent himself. Douglas dissented, admitting that he had been wrong when he voted with the majority in *Goldman*; and Black and Frankfurter dissented in opposition to the lack of fair play involved, which seemed to put a premium on fraud. Vinson, who along with Minton, Jackson, and Reed had voted to deny certiorari in the first place, was convinced that the search was legal. To Vinson, the laundry entered was a public place, and the informer was permitted to enter by OnLee; it was not as if the agent came in and hid behind a box.[40]

The Court broke little new ground in the other criminal cases. In *Jennings* v. *Illinois*, in a Vinson opinion which Burton supported, the Court rebuked the state of Illinois for not having a clear postconviction remedy procedure. A Supreme Court requirement that prisoners exhaust state remedies was useless when it became clear, in case after case, that Illinois either had no such remedy or had a very elusive one. After the decision in *Jennings*, Illinois finally devised what appeared to be an adequate procedure. In *Rochin* v. *California*, Frankfurter, the Court's most consistent defender of the Fourth Amendment, held for the Court, including Burton, that pumping a defendant's stomach to force the disgorging of evidence violated due process because it "shocked" the conscience. Black and Douglas concurred, agreeing that the procedure was illegal because it violated the constitutional privilege against self-incrimination. They did not want the decision in a particular case to hinge on whether the facts "shocked the conscience" of Frankfurter and Burton or some other justice.[41]

In another criminal case during the 1951 term which turned on the issue of jurisdiction, *Madsen* v. *Kinsella*, Burton wrote a "handsome" majority opinion. The defendant, Madsen, was an American citizen who murdered her husband, an American air force lieutenant, in Germany. She was arrested by military police and tried by a United States Court of the Allied High Commission, a court of American civilian judges who applied German law. Procedurally, the court could use both civilian and military judges without a jury. After conviction, the defendant petitioned for release on the grounds that under the Articles of War, only a court-martial or military commission had jurisdiction and that the commission which tried her could not have been a "military" commission because the offense took place after the occupation of Germany and also because the judges were civilians. Burton held that the occupation court had jurisdiction, although a court-martial would also have had jurisdiction if it chose to assert it. To escape this procedural difficulty, Burton simply pronounced the courts as "in the nature of military commissions." A practical difficulty also existed because if the Court decided the commissions were invalid, every past conviction would be upset. Genuine military tribunals would then be required because Congress had not enacted a statute to deal with the problem. In his solitary dissent, Black faced the difficulty head-on by stating that the president had no authority to create the courts which had convicted the defendant and that "whatever may be the scope of the president's power as commander-in-chief of the fighting armed forces, I think that [if] American citizens in present day Germany are to be tried by the American government, they should be tried under laws passed by Congress and in courts created by Congress under its constitutional authority.'' The practical issue in the case was whether a less democratic court system than that in the United States should have been used in Germany. Madsen, of course, was only interested in finding a way to be relieved of the murder conviction.[42]

The cause célèbre of the 1952 term was a criminal case, the *Rosenberg* spy case, involving the convictions of Julius and Ethel Rosenberg for conspiracy to violate the Espionage Act of 1917 by communicating atomic secrets to Russia in time of war. The Supreme Court never really decided the issues, since after the Rosenbergs were tried and convicted and sentenced to death by a district court in New York, a series of unsuccessful motions was filed to delay execution. The court of appeals affirmed in 1952, and the Supreme Court denied certiorari and a rehearing. Justice Black dissented, and Frankfurter added a memorandum to the opinion. The case then went back to the district court, through the court of appeals, and to the Supreme Court; this process was repeated three times on different motions. Eventually, the Supreme Court denied all motions and vacated a successful application for a stay to Douglas individually. The Court then denied a motion to reconsider its own powers to vacate Douglas's stay, and the Rosenbergs were executed on June 19, 1953.

When the justices' views were expressed in conference at a special term convened in June to consider the vacation of Douglas's motion, Vinson seemed especially anxious to have the execution behind him. Black was resigned to defeat: ''whatever might be said would be futile,'' even though he considered it ''terrible to come in and consider these issues'' in this way and concluded that ''no one knows enough about it to decide today.'' Reed, Clark, Minton, and Jackson thought that the case had been held up too long already. Douglas commented that, of course, if the Court thought he had acted for insubstantial reasons, they could vacate the stay. However, he thought there was a substantial question on the matter of the applicability of the Atomic Energy Act. As Burton outlined his position in the case on June 19,1953, the day the Rosenbergs were executed, he had been ready to vote against them on the merits at all times. However, concerning the October 1952 petition, he wanted to grant certiorari in order to hear argument. In conference on June 13, 1953, he voted for oral argument on the motion to stay execution; but when that position lost, he voted in favor of vacating the stay. Again, on June 18, 1953, he was ready to vote against the applicability of the Atomic Energy Act as it stood and was willing to hear argument. But when only he, Black, and Douglas voted for oral argument, he voted in favor of vacating the stay and proceeding with the execution.[43]

One of the cases decided during the 1950 term, *Collins* v. *Hardyman*, sharpened a conflict between Burton's strongly held views concerning race relations and his fervent support of states' rights. A group of American Legionnaires allegedly broke up a meeting in California of persons gathered together to discuss national issues and to petition Congress for a redress of grievances. Those in attendance at the meeting claimed that they should be awarded damages based on the Civil Rights Act of 1871, the Ku Klux Klan Act which provided a remedy in damages for any party injured by any group of persons who conspired to go onto the premises of another for the purpose of depriving their victim of equal protection of the laws of equal privileges and immunities under the laws. In the majority opinion, Jackson narrowly construed the act based on a few late nineteenth century cases and advised the defendants to look to state law for protection.[44]

The majority opinion in *Collins* bristled with an analysis of Reconstruction and post-Reconstruction history consistent with the hostile and reactionary views prepared by historians and read by students during the time when many of the justices were students in high school or college. For example, Jackson asserted that the act "was passed by a partisan vote in a highly inflamed atmosphere. It was preceded by a spirited debate which pointed out its grave character and susceptibility to abuse, and its defects were soon realized when its execution brought about a severe reaction." Burton's dissent, which was joined by Black and Douglas, adhered to the language of the statute and avoided references to the horrors of

Radical Reconstruction. He saved his states' rights position by asserting that the act did not limit its reference to actions by state officials. However, he strongly argued the viability of the statute as creating a federal cause of action in favor of persons injured by private individuals through the abridgment of federally created constitutional rights.[45]

Although still primarily conservative in regards to race relations questions, the Court, along with most of the American public in the aftermath of World War II, increasingly favored whittling away at racial segregation. The Court was ready to continue its forward movement in this area but only at a leisurely pace. This climate presented no difficulty to Burton, who compromised his strong states' rights views in the interest of opposing discrimination against blacks after his single misstep in the *Morgan* case during his freshman year on the Court. Of the three race relations cases which were heard in the 1949 term and were decided for the black petitioners, *Sweatt* v. *Painter* and *McLaurin* v. *Oklahoma State Regents* dealt with access to graduate education, while *Henderson* v. *United States* involved segregation in railroad dining cars. In *Henderson*, the petitioner had been excluded from a dining car because the few curtained-off "colored tables" were taken, even though there were other empty "white tables" in the car.

In conference on the school cases, Vinson elaborated at great length on the history of the Fourteenth Amendment concerning the issue but added that "it may be that now we should expand the Constitution but not on so sensitive an issue when those who wrote the early legislation and the 14th Amendment were not clear on it." Furthermore, he had found no reference to any application of the Fourteenth Amendment to the desegregation of professional schools and believed that "no great harm would come from [racial] association in professional schools." With reference to *McLaurin,* Black stated that he was mainly persuaded by the idea that "it is not *equal* to isolate"; and in the discussion on *Sweatt*, he commented that one "can't set up overnight" a law school, for the "diplomas from the established schools and those from the hurriedly founded will have a different value." Black also indicated that he could not support the decision in *Plessy*. In fact, he believed that the 1883 *Civil Rights* cases in which the rule that the statute based on the Fourteenth Amendment could not prohibit private discrimination should be overruled.

Reed was certain that the defendant in *McLaurin* had been discriminated against; but with reference to *Sweatt*, he could not decide whether the facilities were unequal unless the case was remanded for more evidence. Frankfurter, who had, Burton noted, occasionally acted as a counsel for the NAACP over a period of ten years, told the justices that they should not go beyond what was necessary in deciding these cases: "the court should find [decide in favor] for both students but should not go beyond the scope of the case. [It] should abstain from saying anything about segregation as such." His remarks would probably have come as a surprise to the NAACP, which was arguing for a broader statement on the issues. More support came from Douglas, who quite simply wanted to overrule *Plessy*. Jackson, however, stated that no basis for the desegregation of schools could be found in the Fourteenth Amendment or in any congressional statutes. Furthermore, although he doubted the wisdom of amending the Constitution in order to desegregate, he thought they would have to reverse, narrowly, in the cases at hand. Minton was also in favor of reversal. Clark thought the Court definitely should clarify the fact that there was no way to make segregated law schools equal, in order to avoid continued litigation on assertions that equal schools had been established. However, Frankfurter objected that a clear distinction should be drawn between "equality cannot be obtained in segregated graduate schools" and "segregation is not reasonable when applied to graduate schools," so that the latter would not be taken as the Court's position. Burton simply voted to reverse without recording his comments. His clerks were eager to have these cases decided on as broad a basis as possible, but they realized that to overturn all segregated education was "unwise in this area where feelings run high." Burton noted that resolution of the racial question was within the power of the states, "although an act of Congress would override it if enacted." In the absence of such an enactment, schools which were really equal would be constitutional even if they were segregated.[46]

In conference on *Henderson*, Vinson and Black were certain that the Interstate Commerce Act had been violated; Reed, however, found it "difficult personally" to decide on the issue. Although agreeing with Vinson and Black that the issue should be limited to the statute, Frankfurter also found *Henderson* a "difficult case." He was concerned about whether Henderson had standing to sue; however, he said he would probably vote to reverse. Douglas commented that if there were no statute, "they probably could not reach it [a decision]," for he believed that such segregation in the absence of a statute might be constitutional. Minton agreed. In voting to reverse, Jackson said that he did not know what result to reach because he had never dealt practically with segregation until he came to the Court. This statement implied, of course, that as attorney general he had not concerned himself with the issue. Unlike commentators on the Court, the justices felt the statute, and not the Fourteenth Amendment, was the foundation for the decision. In deciding these cases for the black petitioners, the Court neither overruled nor reaffirmed *Plessy* v. *Ferguson*, in which the constitutional rule of separate but equal public facilities was established in 1896. Both *Sweatt* and *McLaurin* were first assigned to Black, an Alabamian and former member of the Ku Klux Klan, and then later reassigned to Vinson, who wrote as chief for a unanimous Court. In *Sweatt*, the Court held that once black students were admitted to a graduate school, they could not be kept separate and apart. In *Henderson*, Burton, also writing for a unanimous Court, held that the Interstate Commerce Act forbade discrimination in public transportation, a decision which left untouched the constitutional issue of whether the state action had violated the Fourteenth Amendment.[47]

In commenting on Burton's draft, Frankfurter suggested, in *Henderson*, that Burton overemphasized the issue of racial segregation as such rather than the burden placed on the transportation companies in providing segregated facilities. In suggesting to Burton that caution be used in the opinion, Frankfurter stated that:

I doubt whether any member of the court feels more strongly against the racial inequalities than I do. . . . But I also feel very strongly, as you well know, against borrowing future trouble in the exercise of our jurisdiction. Sufficient unto the day is the goodness thereof. No one single cause has got this court into more heedlesss trouble than needlessly deciding issues not before the court or going needlessly beyond an adequate ground of disposing of a controversy, particularly when popular passion is involved.[48]

In order to avoid having Frankfurter write a concurrence, Burton deleted from his draft a statement that the division between the tables on the trains was mostly symbolic, thus focusing on discrimination and not on racial segregation as such. Although he was not able to keep Douglas from concurring, he persuaded him not to file the opinion he had written. Douglas thought that since the case squarely presented the issue of racial segregation in existing facilities, the Court should focus on that issue.

Burton wanted to avoid "any issue of the arguments, etc. in the national election campaign." In November, 1952, after noting that Kansas was not defending in *Brown* v. *Board of Education,* the Court issued an order inviting the state's attorney general to participate or to advise them as to whether he was confessing the unconstitutionality of the statute by not offering a defense. After the order had been issued, Black suggested that the Court read a case in which the attorney general of the United States declined to argue a case before the Supreme Court. Frankfurter looked up the case and told the conference that in calling attention to it, "Black has, I believe, happily reinforced the action we took." The attorney general in that early use had declined not at all as a "courteous act of disrespect" to the Court but because it was asking the attorney general of Kansas whether he wanted to do the same.[49]

In a memo prepared for Burton on the virtues and defects of legal segregation and the *Brown* case, his clerk suggested that "sociology and psychiatry appear to be poor foundations for a decision." Continuing, he asserted that "arguments directed in the briefs which find their basis in either or both of these fields, while not unimportant, in consideration, would . . . be poor bases for outlawing a system as deeply rooted in this country as segregation." He recognized that the decision in *Plessy* v. *Ferguson* was wrong, laboring as it did under the misconception that "segregation is not a pattern imposed by the dominant social and political group on the minority." But if the *Plessy* case were not to be over-

ruled, then, according to the clerk, "immediate relief by way of admission into schools providing equal facilities might be in order."
His recommendation, which was finally put on the bench memo
before oral argument in December 1952, was to reverse in a very
narrowly written decision not overruling *Plessy* as such but
recognizing that "there necessarily is inequality in segregation in
public school facilities since such segregation in present-day conditions precludes proper development of the student." Burton
crossed out the phrase "not overruling *Plessy*" and wrote in
"should overrule."[50]

In conference after the December argument in *Brown, Bolling,
Sharpe,* and other consolidated school cases, not even a tentative
vote was taken. Vinson explained at length, again, that his reading
of Reconstruction legislative history indicated no intention to
desegregate schools. Black was "compelled" to comment that the
reason behind segregation was the belief that black people were
"inferior," to which was added the fear of the possible "mixture of
races," for "it [the mixture] weakens the white race." However, he
would vote with a majority to reverse. Reed's views generally were
in favor of moderation: "Negroes have not [been] thoroughly
assimilated. . . . [We] must allow time—10 years in Virginia
perhaps, every year helps." Frankfurter quickly declared that
discrimination in the District of Columbia violated the Fifth
Amendment due process clause. However, he believed that *Bolling*,
along with the state cases, should be set over for reargument under
the new administration. He continued with the comment that even
though he had never had a close relationship with blacks, he had
"much to do with the problem" as counsel for the NAACP and
believed he had considerable expertise. He thought that his non-
state interventionist views failed him only in conscience; shocking
civil liberties cases such as *Rochin* v. *United States* generally gave
him a firm foundation for decisions on such issues. In these cases,
he did not believe that the states had been shown to be denying
equal protection. Douglas was in favor of declaring segregation illegal but thought the basis for decision was a "maybe" question
that would take a long time to work out. He agreed that the cases
should be set over for reargument. Jackson, who asserted that he

was never aware of segregation before he came to Washington, thought Thurgood Marshall's brief for the petitioners was "sociology" and did not deal with the legal issues; furthermore, he did not think he could say the practices were unconstitutional. He was in favor of holding the cases for a while in the hope that Congress might in the meantime act on the District of Columbia situation. Criticizing the existence of prejudice against the Mexicans in Texas, which he regarded as offensive, Clark asserted that whatever result the Court reached should be the same in the District of Columbia and state cases. However, he would support reargument before decision. To Minton, the hour was getting late; but "segregation is per se unconstitutional [and I'm] ready to vote now." If the votes had been counted, Burton, Minton, Clark, Douglas, and Black would have been in favor of the black petitioners; and Reed, Frankfurter, Vinson, and Jackson would have been opposed.[51]

In setting the cases over for reargument in the next term, the Court listed a number of questions for counsel to address concerning the history and application of the Fourteenth Amendment and the possible decrees which could be issued in the case. In addition, they invited the United States attorney general to argue and file a brief. When the Court was criticized for this invitation, Black told the conference that he believed they should retract it. The remainder of the justices did not agree with him, and the order was issued.[52]

While holding over the *Brown* case, the Court did decide some discrimination cases in favor of the black petitioners. In *Terry* v. *Adams,* the Court continued its efforts to protect the rights of black voters in the South. In decisions made before Burton joined the Court, it had invalidated a statute barring blacks from the Democratic primary, ordered a black voter admitted to a Democratic primary after the state legislature had given the Democratic state committee power to exclude blacks, and condemned discrimination against blacks in a primary conducted "under state statutory authority." The *Terry* case involved the Jaybirds, an all-white association which regularly held its own election some weeks in advance of the Democractic primary regulated by the state of Texas. The winners of the Jaybird election would then enter the Democratic primary, which was open to both whites and blacks, and would generally be successful. The plaintiff, a black man, sought an injunction against the practices which prevented him from voting in the Jaybird primary. Minton, Jackson, Frankfurter, and Vinson had voted unsuccessfully to deny certiorari, which would have left standing the discrimination.[53]

In the conference on the *Terry* case, Vinson could not see where state action was involved, "using the mechanism that they do." In response, to Vinson, Black stated that they should not let words prevent them from outlawing the practice; if the system was approved, it would be "seized upon" by other states to deny blacks their voting rights. Reed agreed with Black about the importance of the right to vote, but he nonetheless thought that Vinson's position was logical. Frankfurter could not decide whether to agree with Black's position that the practice should be outlawed, and Jackson did not think the Jaybird procedure was prohibited by the Constitution. After all, Jackson asserted, "people have some rights." Clark and Burton voted to reverse, with Clark pointing out that "whatever it [the Jaybird primary] was called, it was the only entrance to the Democratic primary." Minton voted to affirm. On March 14, 1953, a second vote was taken. Reed now voted to affirm, which created a 4-4 tie, with only Frankfurter passing. Afterward Clark's draft of an opinion convinced Jackson, Vinson, and Reed that enough state action was involved to support a reversal. Burton also had a series of meetings with Black and Frankfurter in an unsuccessful attempt to work out an opinion on which they could all agree. Douglas and Burton concurred in a Black opinion prohibiting the discrimination on Fifteenth Amendment grounds. Frankfurter concurred separately in the view that the lower court should be ordered to outlaw the illegal primary instead of admitting blacks to it, as the Clark majority opinion held. The only dissenter was Minton, who could find no state action on which to base a complaint of racial discrimination.[54]

In *Barrows* v. *Jackson,* the Court extended the rule of *Shelly* v. *Kramer* against restrictive covenants in housing. Burton and five other members of the Court, in an opinion by Minton, upheld a lower court decision that an award of damages for breach of a racial restrictive covenant would be state action in violation of the Fourteenth Amendment. Vinson dissented on the grounds that the defendant, who did not want to pay damages, had no standing to raise the rights of the unidentified non-Caucasian purchasers as a defense. Reed and Jackson did not participate. In conference, Vinson emphasized even more strongly than in his published opinion his view that "the Negro and his rights is not in this case," although the remainder of the justices were convinced that making restrictive covenants unenforceable would be less useful if damages could be awarded against a white owner who sold to a prohibited minority. Additionally, in a Douglas opinion in *District of Columbia* v. *John R. Thompson Co.*, the Court unanimously held that antidiscrimination laws applicable to restaurants fell within the type of municipal police regulation entrusted to the District of Columbia Legislature of 1871-72 and within the exception of the 1901 code, which repealed all but police regulations and "acts relating to municipal affairs only." The effect of this decision was the desegregation of restaurants in the District of Columbia.[55]

All else during the first four Vinson terms paled beside the widely publicized steel seizure case of the 1951 term, *Youngstown Sheet and Tube Co.* v. *Sawyer.* The case brought the issue of the extent of presidential power squarely before the Court and became the climax to a long dispute between the steel companies and their employees. Burton, as well as Clark, eventually voted with the majority to condemn the exercise of power by the president who had appointed them. On December 18, 1951, the steelworkers' union gave notice of its intention to strike on December 31. Following the intervention and failure of the Federal Mediation and Conciliation Service, President Truman referred the dispute to the Federal Wage Stabilization Board. In taking this action, the president was choosing to act under the authority of the Defense Production Act of 1950 rather than the Taft-Hartley Act. As the president saw the problem, "he had a choice of two alternatives" as provided by Congress. The first was the Taft-Hartley Act, which had a provision for an eight-day injunction. But, "contrary to the claims of some uninformed people," acting under the Taft-Hartley Act was not mandatory. Truman believed that the Taft-Hartley Act was designed chiefly for peacetime disputes and that the Wage Stabilization Board route was better suited to a wartime crisis situation. Having chosen that route, he saw no alternative to seizure when no solution was reached. He believed that he "had to act to prevent the stoppage of steel production which would imperil the nation."[56]

When the board's report was rejected by the companies, and the unions gave notice of a nationwide strike to begin on April 9, Truman ordered Secretary of Commerce Charles Sawyer to seize and operate the mills. The following day, the president sent a first message to Congress reporting his action; and twelve days later, he sent a second. Congress debated but took no action. On April 30, on petition of the steel companies, Judge David Pine of the District Court of the District of Columbia issued an order enjoining the government from taking over the mills. The court of appeals, sitting en banc on the same day, issued an order confirming and continuing the district court order. The Supreme Court, to which the United States appealed, granted certiorari on May 3. Protesting the grant of certiorari without waiting for a full hearing by the court of appeals, Burton and Frankfurter published a dissent in which they maintained that the issues were such as to require all the wisdom the judicial process made available. The majority set oral arguments for May 12, and the decision came down on June 2. Frankfurter and Burton shuddered at the rush toward decision in this significant case.

Burton knew by April 4 that the Court would eventually have to decide the case. In preparation, he began reading Edward Corwin's book on presidential power and the leading case on the inherent powers of the president, *United States* v. *Curtiss-Wright Export Corp.* When the conference met to deliberate the issue of whether to grant certiorari, Vinson opened with the statement that he did not like to bypass the circuit court but that after considering all factors, he thought the Supreme Court should take the case. He continued that the problem involved was not new to him, for he had dealt with such issues in the executive branch during the war. Black and Reed thought the cases should be argued as soon as possible, while Frankfurter, after reciting the history of cases on the powers of the president, asserted that he was opposed to "eagerness to settle"; he did not want the Court "to seize a big abstract issue." No one else commented except Minton, who said, "we [the Court] have to grant certiorari."[57]

Burton, who voted to deny certiorari, had to consider whether he wanted to have himself disqualified in the case. Luther Day, from the law firm in Cleveland where Burton had practiced from 1919 to 1925, was one of the large battery of attorneys representing the steel company. When Day, who was sensitive to this problem, sent a mutual friend to ask whether Burton would find it necessary to disqualify himself if Day stayed on the case, Burton replied that he would not since he felt no "entanglements" at all. Many years had passed since he had been in private practice; and in this case, there were "many other parties and issues quite unrelated to my [his] association with Luther Day."[58]

After the oral argument was heard, Vinson uncharacteristically embarked on a long discussion of the case, explaining that no one was arguing that the president was exercising unlimited power; Truman had asked the Congress to act, but "Congress has done nothing." The president "would have been derelict had he gone the Taft-Hartley route"; and if he had not seized the mills, "the howls would have been greater." Black retorted that "most of what Vinson said is irrelevant." Also, in his opinion, the case was not simply one of which statute to use; the seizure was wrong, but an "injunction is a serious thing for this court to do with no army. It is a serious thing to order the President." He thought the Court could find a solution which did not involve a direct order to give up the mills. Reed elaborated on the necessity for the Court to proceed slowly. He supported the president's power, but he hoped Congress or the president would act so that the Court would not be solely responsible for the resolution of the problem. He would like to "put off the decision . . . [and] simply leave [it] with the President temporarily."

Frankfurter was deeply concerned with the crisis-ridden posture of the case. Even though he was opposed to the seizure, he was more interested in the role demanded of the Court. He hoped "nine opinions . . . [would] be written"; he could not "escape it." He then read aloud an article he had written on the subject of presidential powers some twenty-five years before and outlined the history of government seizures, citing statutes, cases, and other relevant materials. In conclusion, he found that "no cases sustained inherent power in the President." After Frankfurter's lecture, Douglas merely commented that he agreed with Black. Jackson stated that he knew the difficulties a president must have in such crises but that there "were no inherent powers in the executive branch to commit such acts as these." Burton and Clark voted to affirm without comment. After an interval of near silence, Minton, speaking last, discussed the case in terms of his view of the political and economic crisis facing the president: "we have an acute emergency hanging over the world." On presidential powers, he asserted that "if Congress has not prohibited it and the Constitution has not, he need not stand by—he has implied power to act." When the votes were counted, it was 6-3 to invalidate the seizure, with Vinson, Reed, and Minton dissenting.[59]

The Court wrote seven different opinions covering 133 pages. Justice Black wrote the majority opinion, with Frankfurter, Douglas, Jackson, and Burton concurring separately; Clark wrote an opinion invalidating the seizure on separate grounds; and Frankfurter wrote two concurrences and two appendixes. All the justices in the majority agreed that the president did not have the power to take private property in the absence of a statutory basis, at least in time of peace. Burton's opinion rested squarely on the fact that even if the Taft-Hartley Act and the Wage Stabilization Board were read as alternative and equivalent routes, "neither procedure carried statutory authority for the seizure of private industries in the manner now at issue." As a matter of fact, Burton asserted, citing the testimony of the chairman of the Senate committee sponsoring the Taft-Hartley Act, "Congress reserved to itself the opportunity to authorize seizure to meet particular emergencies." Considering the World War II experience with strikes occurring during an emergency and the Smith-Connally Act, which he supported while in the Senate, Burton made it clear that the case did not cover the issue of "what might be the President's constitutional power to meet such catastrophic situations. Nor is it claimed that the current seizure is in the nature of a military command addressed by the President, as Commander-in-Chief, to a mobilized nation waging, or imminently threatened with, total war."[60]

When the Court handed down the decision, the announcement of the opinions preceded all other matters, even the admission of new members to the bar, which usually came first. In addition, all the justices in the majority wrote and orally summarized their opinions. Burton's was the shortest, just five pages including footnotes. Burton explained that "at one time I had feared I might be the only one to reject the seizure and my opinion was written largely while I expected to be in the minority." After certiorari had been granted but before argument, Burton had received the impression from the sympathetic comments expressed by Vinson, Black, Reed, Clark, and Minton, that he would be "largely alone in holding [that] the President was without power to seize the steel plants in the fact of the Taft-Hartley Act providing a different procedure."[61]

Although overshadowed by the *Steel Seizure* case, the most important cases for organized labor during the last four Vinson terms involved the issues of picketing and state legislation which limited the right to strike. The right to picket had been regarded as a freedom of speech granted by the Bill of Rights since *Thornhill* v. *Alabama*, a 1940 case, and *Senn* v. *Tile Layers Protective Union*, a 1937 case, had been decided by the Court. However, in the 1948 term, the Court, including Burton as part of the majority, had held in the *Giboney* case that even peaceful picketing had no protection when it was directed toward an illegal purpose. A state could make certain labor objectives illegal, thereby cutting off the *Thornhill* protection for picketing. Burton's votes still usually reflected a hostility toward union activity which dated from his experience with the antilabor temper of the Senate during his one term there. The $B_2H_1$ resolutions, which he had helped to frame, had been part of the movement toward the Taft-Hartley Act and were efforts to restrict union influence and power.

After insulating one variety of peaceful strike for higher wages from state action because Congress had preempted regulation in this field, in a 1949 Vinson majority opinion which Burton supported, the Court itself cut away almost all of the remainder of the *Thornhill* doctrine. In *Building Service Employees* v. *Gazzam*, a Minton opinion which Burton joined, the Court upheld an injunction against picketing used to induce an employer to force his employees into union membership. According to Minton, "abuse of the right to picket" was unprotected. This case was not as significant, however, as *International Brotherhood* v. *Hanke,* in which Burton joined Frankfurter's majority opinion ordering an injunction against the Teamsters, who were picketing to force a seller of used cars and his family to join the union. In this instance, the ultimate union purpose was to win compliance with a union rule against weekend and evening work which could not be maintained if independents did not comply. A state statute made the union goal illegal; but the Court found, as a matter of public protection and interest, that the union contract interfered with the rights of the community and that the picketing was not protected as a freedom of expression. The opinion applied a noninterventionist theory of due process in which state restraints would be approved if they were based on national interest and concern.[62]

Four of the labor cases involving the strikes that came before the Court during the 1950 term were decided in Burton opinions. *National Labor Relations Board* v. *Denver Building and Construction Trades Council, International Brotherhood of Electrical Workers* v. *National Labor Relations Board, Local 74* v. *National Labor Relations Board,* and *National Relations Board* v. *International Rice Milling Co.* required interpretation of Section 8 (b) (4) (A) of the recently enacted Taft-Hartley Act, which made it an unfair labor practice for any union to engage in concerted activities of which "an object is to force . . . any employer or other person to cease doing business with any other person." In the *Denver* case, the Court had to determine the meaning of the phrase "cease doing business with another person." Using a broad interpretation, the phrase could be construed to mean the prohibition of all labor union activities because all labor union activities were designed to keep customers, non-striking workers, or the like from doing business with the employer. However, Burton, speaking for the Court majority, found that the language was intended to eliminate secondary boycotts. Strikes by union men in situations in which a prime contractor gave employment to a nonunion subcontractor were, Burton asserted, illegal secondary boycotts. Douglas dissented, stating that traditionally, secondary boycotts were attacks on an employer on "a front remote from the immediate dispute"; and the union activity here did not fall in that category.[63]

Burton appeared to be antilabor in the *Denver* case, where there was evidence that union activity was at a comparatively low level. However, he decided in favor of the union, for a unanimous Court, in the *Rice Milling* case. Burton held that the union had not engaged in a boycott when agents of a union picketed a mill with the object of securing recognition as the collective bargaining representative of the employees. During the picketing, the agents told the driver of a neutral customer's truck to turn back from an intended trip to the mill and threw stones at the truck. Burton asserted that the NLRA contemplated something "more than is evidenced by the pickets' request to a driver of a single truck to discontinue a pending trip to a picketed mill."[64]

In the *Electrical Workers* case, the issues were substantially the same as in the *Denver* case except that here the union induced the work stoppage by peaceful picketing rather than by a prearranged signal; hence it did not engage in or call the strike. When Burton found the union activities an unfair labor practice according to the rationale of the *Denver* case, Douglas, Reed, and Jackson dissented without opinion. In *Local 74*, the *Carpenters* and *Joiners* case, Burton again sustained the NLRB's order, finding the union guilty of engaging in an unfair labor practice. In this case, a union employee doing carpentry work in a dwelling house stopped work to force the owner to cancel his installation contract with the supplier of the wall and floor coverings, who employed nonunion men. Reed, Douglas, and Jackson again dissented without opinion.

In the 1952 term, Burton carried the Court further along toward validating state restraints of picketing in labor disputes. For seven members of the Court, he decided that the state of Virginia could validly enjoin peaceful picketing at a construction site by union men against some of the subcontractors who employed nonunion help. The Virginia courts had held that the picketing was being carried on for purposes in conflict with the Virginia "Right to Work" statute, which prohibited any agreement between an employer and a labor union whereby persons who were not members of the union would be denied the right to work for the employer or whereby union membership was made a condition of employment or continuation of employment. Since he could not ascertain from the record whether the picketing was designed for the illegal purpose or was meant only to keep union men away from the job, which would give the picketing constitutional protection, Douglas dissented and asked that the case be remanded for specific findings of fact. Recognizing the inevitability of the decision in the light of recently decided cases, Black dissented without opinion.[65]

Burton wrote opinions in several other less important labor-related cases during the four terms. In *Oakley* v. *Louisville and Nashville Railroad Co.*, he found for a unanimous Court that under the Selective Service Act, in terms of seniority, veterans had a right to reemployment in substantially the same place on the job escalator that they would have been in had they not been in the military service. He wrote a dissent from a verdict for the plaintiff in a FELA case, *O'Donnell* v. *Elgin Joliet and Eastern Railway Company*; and he extended Fair Labor Standards Act overtime compensation to employees of contractors operating government-owned munitions plants on a cost-plus-a-fixed-fee basis in *Powell* v. *U.S. Cartridge*, for a five-member Court majority.[66]

In the 1952 term, for a unanimous Court in *Ford Motor Co.* v. *Huffman*, Burton upheld a collective bargaining agreement whereby an employer allowed employees seniority credit for both preemployment and postemployment military service. Also, he wrote two important opinions interpreting for the first time the featherbedding section of the Taft-Hartley Act. The Court had to reconcile two cases from different circuits which were in conflict on the issue. In *American Newspaper Publishers Association* v. *National Labor Relations Board*, Burton's majority opinion upheld the circuit court decision that the act did not apply to the International Typographical Union's practice of requiring that all newspaper advertisements printed from cardboard matrices supplied by the advertisers be reset by Linotype operators at each paper. This "reproductive" work almost never appeared in print and consumed about 5 percent of the work time of the Linotype operators. In *Gamble Enterprises, Inc.* v. *National Labor Relations Board,* Burton reversed the circuit court and upheld the American Federation of Musicians' practice of refusing to allow traveling name bands to appear at a movie theater unless local musicians were employed to play overtures and intermission music or separate engagements. Both cases required interpretation of that section of the Taft-Hartley Act which made it an unfair labor practice for a union "to cause or attempt to cause an employer to pay . . . any money . . . in the nature of an exaction, for services which are not performed or [are] not to be performed." Upon examination of the legislative history, Burton decided that this section was intended only to prohibit payments where no work was done and that the Congress had rejected language which would have made it necessary for the courts or board to determine the necessity, utility, or desirability of the work actually performed.

In the *Newspaper Publishers* case, Douglas dissented on the grounds that the reproduction of advertising matter set up only to be thrown away was not a service performed for the publisher. In addition, Clark, with the concurrence of Vinson, dissented on the grounds that the act condemned union pay demands for services which the employer was not even willing to accept, such as the contrived and patently useless job operations involved in the case. In *Gamble,* Douglas joined Burton's majority opinion on the grounds that the services of the local orchestra, though unwanted, were not useless; but Jackson, who voted with the majority in the *Newspaper Publishers* case, dissented on the ground that before the enactment of Section 8 (b) (6) of the Taft-Hartley Act, the union had been compelling the employer to pay for standing by and was now accomplishing the same result by compelling the employer to pay for useless and unwanted work. Furthermore, whereas preparing and paying for bogus type was an old and accepted trade union practice to which other terms of employment had been adjusted, the musicians' device was a new subterfuge designed to avoid the effect of the statute.

Although Burton's opinion seemed to be the best way to keep the Court from becoming enmeshed in the thicket of what could increasingly become a by-product of technological unemployment, the use of "make work" problems in times of widespread depression or in depressed industries, the Court did not discuss any of these factors in the conference. When Vinson began by saying that "Congress meant to stop the practice that the NLRB urges here," Black retorted that "[Senator Robert] Taft knew how to write that if he wanted to," and furthermore, Taft never said "that the work must be needed." Unintimidated by Black's rejection of Vinson's point, Clark supported Vinson's position, stating that "Congress intended to stop this." Douglas, Minton, Burton, and Reed voted with Black, as did Jackson, who later changed his mind in the *Gamble* case. Also voting in agreement with Black, Frankfurter stated that "Congress faced up to the problem and then backed away" from outlawing the practices entirely. After reading the opinion which he as senior justice in the majority assigned to Burton, Black commented that "the history backs you up. . . . My own guess is, however, that Congress will take an opposite position in amending the Act."[67]

There were no other greatly significant economic cases during the period, and the few that were decided kept the Court headed in the same direction. In a Clark opinion, the Court shifted the burden of proof from the director to the corporation, in establishing the good faith of the transactions and the business in order to prove his claim as creditor in a bankruptcy proceeding, on a presumption that no actual conflict of loyalties arose. Burton dissented in an opinion joined by Black. Burton denounced such transactions by insiders when a corporation was insolvent and made clear his view that a conflict of loyalties between the stockholders and the director existed in such cases. Douglas, who did not take part in the decision because he was ill, wrote to Burton that he "liked very much" his objection to giving benefits to a wrongdoer who was particularly adroit.[68]

On another recurring issue, Burton decided for four justices, with Clark concurring in the result, that in determining the amount of government compensation to be made to claimants for property damage caused as a result of federal flood control, when flooding took place below the high-water mark, full payment must be made. In his decision for the claimant, Burton found that any uncompensated destruction which affected the agricultural value of the land (even if water was not actually overflowing it) was a taking of private property prohibited by the Fifth Amendment.[69]

A continuing controversy over offshore oil again came before the Court. In the 1947 *United States* v. *California* case, the Court had held that the United States rather than the state of California had control of the offshore minerals of that state in a dispute involving the ownership of offshore oil. In the 1949 term, the Court decided offshore oil cases involving Texas, Louisiana, and the United States. The Louisiana case was readily held to be controlled by the decision in *California*. However, the Texas case was more difficult because Texas had been an independent republic before annexation, and the United States had in the Treaty of Annexation conceded to Texas "all the vacant and unappropriated lands lying within its limits." Decision in the case was made even more difficult since Clark and Jackson could not participate because they had worked on the government case while serving as attorneys general. At first, Frankfurter, Vinson, and Minton expressed the view that the Texas claim should be upheld. Black was faced with the possibility of having to dissent, with an announcement that the *California* case was practically overrruled. Burton, Black, and Douglas were able to obtain Vinson's vote late in May to make a majority of four. The Court, in a Douglas opinion which Burton, Black, Douglas, and Vinson joined, adopted the view that Texas entered the Union on an equal footing with all other states; and under that circumstance, no special privileges, unless expressly reserved, applied to it by virtue of its unique position before admission. Therefore, since no other state could own subadjacent lands, the *California* case rule applied to Texas as well. Reed, Minton, and Frankfurter dissented.[70]

Burton's remaining opinions during the 1949 term included a majority tax decision on a dissent from Jackson's Court opinion declaring invalid a New York attempt to settle the accounts of a common trust fund after giving notice to interested persons by newspaper publication, under a state statute requiring actual notice only where possible. Once again expressing his strongly held philosophy of states' rights, he asserted that "whether or not further notice to beneficiaries should supplement the notice and representation here provided is properly within the discretion of the State. The Federal Constitution does not require it here."[71]

He concurred in a Clark opinion for the majority which denied the claim of a military prisoner that his conviction was invalid because no Judge Advocate General's officer was appointed to hear his case. Also, Burton wrote a majority opinion for four justices upholding the power of the Interstate Commerce Commission, in approving a consolidation of railroad facilities, to extend the period of protection of the railroad employees' interests beyond four years from the effective date of the order. Jackson dissented on his usual grounds that it was unnecessary to resort to legislative history to interpret the words of any statute. Frankfurter also dissented and was joined by Reed, reflecting their opposition to a broad interpretation of the commission's powers. During the 1952 term, Burton's majority opinion in *King* v. *United States* also upheld the ICC's power to order a rise in interstate freight rates to reflect the full amount of a previous increase in interstate rates designed in part to cover a deficit in passenger operations at that time.[72]

During the 1950 term, Burton joined Black in supporting Frankfurter's dissent to Douglas's opinion that fair trade laws which permitted manufacturers to set minimum prices for goods sold by retailers, which would have been illegal under the normal application of antitrust laws, could only regulate the prices of the retailers and manufacturers who were actual parties to any agreement. When Burton, who had at first planned to join Douglas, changed his mind, Frankfurter applauded his open-mindedness, saying, "once more you prove that you are not blocked by having taken a contrary view to begin with." However, the Douglas opinion immediately became the most popular decision of the term when, a few days after the case was decided in May, price wars—especially in cosmetics, drug sundries, and electrical appliances—began among retail stores, resulting in jubilation on the part of consumers."[73]

Burton wrote the majority opinion in a 1952 price discrimination case, *Standard Oil Co.* v. *FTC,* deciding, characteristically, in favor of the corporation. Standard Oil gave its dealers' customers more favorable prices than it charged the customers' competitors, four large Detroit gas jobbers who either retailed the gas themselves or sold it to stations. Discriminatory price cuts to meet competition were forbidden by the Robinson Patman Act, which provided that a showing of price discrimination made a prima facie case of conduct having the prohibited effect of substantially lessening competition. The seller could rebut the prima facie case by showing that the lower price was set in order to meet the lower price of a competititor. The question at issue was: once the prima facie case is rebutted, is price discrimination still illegal? In one of the few instances when he spoke in oral argument, Burton pressed Standard Oil's attorney to discuss his view that the government's description of Robinson Patman was unacceptable because it meant that disproving the prima facie case merely shifted the burden of proof and did not decide the issue. That interpretation would mean there was no real value in a business showing that it had discriminated in order to meet competition and retain its customers; it had to bring forward still more evidence to show that the effect was not to lessen competition within the industry. Satisfied with the attorney's response, Burton's majority opinion indicated that the effect of the rebuttal was to render the discrimination permissible and was a complete defense to a complaint under the act. Burton believed that Congress had not intended "to compel the seller to choose only between ruinously cutting its prices to all its customers to match one price offered to one, or refusing to meet the competition and then ruinously raising its prices to its remaining customers to cover increased unit costs." Reed, who was joined in his dissent by Vinson and Black, interpreted the statute as making rebuttal of the prima facie case not a complete defense but merely a procedural one which left the way open for the commission to determine whether the proven price discrimination injured competition.[74]

Burton's majority opinion in *Spector Motor Service, Inc.* v. *O'Connor* struck down one state's attempt to tax partially out-of-state businesses in order to generate revenue. At issue was a Connecticut tax on corporations which was measured by the net income received from business transactions within the state. The state courts construed this arrangement as a tax or excise upon the franchise of corporations, whether domestic or foreign, for the privilege of carrying on or doing business in the state. In a decision which ended eight years of litigation, Burton held that the tax was invalid when applied to a foreign corporation which engaged exclusively in the interstate transportation of freight by motor truck because it was an interference with the commerce power of Congress. The opinion clearly decided that the tax was unconstitutional because the state characterized it as controlling the privilege of carrying on business. Burton was willing to accept the characterization, but this meant that the act interfered with interstate commerce. As Clark predicted in his dissent, which was joined by Black and Douglas, Connecticut thereafter changed the statute and its characterization and continued the tax. Frankfurter, who was part of the Burton majority, offered consolation when unfavorable comment on the decision resulted. "Contrary to some of the smarties in the law reviews," he told Burton, "your *Spector* was not a formal verbal distinction but a warning that purely interstate commerce could not be taxed for doing business in a state."[75]

Burton's two remaining opinions during the 1950 term were written for the majority. The first case upheld the validity of a Securities and Exchange Commission finding in a corporate reorganization dispute; and the second case held that under the Federal Tort Claims Act, the United States could be impleaded as a third party defendant by a joint wrongdoer. In conference, Burton had agreed that the Tort Claims Act did not require a waiver of immunity and that the government could not be sued, and he had been assigned to write an opinion on that basis. But after researching the cases, he was "convinced to the contrary and . . . drafted an opinion showing why . . . the government should be held liable." He suggested that if he could not get a majority, then "a reassignment will be in order." After circulating his draft in the cases, Burton read a law review article which reached the same conclusion; and he informed the conference that he would cite it in his opinion. Black responded to Burton's change of position by commenting that if no one else dissented, he would "acquiesce" in Burton's disposition of the cases; but he still believed that the opinion represented "judicial hostility to sovereign immunity rather than an interpretation of the Act as written." However, when Douglas indicated he would dissent without opinion, Black apparently decided to join him. Ecstatic at Burton's change of position, Frankfurter told him "you've done it again—demonstrated that it is the essence of the judicial function to pursue research even though the outcome dislodges views frivolously embraced."[76]

In the 1951 term, Burton wrote opinions in seven statutory, one trade regulation, three tax, one civil procedure, and two workman's compensation cases. In the trade regulation case, *Lorain Journal Co.* v. *United States,* he wrote for a unanimous Court, with Minton and Clark not taking part, upholding a Sherman Act injunction against a Lorain, Ohio, newspaper publisher who attempted to strangle a local radio station by refusing to accept advertisements for the paper from clients who also advertised on the radio. In the 1952 term, Burton dissented—joined by Black, Douglas, and Minton—when the Court upheld a tying arrangement for newspaper advertising not in violation of the Sherman Act. At issue was the publisher's practice requiring advertisers to buy space in both his morning and evening papers in order to buy space in either. Despite Clark's effort to distinguish *Lorain Journal,* Burton thought the issues were the same in both cases.[77]

Two of Burton's tax opinions were in cases "each of which was of more than usual difficulty and breadth." In one tax opinion, he declared for a unanimous Court that the third of the retail cost of eyeglasses kicked-back by optical companies to the eye doctors who referred their patients was deductible as an ordinary and necessary business expense. However, lawyers, as a professional group, were not as fortunate as physicians in *Lykes* v. *United States,* in which he found that "legal expenses do not become deductible merely because they are paid for services which relieve a taxpayer of liability." In another straightforward statutory interpretation case during the 1952 term, *Watson* v. *Commissioner of Internal Revenue,* he held for the majority concerning an Internal Revenue Service decision that the profits received from the sale of a commercial orange grove were ordinary income and not capital gains. Furthermore, a taxpayer's legal expenses for contesting a deficiency claim were not deductible merely because the claim, if justified, would consume income-producing property. The legal expenses were not expenses of the company but were personal to the taxpayer.[78]

In the third 1951 term tax case, *Rutkin* v. *United States,* Burton, for five members of the Court, upheld a conviction for willful evasion of federal income taxes. The defendant in this case had failed to include in the tax return money obtained by extortion, which Burton decided was taxable income like any other unlawful gain. During his first term, he had dissented in *Commissioner* v. *Wilcox,* in which the Court majority held that embezzled funds were not income taxable to the embezzler. In conference on *Rutkin,* when there was not a majority to overrule *Wilcox,* Black was assigned to write an opinion which would follow the rule of the earlier case. Still convinced of the validity of his earlier views, Burton prepared a dissent. With the first circulation of Black's opinion on December 18, 1951, Burton circulated his own dissent and asked how many justices would not only embrace it but would also join him in overruling *Wilcox.* When the returns came in, Minton agreed with the dissent but wanted to let *Wilcox* stand; Vinson and Jackson agreed with the dissent and would be willing to overrule *Wilcox;* Clark, Frankfurter, Reed, and Black were in favor of holding to *Wilcox;* and Douglas passed.[79]

As the Court worked to reach a decision, those critics who denounced the length of time necessary to resolve cases might have been more restrained had they had to reckon with Frankfurter, Black, and the other somewhat volatile personalities involved. Frankfurter was up in arms at the suggestion that *Wilcox* be overruled, even though, as he wrote to the conference, he "did not give a tinker's dam about the *Wilcox* case" as such; "but the whole point about stare decisis is that a case should not be overruled merely because it is later deemed wrong and particularly by a court differently composed." He was not, of course, "talking about stare decisis in relation to constitutional issues," which were always open to reexamination because legislatures could not displace a constitutional adjudication. But, Frankfurter continued, even with constitutional issues, "one ought to pause long before overruling a prior line of contitutional adjudication." When it came to overruling a case of statutory construction, Frankfurter added, the whole philosophy of law was drawn into question, for "the most influential factor in giving a society coherence and continuity is Law." Overruling cases "when new men have come on the Court

. . . encouraged the notion of law as the caprice of individuals.''
The tests Frankfurter thought the Court should use in deciding
whether to overrule were time, chance, the flow of history, questions of constitutional power, or other large public issues. They
should beware of ''wantonness'' which ''adds to the potential
chaos of society.''[80]

Frankfurter repeated his concern to Burton in January, while ap-
plauding Burton's ''open-mindedness.'' He criticized Burton's
statement in conference that more people such as Rutkin ''could
hardly have relied on the decision in *Wilcox*'' on the grounds that
''adherence to stare decisis did not call for observance.'' However,
Frankfurter insisted that point was not the most important reason
for adhering to the doctrine. Flattering Burton while criticizing
Black, he noted that ''Hugo [Black] would be genuinely delighted
to have *Wilcox* overruled, although he is against doing so, because
he really doesn't care for stare decisis; he takes very little stock in
the considerations of social policy that you and I care about, that
is, the importance of not shaking, or at least not jostling, the fabric
of law by making people feel there ain't no such thing.'' However,
Burton remained unpersuaded and continued his attempt to obtain
votes for his position.[81]

By January 9, Burton was writing the majority opinion, with
Clark having shifted his vote after further research. At this point,
Clark was even willing to overrule *Wilcox:* ''personally I am willing
to stand anything the dissenters might say.'' Since Minton and Vinson seemed agreeable, it seemed that Burton might get a majority
to overrule by February. However, Frankfurter's protestations and
the prospect of Black's ''gloating'' must have had their effect, because *Wilcox* was not overruled but was limited to its facts. After
the vote was taken, Jackson told Burton, with reference to the de-
nunciation of the majority in Black's dissent, ''I had no idea you
were so cruel, anarchistic, totalitarian and lawless. I thought you
should only be jumped on once this morning and so laid off. [I]
hope you suffered no deep bruises.''[82]

In the civil procedure case of *Perkins* v. *Benguet Consolidated
Mining Co.,* Burton wrote for the majority that doing business in
Ohio did subject a foreign corporation to the service of a summons
in an action, in personam, in Ohio without violating due process;

and he took a proworker position in opinions in two statutory liability cases. He held for the majority in a seaman's statute case that
it was not permissible under the applicable statute for an employer
to offset, against a seaman's claim for wages, the cost of medical
care and hospitalization for another crew member who was injured
by the seaman without justification during the voyage on which the
wages were earned. Furthermore, he held that congressional legislation had preempted the field. He also dissented, with the concurrence of Douglas and Black, from a Minton opinion in which six
members of the Court agreed with the courts below that the time
for filing claims under the Longshoremen's and Harbor Workers'
Compensation Act ran from the date of the accident rather than
from the date of the beginning of the disability, even if the disability did not result until one year later.[83]

Among the normal grist of statutory and jurisdictional cases
decided by the Court during the 1952 term were Burton's majority
opinions in a Full Faith and Credit case, one tax case, one administrative law case, one Interstate Commerce Commission case, and
four labor cases. He concurred in a case interpreting the National
Service Life Insurance Act, concurred in part and dissented in part
in a civil procedure case, and dissented in an antitrust case. In the
Full Faith and Credit case, *May* v. *Anderson,* Burton decided for
four other members of the Court that the Constitution did not require one state to follow the child custody decree rendered by
another state which had personal jurisdiction over only one parent.
Burton, in upholding custody by the mother, characterized her interest in the custody of her children as "far more precious . . . than
a property right." Burton cited appropriate prior authority in
reaching the decision; but as Black indicated in noting his agreement, "I construe your opinion as not holding that Full Faith and
Credit must be accorded to a judgment fixing the custody of children. The best interest of the child must always be the determining
factor."[84]

In *Transcontinental Western Air, Inc.* v. *Koppal,* Burton held
for the majority that a discharged employee of a carrier subject to
the Railway Labor Act was not precluded from resorting to a state-
recognized cause of action for wrongful discharge as long as he
showed exhaustion of his administrative remedies under his con-

tract of employment, if the applicable state law so required. In
*United States* v. *Henning*, Burton and Vinson concurred in a Clark
opinion that under the National Service Life Insurance Act, the
proceeds of a policy on the life of a deceased serviceman should,
since his father, as beneficiary, had died without receiving any part
of the proceeds, be awarded to the natural mother of the serviceman instead of being divided between the natural mother and the
stepmother's estate. In filing his concurrence, Burton rejected Vinson's suggestion that he include "a paragraph setting forth that we
concede to no one a greater love for our parents. Such affection or
its degree is not involved in this case. It is simply a question of construing an act of Congress passed by Representatives and Senators
who had fathers and mothers whom they either loved or revered
dearly."[85]

When Minton, for all members except Frankfurter and Douglas,
who did not participate, reversed a lower court decision dismissing
the case of a foreign corporation sued for libel in a Florida state
court, which removed the action to the federal district court, on the
grounds that the corporation was not doing business in Florida,
Burton concurred in part and dissented in part. He believed that the
Court ought to announce whether the corporation was doing business in the state in order to avoid further litigation on that issue.[86]

As the Truman period came to an end, so did Vinson's tenure as
chief over a controlling bloc of Truman-appointed justices. By this
time, Burton had fully developed the positions he would generally
follow throughout the duration of his service on the Court. His
tendency to support assertions of governmental authority was reflected in his role in civil liberties cases. He supported rejecting the
clear and present danger test in freedom of expression cases but
would uphold test oaths only if they were reasonable and scienter
was required. He believed there was no right to government employment and that the attorney general's listing of subversive
organizations was permissible but that the attorney general must be
able to defend a listing when challenged. He also strongly supported the exclusion, denaturalization, and deportation of
suspected subversive aliens as a matter of national policy.

In criminal procedure cases, he continued to favor police
authority and state control. He was willing to approve warrantless

searches and seizure as incident to arrest and to insist that state prisoners exhaust state remedies before seeking relief in federal court. However, he drew the line at surreptitious wiretapping and stomach pumping, which he felt were unacceptable police procedures.

In race discrimination cases, he voted an end to racial segregation in education, in interstate railroad transportation, and in exclusionary devices at the polls; and he wanted to overrule *Plessy* v. *Ferguson.* Toward labor, he opposed protection for picketing that was not peaceful, favored application of national law without interference from the states when the NLRA and Taft-Hartley Act had preempted the field (such as the regulation of secondary boycotts), but permitted state prohibition of labor union activity, including strikes and picketing directed toward illegal ends (for example, forcing someone to join a union or to violate state right to work laws). However, he favored a broad interpretation of workmen's compensation statutes in order to provide protection, if at all possible, for the workers. In ICC cases, he usually voted to uphold the authority of the commission; and in antitrust cases, he preferred interpretations that would not interfere with business unless a practice in fact had an anticompetitive economic effect.

On federal tax issues, he increasingly preferred to decide cases in favor of the Internal Revenue Service unless the statute clearly precluded it. To this end he declared that claimed capital gains were ordinary income, disallowed deductions, and insisted that embezzled and extorted funds were taxable income to the miscreant.

He opted for congressional authority while joining the majority to denounce the president's abuse of power in the steel seizure case. Even though he had easily taken an expansive view of the president's authority in time of war and the president had appointed him to the Court, the determining factor seemed to be less a concern that the chief executive was overbearing than an opposition to any diminution of the power of Congress, which was one of the values he held most dear.

In most of his views, Burton was ensconced comfortably as a member of the controlling bloc on the Court. He, Vinson, and Reed were most often joined by Minton and Clark. In the 1949 term, Clark, without judicial experience, tagged along behind Vinson more closely than Minton, who had come from the court of appeals, although they usually voted as a group. In the 1950 term, Burton voted with them less often because he had become slightly more libertarian, voting seven times in favor of and nine times against the claim right in the non-unanimous cases.

The work of the Court was enlivened by controversy within and continuing criticism from without. Frankfurter, who never had much respect for Vinson as chief, did not endear himself to his less-learned brethren by taking as much time as he wished in the conferences—sometimes including elaborate diagrams, charts, and the like—to lecture to them on points of law. However, he and Burton got on very well since Burton accepted his flattery, sometimes voted with him, and had nothing but praise for Frankfurter.

Although commentators on the Court felt the small annual dockets of the period resulted from the denial of certiorari in too many significant cases, the denials that occurred were issued after full-dress discussion. For example, *Koons* v. *Kaiser, Koons* v. *Kaufman,* one of the cases in which some commentators believed certiorari should have been granted during the 1950 term, presented the issue of how and where cases could be transferred from one district court to another under the new transfer provisions of the judicial code. The case turned on whether a court order could be reviewed in both or either the transferor or transferee circuit. The justices discussed the issues and agreed with Frankfurter's position that the Court should avoid deciding the issues until there was a clearer impression of what the circuit courts might do in such cases. In the cases that had been decided, there was no real conflict. Although he felt there was "some unsatisfactory language" in one case written by Justice Learned Hand, he thought "this [is] one of those rare bits of fancy talk in which Judge Hand was thinking out loud with nobody by his side to correct him." However, he thought the Court should wait for other circuits to act and "for the present . . . leave the lily lay." Burton's clerk suggested that Frankfurter's comment about Hand was incorrect since "there was in fact somebody sitting by Judge Hand's side to correct him for Judge Jerome Frank dissented sharply on that very issue" and that there was already enough of a real conflict to decide the issue. However, when Burton presented that view in the conference, the members agreed that the issues were not yet ripe and denied certiorari.[87]

In taking the long view, the most distressing effect of the denial of certiorari or appeal was that a number of litigants whose appeals were dismissed for failure to raise a federal question presented issues which, years later, the Court decided in ways which could have benefited the earlier unsuccessful petitioners. For example, in many of the coerced confession or illegal search cases, in later years the Court would have excluded the evidence and acquitted the defendants or would have ordered the holding of new trials.

In any case, the Court's docket was small and its critics, not having to contend with a group of strong-willed justices, were large in number. Frankfurter, who rarely seemed interested in actually deciding cases, often attempted to impede the decision-making process even when certiorari had been granted. The Court, upon the passage of the 1925 Judiciary Act, had agreed that whenever four justices wanted to grant, the writ would be granted and the case decided on its merit after argument. However, Frankfurter continued to insist that when only four voted to grant, the five who had opposed certiorari could then quickly vote that certiorari was improvidently granted and could thus dismiss the case without deciding it on the merits. In two cases in the 1951 term, Frankfurter refused to vote, for he thought the writs should have been dismissed as improvidently granted rather than announcing decisions in the cases.[88]

The most persistent critic of Burton and the Court was still Fred Rodell, who was called the "Westbrook Pegler of legal education" by Burton's first clerk. In articles in the *New Republic* in December 1949 and in *Look* in July 1951, he criticized the Truman justices in general for ineptness and castigated Vinson for not healing the Court's factional disputes, for not writing his fair share of majority opinions, and for letting cases back up until the end of the term. Clark, according to Rodell, was a "smiling superficial, opportunistic man on the move," while Minton wrote "usually sloppy or off-the-beam or just plain pedestrian" opinions. Even Frankfurter did not escape criticism for being "the Court's great expert at legal needlework who purports to reach his almost invariably conservative results by the use of impersonal ineluctable logic." But the "bumbling Justice Burton," according to Rodell, was "an old-fashioned, narrow-gauged, precedent-worshipper who tries interminably to match cases as a woman shopper matches colors. His meticulous and rigorous concern with irrelevances and trivia makes much of his work almost a parody of the judicial process."[89]

Rodell's assessment of the justices was partially accurate; but what he failed to note was that no chief justice could encourage Frankfurter, who believed passionately in writing opinions, to stop writing dissents, or make Black and Douglas stop dissenting when there was a solid majority for some very anti-libertarian opinions. The dissenters viewed their task as paving the way for a new elaboration of law once they achieved a majority. As a member of the controlling bloc on a Court where fewer cases came up and even fewer were taken, Vinson did scatter the cases in such a way as to leave the impression that he had written too few opinions. Also, his procedure for assignment in divided cases was to give the task of writing to a wavering justice in order to hold him firmly with the majority. The waverer might be any one of the justices, regardless of ideology. Often, it was simply inexpedient for the chief or one of the other anti-civil libertarians to write the opinion.

Rodell's description of Burton as being ploddingly conscientious struck at what was regarded by others as a great strength. From Burton's point of view, he had to be careful and meticulous for he recognized his own weaknesses. He also believed passionately in the significance of even the small cases and thought it was necessary to unearth every possible precedent before deciding cases. Too, he was concerned about the ordinary practitioners of law who may not have been as sophisticated as the law professors who were Frankfurter's audience. Knowing that he was not brilliant and that writing came hard and was not likely to be filled with flowing phrases, Burton thought the best he could do for the practicing lawyers was to outline every precedent that he had considered and rejected and the process by which his result had been reached. His enthusiasm undampened by his critics, he indulged his interest in the history of the Court by writing an article on the Aaron Burr trial, "Justice, the Guardian of Liberty," during the 1950 term, and a speech for the Tenth Judicial Circuit Conference, "Dramatization of the Dartmouth College Case," during the 1951 term, both of which were published in the *American Bar Association Journal*.[90]

Although Burton was not interested in answering Fred Rodell's criticism, his first clerk suggested that "some of us should do some answering to Rodell in public." Burton's secretary, Tess Cheatham, told Mann that she had sent a Supreme Court envelope to Rodell addressed to "Professor Fred Rodent [sic]," in hopes that a few people would see the envelope before Rodell and that "somebody would . . . [laugh] at him for a change." She added, "I would love to get my little pink mitts around his throat and just squeeze."[91]

Still very much the politician, Burton received and answered letters on a great variety of subjects. To an inquiry about his interest in investments, he responded. "I am quite out of the field not only because of lack of the primary essential of funds for making investments but because as a justice of this court, I have found it necessary to eliminate all kinds of investments except U.S. securities and an investment trust, which does away with all consideration on my part of the securities in which that trust places the funds." Most of the letters he received concerned his opinion in *Henderson*. One correspondent asked "are these United States becoming a quadroon second Africa with a future quadroon Supreme Court?" His minister, however, told him that he was "proud and happy" that Burton wrote the opinion; not only was the decision right, "but it deprives Communist agitators of one more weapon in their war upon our free society."[92]

Before the 1953 term commenced, Chief Justice Fred Vinson died, after serving only seven terms; and an era came to an end. In summing up his contributions, commentators who faulted the Vinson Court for being antilibertarian were correct, if a bit too simplistic in their appraisals. Douglas and Black almost always voted for libertarianism without disposing of the competing claims of authority in rational legal terms. Although he never failed to rationalize the legal issues in a case, Frankfurter voted on the side of liberty only when it was "shocking to the conscience" to do otherwise. Burton and the other members of the Vinson controlling bloc always attempted to balance liberty and authority in their opinions, even though they eventually voted on the side of governmental authority and order. As records of the internal affairs of the Court demonstrate, the Vinson Court took seriously its duty to consider the competing claims of liberty and order in society and to decide the difficult issues of the day, from the steel seizure case and the Communist trials to the mine workers trials and the important labor interpretation cases. The commentators who disagreed with the Vinson Court took this position primarily because they disliked the Court's decisions. There was no conscious effort on Burton's part to be anti- or pro-civil libertarian, but there was an effort to take seriously the task of judging.

# 5

## Transition to the Warren Court

B U R T O N and the Supreme Court passed through a period of transition from 1953 through 1954. New appointments, including that of a new chief, led to the development of a new controlling activist bloc. Burton, now a mature justice, found himself gradually in the minority as he held to his non-interventionist views. The Court, once attacked for its anti-civil libertarian views, became more libertarian, raising the ire of its former defenders. But at the beginning of the 1953 term, the storm clouds were barely visible on the horizon.

In the fall of 1953, the Supreme Court commenced the term under the leadership of a new chief justice, Earl Warren of California. Appointed by the newly elected president, Dwight D. Eisenhower, as a concession to the liberal wing of the party, Warren became the nation's fourteenth chief justice. A Republican, Warren had spent his entire career in public life. He had sought public office on eight occasions, from the district attorneyship of Alameda County, California, to the vice-presidency of the United States; and he had won every office except the vice-presidency. During the 1952 preconvention campaigning for the national Republican ticket, Warren, as governor of California, became a dark horse candidate for the presidency, the favorite son of the California delegation. However, it was understood that the only way Warren could be nominated was if there were a deadlocked convention. The convention was not deadlocked; and after Eisenhower was nominated, Warren agreed to campaign for the ticket. In a series of interviews, Warren made it clear that he would be open to an offer of an acceptable position in the new administration. Still in his third term as governor of California, Warren did not think he could be reelected because of the divisions in the state Republican party.

After the election, there was much speculation about Warren's future. Most of the rumors focused on a Supreme Court appointment which might result from the retirement of Frankfurter, who had been ill during the previous term and who was past retirement age. One reporter even called a shocked Frankfurter to ask whether he was going to retire. He did not, of course; but the swirling controversy might have reduced the warmth of Frankfurter's reception of Warren on the Court. When Fred Vinson died, Eisenhower would have appointed John Foster Dulles or Thomas Dewey chief; but they were not interested. Two available Republican circuit judges were considered too old. In addition, there was a possibility that Burton could have been elevated to the chief's position and Warren appointed as an associate justice. Unfortunately for Burton, the publicity regarding his output and the quality of his work on the Court, much of it unfair, had created an image of him as a middling justice who had not gained prestige while on the Court. Although Eisenhower had believed he was only committed to appoint Warren to an ordinary vacancy, after exhausting other alternatives, he made the appointment, which evoked both widespread approval and discontent in the press. Liberal journals emphasized that his responsibility for the evacuation of Japanese Americans in 1942 was a sign of his bigotry and also voiced their disapproval of his support of a loyalty oath for California state employees. Conservative journalists decried his lack of judicial experience, his support of civil rights for blacks, and his leniency with communism in his rejection of a special oath for teachers at the University of California which differed from the oath for other state employees.[1]

In the first year of the Warren Court, the question most often raised by observers was whether the new chief justice would align himself with Reed, Minton, Burton, and Clark to retain the center controlling bloc or would join with Black and Douglas to form a new libertarian bloc, which might be able to obtain Frankfurter's vote occasionally for a grant of certiorari in those civil liberties cases which had recently been continually denied. His background gave little hint as to his philosophy concerning the role of courts, and an analysis of his political activities produced mixed results. In fact, during Warren's first two terms, the already large percentage of cases denied certiorari became even larger. During those first two years, except for the school segregation cases, the pattern of decision in civil liberties cases remained approximately the same, with Warren voting with the controlling center bloc.[2]

During the 1953 term, there was a noticeable decline in the Court's business. Although Warren was appointed in October, he was not confirmed by the Senate until March; and it also took some time for him to adjust to running the Court and for the other justices to adjust to him. A great deal of effort was devoted to the most publicized action of the term, the long-awaited decision in the school segregation cases, *Brown* v. *Board of Education et al.* The Court received and postponed a number of segregation cases during the term until it could resolve the issues for decision in *Brown*, which would then be controlling as precedent. Reargument in the segregation cases held over from the previous term was originally set for October but did not actually occur until two months later. The Court gave the impression, which was accurate, of proceeding slowly, carefully, and deliberately toward a decision in the cases, which finally resulted in Warren's May 1954 unanimous opinion overruling *Plessy* v. *Ferguson* and declaring separate education inherently unequal.[3]

In preparation for the argument and decision in the case, Frankfurter, becoming convinced of the unreliability of the most frequently quoted account of the Fourteenth Amendment, had "one of the most dependable law clerks I have found [Alexander Bickel]" devote some weeks during the 1952 term to reading every word of the *Congressional Globe* relating to the history of the amendment and related measures. Apparently, Frankfurter believed reading public documents would produce a more reliable historical account. In any case, Bickel's history was "inconclusive in the sense that the Congress as an enacting body neither manifested that the amendment outlawed segregation to that end, nor that it manifested the opposite."[4]

In the conference after reargument in December, the justices agreed to the suggestion that they simply discuss the case without taking votes. When Frankfurter commented that he felt like Benjamin Franklin at the Constitutional Convention, it is not clear whether he was referring to the opportunity to make new law or to Franklin's suggestion that the convention begin with daily prayer. Burton remarked that regardless of the holding, they should decide the case that term. In a straightforward fashion, Warren indicated that *Plessy* was based on the inferiority of black people; and if the Court were to sustain that decision, it would be sustaining that point of view. He "personally could not see how today [one] can justify segregation based solely on race. . . . [But] it would take all the wisdom of this court to do this [solve the problem] with a minimum of . . . strife. How we do it is important." Reed understood Warren's position that equal protection had not been satisfactory; but he believed that the issue was not whether blacks were inferior, because "there is no inferior race." To Reed, the issue was a matter of long-exercised state police power, and he would leave the "entrenched aspects and wait to see what the rest of the court does."

Frankfurter made it clear that he was in no hurry to reach a decision and was not really concerned about the number of opinions that might result. To him, the difficulty was that in the United States' legal system, the Court was the "trustee of due process," which placed a heavy burden on the judiciary. He felt that the Court should proceed with care so that regardless of their decision, they would not sound "self-righteous" or like the "Lord Almighty." He accepted the notion that even if the framers' intention with the Fourteenth Amendment could not be clearly ascertained, "time works changes" in interpretation. Douglas favored ending segregation and supported Warren's reasoning in the *Brown* case that the study of history only threw a "mixed light" on how to interpret the Fourteenth Amendment. However, in *Bolling* v. *Sharpe*, the District of Columbia case in which the Fifth Amendment applied, he was unsure of the constitutional authority for a decision concerning segregation and did not understand clearly whether it was mandatory or merely permitted. If he had to vote at that point, he would vote to have the District of Columbia case sent back to the court of appeals. Otherwise, he needed more time to consider the point. Jackson saw the issue before the Court as clearly one of politics. He did not really know how "to justify the abolition of segregation as a judicial act" and was searching for a legal basis for an essentially political conclusion.

Clark, a Texan, asserted that he was probably closer to the problem than anyone else on the Court except Black, who, after hearing the oral argument, had gone home to Alabama on December 10 to visit his sister, who was seriously ill in Birmingham. Clark believed since there were "dangers of violence" from a decision ending segregation, the Court, in framing a decree, should be careful not to treat the entire South the same but should allow for local differences. He stated further that he was surprised to discover that the legislative history was unclear, for he had always assumed that one of the purposes of the Fourteenth Amendment was to abolish segregation. At this point, Jackson warned that there was "no great loyalty" to the public school system in the South and that if a decision ending segregation was made, public education might be abandoned. When it was his turn, Minton commented that in Indiana there was a choice of schools that could be attended but that segregated schools still existed. Clark described a similar problem of prejudice against the Mexican-Americans in Texas and asserted that he would go along with a decision ending segregation as long as the remedy was carefully outlined. Minton interjected that he did not foresee trouble if segregation was ended, because no matter what the framers of the Fourteenth Amendment thought, "it is a different world today." He thought it was not necessary to frame a specific remedy and that the Court should let the district courts "have their heads."[5]

There was a clear majority for Warren's position in the conference. However, at this point, Reed was reluctant; he did not want to announce his decision until the remainder of the justices had indicated firm positions. Frankfurter was tentatively with the majority, and Jackson would go along with the majority if a rational legal opinion could be worked out. Warren, Douglas, and Burton, who had been in favor of reversal from the beginning, were certain Clark would go along as long as a carefully drawn decree resulted; and Minton was clearly supportive. Black was absent, but he too had from the beginning indicated a desire to reverse. The change of the justices' positions to a single unanimous opinion resulted from the oral argument, the passage of time, and discussion, as well as Warren's persuasiveness.

By January 15, 1954, the issues were resolved; and the justices were concerned mainly with the decree. All the justices on the Court were trying their hands at fashioning decrees as Warren was writing his opinion. Among the more simple decrees that he and his clerk prepared, Burton preferred one which stated that

it is accordingly rendered, adjudged, and decreed that the defendants proceed at once to furnish the plaintiffs and other Negro pupils of said district educational facilities, equipment, curricula and opportunities equal to those provided white pupils; and it is further ordered that the defendants make report to this Court within six months of this date as to the action taken by them to carry out this order.

The language in Burton's sample would leave the way open for the localities to replace "inherently unequal facilities" in whatever way they saw fit, with no guidelines established by the Court; but requiring them to report in six months would indicate that the Court was serious about expecting change and could make further orders in conformity with its objectives. One concern of Burton's was to keep the language of the decree general and to avoid "particularizing," which would "inadvertently appear to give sanction to any one particular delaying device."[6]

In his January 15, 1954, memo to the conference concerning the contents of a possible decree in favor of the appellants, Frankfurter assumed that a decision had been made and then dealt with the specifics of how to "transform state-wide school systems in nearly a score of states. . . . A clear appreciation of what result is required is indispensable. The aim is summarized in the phrase 'integrated school'." To Frankfurter, the major task for the decree was the finding of facts about conditions in different school systems. He envisioned future litigation on the subject but thought the Court should avoid "a mere declaration of unconstitutionality [which] will be the most prolific breeder of litigation and chaos." However, he knew an initial decree would be in general terms, namely, "that the inequalities which any segregated school system begets cannot stand and must be terminated as soon as this can be done with due regard to the requirement that school systems be not disrupted and that no substantial lowering of standards over present ones result for any sizeable group." Therefore, Frankfurter suggested that the Court should announce a general decree requiring desegregation of school systems and that it should appoint a master for each of the appropriate states or direct the district courts "to proceed in molding decrees through the inquiring and hearing of a master in the first instance."[7]

During the period after oral argument and before the decision came down in May, the members of the Court engaged in frequent informal discussion on the cases. Warren and Burton discussed the opinion on numerous occasions. The clerks were told very little about the discussions in order to minimize the danger of the information leaking to the public. When Warren circulated his draft in May, Burton thought it was a "magnificent job that may win a unanimous court," a result which would have been impossible the year before with Vinson, Jackson, and Reed in opposition and with Frankfurter wavering. After Warren's opinion was accepted in final form by the conference, the justices personally handed back the circulated drafts, again to avoid possible leaks. Burton gave Warren the rehearing and the passage of time credit for the result, commenting that the unanimous result was "a major accomplishment of his leadership and an evidence of the value of time in its consideration." However, it was clear to most members by May that formulating a decree would be no easy task. Therefore, the decision announced on May 17, 1954, held the cases over for reargument on the substance of the decrees until the 1954 term. The contending parties, as well as the attorney general, were invited to address themselves to the scope and substance of a decree in the reargument.[8]

In November 1954, after the Senate Judiciary Committee decided to postpone acting on the confirmation of Justice John Marshall Harlan, the Court ruled to delay argument on the decree in *Brown* until spring. Harlan, the grandson of the late nineteenth century antisegregationist associate justice, was a Republican New York lawyer who had been appointed to the second circuit in January 1954, and was appointed to the Supreme Court upon the death of

Jackson one week after the term began. Meanwhile, the Court assigned six law clerks, including one of Burton's, to prepare a Segregation Research Report for their perusal, along with a paper containing their recommendations for a decree in the cases. In their report, in which they suggested that the Court should remand the cases to the court below, the clerks asserted that these courts could decide for themselves whether to appoint masters. All but one of the clerks, not Burton's, thought the Court's decree should announce some general guidelines for the district courts to use in determining whether the plaintiff in a particular case was being segregated on the basis of race and whether specific defendants were making good faith efforts to end such segregation. They thought the guidelines would "enable local judges to point to a superior authority in undertaking what will often be unpopular action." In addition, the guidelines would "give them some standards for evaluating the states' plans in determining whether they represent bona fide compliance, rather than being left wholly at sea when faced with the jargon of educators which may or may not be a guise for evasion."[9]

When it came to actually establishing what the guidelines should be, the clerks suggested that attendance districting must not be designed to perpetuate segregation, that optional voluntary choice (freedom of choice) would be "valid if the choice is open to children of both races unless the plaintiff is denied admission to the school of his choice," and that individual assignments by school authorities would not be "presumptively invalid." The timetable for compliance offered difficult problems. Five clerks agreed that it would be "impractical to demand immediate compliance"; but "the mere passage of time without any guidance and requirements by the courts produces rather than reduces friction. It smacks of indecisiveness and gives the extremists more time to operate." One clerk wanted the district courts to set a timetable; but the remainder disagreed because "this would put a premium on local hostility to demonstrate the 'impracticability' of immediate action." Another clerk believed a twelve-year limit for compliance was necessary in order to minimize the "extreme injustice of condemning half a generation of Negro children to a segregated system." However, the majority thought that a reasonable time limit coupled with good faith compliance might be a compromise solution.[10]

When the Court discussed the decree in conference after argument, only Burton, Harlan, Clark, and Warren expressed the view that the suit should be regarded as a class action and that the decrees should run not only for the benefit of the named plaintiffs but of others similarly situated. Black and Douglas were strongly in favor of limiting the effect of the decree to the individuals suing, while Reed thought the decree could be regarded as a class suit in terms of widespread effect but that the Court need not overtly announce that it was. Minton and Frankfurter understood that even if the decision were restricted, as it ought to be, to named parties, others would seek to benefit from the decision. All the justices agreed that the cases should be remanded to the district courts. Warren asserted that the decree should state what factors the district courts could take into account, excluding mention of "psychological or sociological attitudes." In addition, he believed it should be a short opinion and a "bare bones decree," with the district courts given as much latitude and as much support as possible. Black agreed, stating that "the less we say the better off we are. . . . To issue orders that *cannot* be enforced would be a great disadvantage." Reed thought they should leave the implementation of their decree to the district courts, but Douglas thought the decree "should give a push" and suggest desegregation "as fast as circumstances permit." Clark added that he thought a broadly effective decree could be enforced in Texas without too much trouble. Minton warned the Court to be mindful of not revealing the "inner weakness" of the judiciary by rendering a "futile decree," while Harlan suggested the issuance of a simple opinion without a time limit with the decree. Burton's position was that the decree should remand the cases to the district courts with an order to desegregate school systems as soon as possible. Local officials should be required to submit plans to the appropriate district court, which would retain jurisdiction and would enter further orders from time to time to effectuate the decree. Frankfurter stated his disagreement with Thurgood Marshall's assertion for the petitioners that hostile "attitudes are to be left out of consideration." Additionally, he argued persuasively that Holmes's use of the equity maxim, "with all deliberate speed," in a 1911 case which enforced a money judgment against the state of Virginia, could reflect their position that enforcement should take place only as rapidly as possible and not immediately. His success in obtaining this use of language in the decree helped to overcome his reluctance to support the decision in the first place.[11]

Most of the Court's other work in the first two Warren terms faded into insignificance alongside the school segregation case. Only a few civil liberties cases were decided in the 1953 term. Burton voted with the majority in holding that the Federal Regulation of Lobbying Act of 1946, which required registration and financial disclosure by those persons attempting to influence federal legislation, was not void for vagueness in violation of due process but that New York and Ohio statutes censoring two motion pictures were unconstitutionally vague. He joined Frankfurter's dissent when the Court, in a 5-4 decision, admitted evidence obtained by surreptitiously placing microphones in the home of Irvine, a suspected violator of California's antigambling laws; and he wrote the majority opinion upholding the use of evidence procured without a warrant in *Salzburg* v. *Maryland*, another search and seizure case. In *Salzburg*, the issue was whether Maryland had violated the equal protection clause of the Fourteenth Amendment by authorizing its courts to admit evidence procured by illegal search or seizure in prosecutions for certain gambling misdemeanors in Anne Arundel County. The defendants convicted for gambling raised the constitutional issue because Maryland at that time prohibited the admission of such evidence in like prosecutions in other counties and even prohibited its admission in prosecutions for many other misdemeanors in Anne Arundel County. Burton held Maryland's action valid because each state could set its own rules of evidence. Furthermore, he asserted that the equal protection clause related to equality between persons as such rather than between punishments for categories of offenses. The clause did not prohibit classification into categories as long as it was reasonable; and "the state government might well find reason to prescribe, at least on an experimental basis, substantial restrictions and variations in procedure that would differ from those elsewhere in the state.'' Additionally, Burton asserted that there was no due process violation because the Maryland statute offered "to offending searchers and seizers no protection or immunity from anything be it civil liability, criminal liability, or disciplinary action.''[12]

Chief Justice Warren did not understand how Burton could dissent in the *Irvine* case, in which Warren had supported the use of the evidence, and yet was of the majority view in *Salzburg*. Burton responded that he distinguished between "an ordinary, but violent, search and seizure made with no warrant," as in *Salzburg*, and evidence obtained "by what I regard as the 'shocking' procedures of surreptitiously, and illegally, inserting a listening device within the home (or even private business premises) of the suspect and for a long time (30 days in the Irvine case) recording whatever occurs there." Burton apparently accepted the procedure of examining each case on the facts and only excluding evidence on due process grounds when his conscience was "shocked." Frankfurter, in congratulating Burton on the *Salzburg* opinion, explained that it was comforting to know that Burton shared his views and that their decisions in search and seizure cases were based on a philosophy of law and "not personal matters." Burton's position in *Salzburg* was essentially that in the absence of physical coercion, the Court should permit the fruits of an illegal search to be used against a defendant in state courts.[13]

The new chief justice was part of the majority which supported Burton's opinion in *Barsky* v. *Board of Regents*, another civil liberties case which developed during the paranoia over subversion in the 1950s. Barsky, a physician and resident of New York, was convicted in a federal court in the District of Columbia for violating a federal statute by refusing to produce before a congressional committee subpoenaed papers belonging to the Joint Anti-Fascist Refugee Committee, of which he was the chairman. After he had served his sentence, disciplinary proceedings were instituted against him under a New York statute authorizing such action against a "physician who has been convicted in a court of competent jurisdiction, either within or without this state of crime."[14] In this proceeding, the subcommittee on grievances, which held the original hearing, allowed the prosecutor to introduce evidence that the organization headed by the physician was listed by the attorney general as a subversive organization; and the subcommittee made a specific finding to this effect in its report. The subcommittee recommended a suspension for three months, and the full committee recommended six months. However, a reviewing committee recognized that, in view of the holding in Burton's opinion in *Joint Anti-Fascist Refugee Committee* v. *McGrath* during the 1950 term, no evidentiary weight could be given to the attorney general's list and recommended that the physician should simply be reprimanded. Despite this recommendation, the deciding agency, without stating any reasons, suspended the physician for six months.[15]

After the court of appeals upheld the suspension, Burton affirmed for six members of the Court, holding that there was no violation of due process. To Burton, the statute was not unconstitutionally vague; and it was proper for the state to revoke the physician's license, even though the offense involved no moral turpitude and was not criminal under New York state law. The physician's objections, based on the introduction into evidence of the attorney general's list of subversive organizations, was rejected by the majority on the grounds that they could find nothing sufficient to sustain a conclusion that the administrative agency relied upon such evidence. Controlling was the state's legitimate concern "for maintaining high standards of professional conduct," and the procedures involved were "well within the degree of reasonableness required to constitute due process in a field so permeated with public responsibility as that of health."[16]

Douglas concurred in Black's dissenting view that New York had violated the Constitution by using the attorney general's list and by permitting trial by an agency vested with arbitrary powers. In a separate opinion joined by Black, Douglas also dissented on the grounds that Barsky's crime consisted of no more than a justifiable mistake regarding his constitutional right to refuse to produce papers for the congressional committee and had no relation to his fitness as a physician. Frankfurter dissented solely because, on the facts, it appeared that the attorney general's list was used and relied upon by the agency in making its decision. However, Burton disagreed, asserting that Frankfurter's view of the facts was based on an assumption not in the record. While Frankfurter would remand to the lower court for more evidence on the facts, Burton believed that the absence of such evidence in the record was a sufficient basis to conclude that there was reason for the suspension.[17]

In the non-civil liberties cases, there was little opportunity for Burton to exhibit his judicial skills. The Court unanimously reversed a Civil Aeronautics Board decision refusing to permit an air carrier to offset excess earnings in its domestic flights against the carrier's need for a subsidy in its foreign operations. The Court rejected the CAB's argument that the Court should respect the administrative judgment of the agency. Burton agreed with his clerk that "what particular 'expertise' the defeated exCongressmen who comprise the bulk of the CAB bring to bear on this problem or any other has long been a mystery."[18]

Since he had in previous terms written three opinions on the subject, Burton was assigned the Court opinion in a Federal Water Power Act case involving the computation, under state law, of payments made to a power company by its licensees for use of a navigable stream for power purposes. He decided for four members of the Court that a state law permitting the deduction of expenses paid by power company licensees for the use of such rights, in computing the licensee's surplus earnings for amortization reserve payment purposes, was a valid exercise of state power and did not interfere with federal law. The payments were used to depreciate the power company's net investment in the project. Even though the federal government had a propriety right to free use of navigable streams, this fact did not prohibit a state from permitting private companies to establish profit-making facilities on such streams. Joined by Black and Minton, Douglas dissented on the grounds that the ultimate effect of the majority's ruling to permit the deduction would be to require the federal government to pay for using waters of a navigable stream if it had to take over the property and compensate the owners. In effect, the decision permitting the deduction benefited the power corporation by reducing its expenses for water. Without such clear authorization, there could be no taking of private property for public purposes. Ever the flatterer, Frankfurter told Burton that his opinion was "a good illustration of the difference between starting with a problem to be solved instead of a predetermined conclusion to be justified."[19]

Burton wrote opinions in two other federal statutory cases and one admiralty case. He dissented, joined by Jackson and Frankfurter, when the Court held, in a per curiam opinion, that a shipowner was liable for injuries suffered by a stevedore on his ship resulting from the unseaworthiness of equipment, even though the equipment was not shown to belong to the shipowner or to be part of the ship's equipment. According to Burton, if the statutory liability of shipowners was to be expanded, there should be "legislative authorization rather than mere judicial recognition."[20]

In a statutory case involving an accident at sea, he concurred separately to a per curiam decision that an administrative ruling that a death which occurred on a barge drawn up for repairs on a marine railway was compensable under the federal Longshoremen's and Harbor Workers Compensation Act. He also decided for the majority that an employer, charged with violation of the wage stabilization provisions of the Defense Production Act of 1950, could not enjoin the administrative proceedings designated to determine his guilt. Burton's concise handling of the issues gathered the support of his colleagues. Douglas wrote to Burton, "I voted the other way. . . . But if you have the others and no one writes in dissent, I will quiet my doubts and go along with you." Frankfurter, who had passed in conference, was exultant: "good! How absurd it seems for any of us to have voted in our state of ignorance in this case instead of having someone make precisely the thorough investigation that you made and report the result as this opinion does."[21]

Burton, who had already written a number of leading labor law decisions, wrote two majority opinions interpreting the Taft-Hartley Act. In one case, technicians employed by a broadcasting company were discharged when, during a dispute between the company and the union to which the technicians belonged, they distributed handbills attacking the quality of the company's television programming. The NLRB refused to order their reinstatement, ruling that the employer was not guilty of an unfair labor practice in discharging them because, in view of the indefensible character of their activities, the discharges had been for cause. The court of appeals, although refusing to order reinstatement of the technicians, remanded the case to the board on the ground that the board had failed to state whether the technicians' activities were unlawful as distinguished from indefensible. Speaking for six members of the Court, Burton reversed the court below, announcing that the evidence showed clearly that the employees had been guilty of such disloyalty to the employer as to constitute cause for their discharge regardless of the connection of their activities with the labor dispute. Frankfurter dissented, joined by Black and Douglas, and took the view that the court of appeals had made the proper ruling regarding the board's order. In addition, the dissenters felt that employee "disloyalty" in a labor dispute situation is not in every case the kind of "cause" for discharge contemplated by the Labor Management Relations Act. However, Burton agreed with the employer that when the employees "launched the [vitriolic] attack on the quality of the company's television broadcasts," that action was "a demonstration of such detrimental disloyalty" as to provide "cause" for its refusal to continue to employ "the perpetrators of the attack." To Burton, the Taft-Hartley Act did not require reinstatement of employees fired for "cause. . . . There is no more elemental cause for discharge of an employee than disloyalty to his employer."[22]

The other labor case assigned to Burton involved a construction corporation which was performing work in Kentucky. During construction, agents of the defendant labor union demanded that the corporation's employees join one of its locals. The corporation and many of its employees refused, whereupon the union's agents made threats of violence to such a degree that the corporation was compelled to abandon all its projects in the area. The corporation then sued the union for damages in state court and obtained a substantial judgment. Assuming that its actions constituted, if anything, an unfair labor practice, the union contended that the state courts were excluded from entertaining common-law tort actions for the recovery of damages caused by such conduct.

Again for six members of the Court, Burton rejected the defendants' contention on the grounds that a favorable decision would, in effect, immunize them from liability for their conduct. The Labor Management Relations Act authorized the NLRB to enjoin unfair labor practices prospectively but made no provision for damages for past acts of the kind involved. Burton announced that "Congress has neither provided nor suggested any substitute for the traditional state court procedure for collecting damages for injuries caused by tortious conduct." For the Court to cut off the corporation's right to recovery "will deprive it of property without recourse or compensation." He saw "no substantial reason for reaching such a result."[23]

Burton dissented, joined by Reed, from a per curiam opinion in *Toolson* v. *New York Yankees*. In this case, a complaint that organized baseball was in violation of the Sherman Anti-Trust Act was dismissed because the business of providing public baseball games for profit between clubs of professional baseball players was not within the scope of the federal antitrust laws. The majority, citing a similar holding in a 1922 case, pointed out that Congress had had that earlier ruling under consideration but had not seen fit to enact legislation subjecting baseball to the antitrust laws. Burton disagreed, asserting that it was "a contradiction in terms" to say that baseball was not engaged in interstate trade or commerce.[24]

In the 1954 term, the Court was confronted with a similar issue when it considered whether the business of producing, booking, and presenting legitimate theatrical attractions or boxing on a multistate basis was interstate trade or commerce within the Sherman Act. Burton and Reed joined the Court's opinion that the Sherman Act was violated but repeated the views they had expressed in their dissent in *Toolson*. In conference, after Warren and Black had both denounced any attempt to extend the baseball case decision, Frankfurter commented that it was difficult to believe that Congress had exempted baseball and not other sports. Black interjected that Congress did not exempt baseball; "the Court did." Douglas and Clark were sure about the theater case but uncertain about boxing, since it seemed odd to exempt one sport and not the other. At this point, Minton stated that the Court should not let the "tail wag the dog."[25] To him, the enterprises only incidentally involved interstate sports. Burton discussed the case at great length with the other members of the Court. At various times, Warren, Douglas, Jackson, and Clark expressed "sympathy" with his point of view; but they "apparently felt obliged because of its probably retroactive effect on law suits to vote the other way." However, Burton's clerks reported to him that the law clerks favored the dissent about seventeen to two, the two being Frankfurter's.[26]

During the 1953 term, the Court again considered the offshore tidelands oil problem that they had decided in 1947. The 1947 decision that California was not the owner of a three-mile offshore strip and that the federal government had "paramount rights in and power over" the three-mile coastal area of California was supported by Burton and four others in a Black opinion, to which Reed and Frankfurter dissented. The Court decision was hotly contested, but negotiations continued between the United States and California on its implementation. In Congress, bill after bill had been introduced to give control of the valuable lands to the states, but none had passed. In addition, the attorney general, basing his action on the California decision, brought suit against Louisiana and Texas to take over their offshore oil. In 1950, Douglas's decision for the Court applied the California rule to Louisiana, with Frankfurter dissenting, and to Texas, this time with Minton and Reed also dissenting. Since there was no congressional legislation on the subject, the Court decrees that the states involved owed money to the national government were to be enforced by the Department of the Interior based on a presidential order.[27]

Critics of the Court decisions insisted that there should be state control of the offshore oil. The movement to enact a bill giving title to the states gained momentum in Congress. When the bill was passed, Truman vetoed it, explaining that federal ownership had been affirmed and reaffirmed by the Supreme Court and that he would not turn over to certain states as a "free gift" that which belonged to all the people. The veto and the whole issue became a major part of the 1952 presidential campaign. When Eisenhower, who favored state ownership against Stevenson's opposition, won the election, hearings began in Congress on a new state possession bill. The bill, the Submerged Lands Act, was passed in May 1953, and it was immediately signed by President Eisenhower. But concurrent with the act's passage, Congress enacted the Outer Continental Shelf Lands Act, providing for federal control of lands and resources beyond state boundaries and extending to the edge of the continental shelf. This legislation, which seemed to imply a limitation on the broadly drafted Submerged Lands Act, was passed, in part, to offset charges that the Submerged Lands Act was a "giveaway" in exchange for Eisenhower's victory and, in part, to minimize the constitutional questions raised by the act.

Naturally, some of the states decided to challenge the constitutionality of the new acts. Alabama and Rhode Island, in *Alabama v. Texas et al.*, argued that *United States v. California* precluded Congress from disposing of the rights of the people in other states to their offshore lands. According to this argument, Congress was treating states unequally. In a brief par curiam opinion, the Court majority of six justices, including Burton, denied the motions of Alabama and Rhode Island to file bills of complaint. The new chief justice from California, who had announced before joining its bench his support of state control, did not participate. The Court upheld the unlimited power of Congress to dispose of property belonging to the United States. Black and Douglas dissented. Of course, those state control advocates who had previously criticized the Court now praised it and vice versa. As a practical matter, only in California did most of the valuable oil lands remain under state control by virtue of the Submerged Lands Act. In other states, the Outer Continental Shelf Act placed control of the oil in question in the hands of Congress. More litigation over the meaning of the two acts continued until 1965, when the Court announced that even California's jurisdiction only extended to within three miles of the coastline.[28]

In the 1954 term, with a small Court docket, Burton again wrote few opinions. The most exciting event of the term was the fashioning of the decree in *Brown*. But the unanimity that the Court had exhibited in deciding the *Brown* case did not extend to a case involving discrimination against Indians. In *Rice* v. *Sioux City*

*Memorial Park*, the Court refused to decide that a deceased Indian soldier killed in combat in Korea should be permitted burial in a plot purchased by his wife in a cemetery for whites. When Mrs. Rice sued the cemetery for damages, the Supreme Court of Iowa denied relief because of a clause in the burial lot contract which limited burial privileges to "members of the Caucasian race." The Supreme Court, after granting certiorari, affirmed the opinion below by an equally divided Court. After argument, on petition for rehearing before a full Court, the Court disposed of the case by written opinion. In a Frankfurter opinion supported by Burton and three others, the Court dismissed the writ as improvidently granted. Frankfurter had argued persuasively in the conference that the Court would have to overrule the civil rights case of 1883, in which the Court had decided that the Fourteenth Amendment did not proscribe private discrimination, in order to decide the case for Mrs. Rice. Frankfurter announced for the Court that Iowa had enacted a statute during the litigation which made it a crime in the future to refuse burial under the circumstances of the *Rice* case. The case was "academic or episodic," not likely to arise again, and therefore ripe for dismissal.[29]

Burton was able to distinguish this case from the school segregation case because he believed that the Fourteenth Amendment was directed toward affirmative state action and not instances in which the state left the parties where it found them. Otherwise, he asserted, "almost all private agreements" would be illegal. For example, an individual would be able to sue successfully for damages when a private club to which he belonged refused to serve his black guest. Burton felt that such action would run nondiscrimination into the ground. He wrote that another point which bothered him about the case was that, on simple principles of contract law, to enforce the contract *without* the limitation made by the parties would be to enforce a contract they had not made.[30]

In another civil liberties case, Burton concurred in Reed's dissent when six members of the Court held in a Warren opinion that a presidential Loyalty Review Board had exceeded the powers conferred upon it by the executive order when it barred a special consultant to the Public Health Service from federal employment for three years as a result of disloyalty. He and Reed believed that the board's action was in conformity with the executive order and that the Court should review presidential orders concerning the internal operations of the executive branch.[31]

During the term, eighteen cases dealing with various aspects of federal criminal law and procedure were decided with full opinion. Decisions in six cases were unanimous. However, in the non-unanimous cases, the discussion shed some additional light on the views of Burton and the other justices on such questions. The claims of the accused were sustained in eight cases and denied in four. Still at one end of the spectrum, Douglas voted in favor of such claims in all cases, Black in ten, and Frankfurter in nine. Burton voted against the claimants in six cases. In the five cases involving state criminal law and procedure, two dealing with the right to counsel were decided unanimously in favor of the defendants; and the Court was divided in the remaining cases, of which two were decided in favor of the accused. In all three cases in which there was division, Black and Douglas voted in favor of the defendant, Warren and Frankfurter did so in two cases, Burton and Clark in one, and Reed and Minton in none. Harlan voted with the majority in favor of the defendants in the two cases in which he participated. Although the voting patterns indicate a moderately libertarian trend, they were as usual only the tip of the iceberg.[32]

Among the non-unanimous federal criminal cases, the Court, including Burton, decided in favor of recalcitrant witnesses before congressional investigating committees in three companion cases— *Quinn* v. *United States, Emspak* v. *United States,* and *Bart* v. *United States.* Quinn and Emspak were union officers; and Bart was the general manager of Freedom of the Press, Inc., which published *The Daily Worker* and *The Daily Worker Newspaper.* Each of the defendants had been convicted of contempt of Congress for refusing to answer questions propounded by a House subcommittee on un-American activities. In three opinions by Warren, the Supreme Court reversed the convictions. The chief justice asserted that, particularly in a period when fear of adverse public opinion tends to cause a witness to make a "veiled claim of privilege," the burden of forcing clarification of the ambiguities in a witness's position was on the interrogator. The committee had failed to make it sufficiently plain that it was not willingly abandoning those questions to which objections had been interposed, and the committee's failure to rule on the objections was fatal to a citation for contempt.[33]

In conference, Warren commented that he had changed his mind since the first argument of *Emspak* during the previous term, when he thought that Emspak was attempting to have his cake and eat it too; "he did not want to testify and yet he did not want to look guilty." However, Warren had since decided that he would avoid the other issues in the cases, for example, the incriminating nature of the questions, and "focus on the necessity for the committee to clarify the possible usage of the privilege against self-incrimination." He could see that at least one of the defendants had not clearly claimed the privilege, but "any indication of a claim should be enough to make the committee alert as to whether it is claimed or not." Black stated that he would be willing to reverse the convictions on all grounds but thought the narrow basis sought by Warren would be acceptable. However, Reed thought that one of the defendants had clearly claimed the privilege but that "the interest of the government in full and free disclosure" was most important. Furthermore, he believed it was a citizen's duty to "disclose what he knows."

In declaring his agreement with Reed, Clark voted to affirm *Emspak*; but he stated he would reverse in the Quinn case. He and Minton, who also agreed with Reed, thought the important issue was whether the questions were incriminating. The recently appointed Harlan, who immediately began taking up as much time in the discussions as Frankfurter, gave a lengthy speech on the constitutional protection against self-incrimination, concluding with the statement that he thought that it made no difference what the motives of the defendants were; they were entitled to claim the privilege and did not. He would reverse *Quinn* and affirm *Emspak* and *Bart*. Frankfurter, Douglas, and Burton agreed with Warren, even though the first time *Emspak* was argued, Burton had voted to affirm and Douglas had passed. In his opinion, Warren was able to reconcile the Clark and Minton views by agreeing with them that Quinn's claim was not clear. But he still shifted the burden of inquiry to the committee in order to lay down guidelines for future action in what was "relatively virgin territory."[34]

In *Gonzalez* v. *United States*, when the Court decided in favor of a Jehovah's Witness seeking relief from a criminal conviction in a conscientious objector case on the grounds of unfair notice and opportunity to defend, Burton joined Reed's dissent, which sanctioned the fairness of the procedure.[35]

The *Gonzalez* case was one of three conscientious objector cases decided that term in favor of the claimants in which Reed and Minton dissented, but it was the only one in which Burton joined a dissent. Burton was strongly in favor of fair procedure in the Selective Service System. He believed that

a full and fair hearing where it is important . . . before a hearing officer was important but he believed that arguing the facts at each stage of the appeals process would place too heavy an additional burden on the Court. Additionally, in balancing the requirements of the draft against due process, he concluded that the Courts may have interfered too much already in the Selective Service process.[36]

Among the non-unanimous cases involving state criminal procedure was *Regan* v. *New York*, in which a New York City policeman waived the immunity from prosecution he would otherwise have had under state law concerning information he might give before a grand jury. Provisions of the New York Constitution and the city charter required him to sign the waiver or lose his job. Long after he had resigned as a policeman, he was brought before a grand jury and asked whether he had ever accepted bribes while a policeman. When he refused to answer the question, claiming a federal constitutional and state privilege against self-incrimination, he was convicted of criminal contempt; and his conviction was affirmed by the state appellate courts. The issue was whether his conviction deprived him of his liberty without due process. Only a bare minimum of four—Burton, Douglas, Reed, and Black—voted to grant certiorari in the case. The remainder voted to deny, which would have left the decision below standing. In conference, there was little discussion. Warren asserted that the statutes were clear and that the constitutional testimony was voluntary. To Warren, the waiver provided "merely that he can't hold his job if he refuses." Frankfurter agreed that there was "nothing in the Fourteenth Amendment to bar this or to bar the withdrawal of the privilege" against self-incrimination; and Burton noted that Regan was not coerced into signing the waiver, for he admitted it was voluntary. In Burton's view, the necessity for keeping a job was not the kind of coercion which rendered a waiver involuntary; he did not see a due process violation. In a Reed opinion, which Burton supported, the conviction was sustained by six members of the Court.[37]

Another non-unanimous state criminal case was *Williams* v. *Georgia*, which questioned the adequacy of the grounds upon which the state denied an appeal. Williams, a black man, was convicted of murdering a white man and was sentenced to death. After his conviction was affirmed upon appeal, his counsel filed an extraordinary motion for a new trial, alleging that there had been a denial of equal protection through the jury selection process. Counsel claimed that during the selection of the jury, the names of the prospective jurors were placed on tickets, white tickets for names of white persons and yellow tickets for black persons. In addition, he asserted that he had not challenged the "array" at the time of trial because he did not know and could not have known of the procedure. The appeal was based largely on a 1952 case in which the Supreme Court had ruled unanimously that this use of tickets was unconstitutional. Williams's lawyer did not rely upon the 1952 decision in his appeal until some six months after the case was decided, when he filed his extraordinary motion for a new trial. The Georgia Supreme Court ruled, the second time the case reached it, that not only had the defendant waived any objections to the jury's selection by failing to challenge the array, but its own ruling in the earlier case had fully explained the jury selection procedure, and the defendant's court-appointed counsel should have known it.

In conference, Warren expressed the view that the Georgia court did nothing even after they knew their selection procedure was unconstitutional and that "to let Williams do without a fair trial would be discrimination." Furthermore, he did not believe the defendant had competent counsel; the Court ought to reverse and order a new trial. While agreeing substantially with Warren, Black stated that he feared a new trial for Williams as the decision would simply "be patched up." Reed, Clark, and Minton wanted to affirm on the sole basis that the objections to the array must be timely; and at most, stated Clark, they could sent it back to see if the lower court wanted to use its discretion to reverse. Again, Frankfurter explained his "strong views on the duty of this court not to take over [the] administration of the criminal law of the states" and noted his agreement with a memo circulated by Harlan stating that there should be no hard and fast rule on challenges to the array so that if there was discrimination, it could be denounced. In Frankfurter's view, the Court should proceed in an orderly way, enlisting and molding the understanding of the lower courts; they should remand the case to give the Georgia court the opportunity to work the case out in a fair manner. Douglas commented that he would not reverse on the ground of incompetent counsel because he believed the attorney was "just slow," but he did not want Georgia to have "another crack" at executing Williams. Burton expressed agreement with Frankfurter's reasoning and Harlan's memo and was also concerned about federal interference with state courts. Douglas and Black were in favor of complete reversal; Frankfurter, Harlan, and Burton were in agreement on remanding the case; and only Warren was in favor of a new trial. Therefore, it was decided that one of the three who desired a remand would write the opinion, reconciling the views and gathering a majority on the same grounds. Frankfurter, as the senior of the three, was given the task.[38]

When the case was remanded, the Georgia Supreme Court unanimously ignored Frankfurter's attempt to cajole it into reversal and upheld its prior decision. The Georgia court asserted flatly that challenges to the array must be made at the time of trial and that the Tenth Amendment prohibited such attempted interference with the state's jurisdiction.[39]

Again, many of Burton's opinions were written in the statutory interpretation cases of interest to specialists and practitioners. A tax case in which the Internal Revenue Service had denied a deduction for a conditional bequest to charity was an example of a case in which the minority ended up being the majority.[40] The decedent had provided that one-half of his estate would be given to charity if his daughter, who was twenty-seven at the time of his death, remained childless. Only Clark, Reed, Burton, and Warren had voted to grant certiorari. In the conference on the merits, only

Burton, Black, and Warren voted to reverse; the others would affirm. Reed prepared a majority opinion which, when circulated,
received the approval of everyone except Black and Burton. In a
note to Burton, Black wrote that he was "certainly not going to
agree to Stanley's opinion" and that he intended to write a dissent
but would be pleased to have Burton write the dissent if it suited
him. In addition, Burton's clerk, who had thoroughly discussed the
precise issue involved in a law school tax course and had some
strong views on the trust provision as a tax evasion device, urged
him to write a dissent.[41]

When Burton's dissent was circulated, the Reed majority
crumbled, leaving Reed and Douglas in disagreement with the new
majority. Upon reading the dissent, Frankfurter informed Burton
that "as a rule I do not deem it desirable to dissent in a case turning
merely on disputed statutory construction . . . but I cannot escape
the force of your views in that case and so I'm advising Stanley that
I'm leaving him and joining you." To the disappointed Reed
Frankfurter declared, "it will not be news to you that this is the
kind of case in which normally I do not invest my guts." Additionally, he commented that "for me the presumption is strong in
favor of the correctness of a doctrine sponsored and adhered to by
the Second Circuit. But Harold's opinion put me on my intellectual
conscience to exercise an independent judgment." Even though he
was disagreeing with Reed, Frankfurter told him that "I cannot
honestly say that I regret having nudged you to improve your opinion at least in form." Warren was already in agreement. With only
eight members, the decision would have been affirmed 4-4; but
Clark and Minton finally capitulated to make the Burton majority.
For six members, Burton upheld the Internal Revenue Service and
denied the deduction.[42]

In the other routine cases, Burton decided for a unanimous
Court that an American importer of Canadian seed potatoes did
not have to pay damages to the United States government resulting
from the use of the potatoes for table stock as opposed to seed purposes; and he held for six members that deficiencies exacted in as-
sessing excess war profits taxes had to be paid from the due date
and must include interest.[43] He also wrote unanimous majority
opinions in two Federal Power Commission cases upholding the

commission's authority. In one case, he held that on a petition to review a natural gas rate reduction order of the commission, the court of appeals could not on its own motion consider an objection which had not been urged before the commission in the application for a rehearing. Burton strongly affirmed the primacy of administrative power because "it is not the function of a court to itself engage in rate making."[44]

In the other case, a power company in Oregon was granted a license by the FPC, over the objection of the state fish and game commission, for a power project involving nonnavigable waters on a federal reservation in that state. Over Douglas's dissent, Burton decided that not only did the commission have the power to issue the license but adequate provisions had been made to prevent injury to the fish affected by the project. When Burton's opinion was circulated, Frankfurter commented, "a characteristically careful piece of work. I do not believe that Douglas can dislodge you." In fact, Douglas's opinion did not "dislodge" him. Furthermore, as Burton's clerk asserted, two of the cases relied on by Douglas were "totally different from the instant situation" and did not even need to be distinguished in Burton's opinion.[45]

Burton, for a majority, upheld a decision by the Supreme Court of Washington that had required a union to deliver goods owned by the union in California to the Court for security until a damage claim brought by employees for black listing had been decided. Although the issue was procedural, the resolution reflected his hostility toward the abuse of power over employees by unions.[46] He dissented from a Fair Labor Standards Act decision in *Manejo* v. *Waialua Agricultural Co.*, which extended coverage to processing plant employees of an agricultural company. Believing that they were exempt from coverage because they were "employed in agriculture" under the terms of the act, he continued his opposition to a broad interpretation of the FLSA.[47]

Burton also wrote dissenting opinions in two admiralty cases relating to the waiver of negligence in towage contracts, and he joined the dissent in a third. It had long been settled in American maritime law that contracts exempting common carriers from liability for negligence to their customers were against public policy. However, tugs were not usually classified as common carriers; and the continued use of negligence exemption clauses in towage contracts had been encouraged by the ambiguity of Supreme Court precedents and the enforcement of such agreements in the second circuit. In three cases during the term, the Court, through Black, sharply limited the effectiveness of such clauses by strictly construing them. Burton's opposition to limitation on the exemption clauses was based on unwillingness to make changes in long-standing commercial law and a belief that whatever terms the parties to a contract agreed to ought to be enforced.[48]

Burton had come into his own by the end of the first two Warren terms. He was confident, in complete mastery of the technical aspects of his discipline, and sure of his matured philosophy of law and judging. He was still his own man, admired for his independence of mind and strength of character by the other justices and the law clerks. When the clerks polled themselves that term to decide which justice they would choose to decide a case if they were on trial or, in general, who was the best justice, they picked Burton, who lost only one vote, that of one of his own clerks who was a great admirer of Frankfurter. Burton maintained close relationships with Reed and Warren and was greatly admired by Harlan when he came to the Court. He was highly regarded for not being result oriented; and his judicial behavior endeared him to moderate and conservative commentators, who increasingly distinguished him as an example of what the Warren Court should be. As he approached the tenth anniversary of his appointment, Burton believed that he had "given the work the best of whatever abilities and qualifications I have had and, in doing so, I trust that with the years I have gained in my capacity to perform the unique duties of the office."[49]

# 6

# Burton After Ten Years: From Majority Justice to Minority Justice

AS BURTON began the second decade of his service on the Court with the good wishes of his colleagues, his secretary, Tess Cheatham, surprised him with a reunion party of former law clerks. His first clerk, Howard Mann, acted as master of ceremonies and conducted a seminar in which each former clerk read a brief résumé of his experiences and gave due praise to the justice. The Court convened amid continuing attacks from critics for its decree in the segregation cases. In March 1956, ninety-six members of the South's congressional delegation issued a Southern Manifesto, criticizing the Supreme Court decision on constitutional grounds; and declarations of interposition and nullification were issued by the legislatures of five states.[1]

Internally, the work of the Court began with another Frankfurter memo decrying the lack of time available for the decision-making process. Although commentators still criticized the Court for the small number of cases decided and length of time expended in deliberation, Frankfurter wanted more time and thought that the Court should find some means of "assuring due deliberation" of its decisions. He believed that the justices had often been inadequately prepared for discussion in conference and that they had been "denied, in the very nature of the customary conduct of our business, adequate opportunity to reach a solid judgment before we vote on a case." He cited the length of time devoted to the segregation cases, in which the maturing process was "fully explored," as an appropriate pattern to follow. As further support for his complaint, he pointed out that on more than one occasion, a justice to whom an opinion was assigned changed his vote after further study. Frankfurter asserted that he was not "so foolish" as to think they "should aim at perfection"; but "the job of adjudicating the most exciting cases that come before this court is not unlike the work of scientists and philosophers. It is rarely accomplished in a brief spurt of inspiration. Ideas have to be incubated and brought slowly to maturity." Specifically, he suggested that no vote be taken in conference, that the cases be assigned to one justice for a full report on the issues before a vote, that two or three days should elapse between argument and conference on a case, and that more time should be made available after an opinion was circulated for potential dissenters to note their intent. Since the other justices believed that the time available was already sufficient and in some cases too long, the Court continued to follow its usual procedure.[2]

For the first time in three years, the issues of racial segregation and discrimination did not occupy a large part of the Court's time. The justices summarily disposed of these issues in the cases that did come up and remanded a case involving the legality of the Virginia antimiscegenation statute. The Court was not yet ready to decide the issues. With the time-consuming segregation cases concluded, the Court disposed of many more cases with full opinions. A significant part of their output dealt with interpreting statutes and administrative procedures instituted to suppress alleged subversive and seditious activity during the McCarthy era, and their decisions were not always greeted favorably.

For example, in *Pennsylvania* v. *Nelson*, a storm of criticism resulted when the Court held that federal legislation regulating Communist activity, the Smith Act of 1940, had superseded the Pennsylvania sedition statute. Burton and Minton concurred in Reed's dissent to the majority decision which invalidated similar statutes in forty-two states and raised serious doubts as to the validity of other state regulatory measures in this field. Criticism of the decision led to the introduction into Congress of several bills disavowing an intention to occupy the field so that states could continue their independent efforts to ferret out sedition. Warren had stated that he believed there would be no loss to the United States if the states were preempted in the field. Black, who had been the only one to vote to deny certiorari, voted to affirm without comment. Reed asserted that as a matter of personal feeling, he would be happy to see the state sedition acts outlawed; but he could see no reason to do so in this case. In agreeing with Warren, Frankfurter said that he would even be willing to disallow all state treason laws. Douglas voted to affirm and Burton to reverse without comment, while Clark voted to reverse because he believed that state and federal laws could both operate in the field. Minton voted to reverse; and Harlan, who was "not ready to vote," stated that he had "no doubt as to the wisdom" of such state sedition laws. However, Clark changed his mind after seeing the Warren opinion; and Harlan eventually voted to affirm, giving Warren the six-man majority.[3]

In *Slochower* v. *Board of Higher Education*, the Court considered the dismissal of a state employee, a Brooklyn college professor, because of his use of the privilege against self-incrimination. At issue was a New York City charter provision requiring the discharge, without notice or hearing, of a municipal employee utilizing the privilege against self-incrimination in refusing to answer legally authorized inquiries concerning his official conduct. The professor refused to answer questions relating to past Community party membership, although it appeared that in previous sessions before a state investigating body, he had testified fully in response to similar questions.

In conference, Warren, who with Reed and Minton had been the only members who had voted not to hear the professor's appeal, expressed the view that the decision should be reversed. Although he believed the New York action violated the Constitution, he wondered aloud whether some of the cases coming up might not be clearer vehicles on their facts for striking down the excesses of government efforts to pursue subversion. Such cases might include *Communist Party* v. *SACB* and *Ullman* v. *United States.* Frankfurter asserted that on the merits, "oceans of ink" had been spent on the issue of the right to government employment; but no one had said more than Holmes had in the 1892 Massachusetts police case, in which he laid down the dictum that "there was no constitutional right to be a policeman." However, Frankfurter saw the question in this case as being whether Slochower's membership in the party in 1940 was related to his job in 1955, and he found no such relationship. Douglas insisted that "there is a constitutional right to have a job and not to be withheld from it." Additionally, Douglas felt the New York charter section was an unconstitutional bill of attainder. Clark believed they could reverse per curiam by simply citing *Wieman* v. *Updegraff* from the 1951 term. Reed commented that his views were "well known, that it was within the power of the city to do this," while Minton asserted that when Slochower took the Fifth Amendment, he waived his right to a hearing before being dismissed. Harlan stated he would rather not express his views until he heard the arguments in the other Fifth Amendment cases coming up. As for Burton, he expressed his usual view that information needed by appropriate public bodies ought to be provided by citizens and that fitness for holding a professorship could in part be determined on the basis of information concerning one's associates, past and present. However, he was one of an unsuccessful minority which agreed that a rehearing should be ordered on the point of whether Slochower could have known that he could be dismissed for invoking the Fifth Amendment. In a Clark opinion, five members of the Supreme Court found that Slochower's dismissal had been a denial of due process. Minton and Burton joined a Reed dissent on the grounds that a city could require its employees either to give evidence regarding the facts of official conduct within their knowledge or to give up the positions they held.[4]

In *Cole* v. *Young*, Harlan, supported by Burton and four others, held for the Court that the summary suspension powers of department heads under the Internal Security Act of 1950 applied only to employees in "sensitive positions." Clark dissented, joined by Reed and Minton, on the grounds that Congress intended summary dismissal of employees whose retention would be harmful to the national interest, regardless of the sensitivity of their positions. Additionally, the Court upheld the constitutionality of the Immunity Act of 1954, which provided that witnesses before federal grand juries investigating matters relating to national security could be compelled to give incriminating testimony in return for immunity from subsequent prosecution. Frankfurter's majority opinion, which was supported by Burton and five others, rejected the petitioner's claim that the immunity granted was not as broad as that provided by the Fifth Amendment and therefore should not displace its protection.[5]

In three decisions during the term, the Court dealt with long-standing controversies over two articles of the Uniform Code of Military Justice. Congress enacted the articles in 1950 in order to subject servicemen and their dependents to court-martial for crimes committed abroad. The Korean War brought before the Court the issue of the constitutionality of these code sections. Robert Toth was apprehended in Pittsburgh, Pennsylvania, by military authorities in May 1953 and was charged with having committed murder while an airman in Korea. His arrest took place five months after Toth had received an honorable discharge from the air force and at a time when he had no affiliation of any kind with the military. Toth was flown to Korea and was awaiting court-martial there when the United States District Court for the District of Columbia, on petition of his sister, granted a writ of habeas corpus on the grounds that the military had not complied with certain legal procedures necessary for Toth's removal to Korea. The court of appeals found these procedures unnecessary and reversed. When the case reached the Supreme Court, the majority voted to reverse the court of appeals decision, with the dissent of three justices. The Court had great difficulty in reaching a decision. After it was first argued in February 1955, a majority—including Warren, Burton, Reed, Minton, Harlan, and Clark—wanted to affirm. Douglas was also leaning in that direction. Warren believed that Congress had made a "reasonable" grant of power that could be discharged by the armed forces. Furthermore, he felt that the relevant legislation which empowered the air force to act in the case was less objectionable than some earlier acts, such as the 1863 act which was designed to punish fraud under military regulations and which was extended to apply to civilians. Black admitted the relevance of the history of the fraud act but did not believe its principles ought to be extended. Reed noted his agreement with Warren and commented that the Constitution permitted treatment of Toth as if he were still in the air force. Frankfurter, who with Black wanted to reverse, asserted that the usual presumption that an act of Congress was constitutional could not apply in this case. To him, trying a civilian in a military court clearly violated the Bill of Rights.

After Reed, who was assigned the majority opinion, circulated it and Black circulated his dissent, the majority crumbled. Burton's clerk tried to persuade him to join Black, but Burton adhered to the Reed position. However, no decision was reached, and the case was set over for reargument in the 1955 term. After reargument, Black's dissent was rewritten and circulated as the majority opinion. In the second conference, Warren explained that he now thought the statute conflicted with the Fifth Amendment and that the "necessary and proper" clause cited by Reed did not cover the issues involved. Furthermore, he did not think the case was as significant as the government urged; and he added that if Congress did not like the decision, it could enact a statute providing for such trials. Burton and Minton concurred in Reed's dissent to Black's majority opinion.[6]

Despite the decision in *Toth*, the Court upheld military jurisdiction over two military dependent wives who murdered their husbands, members of the armed forces, outside the United States. The cases involved were *Kinsella* v. *Krueger* and *Reid* v. *Covert*. Citing cases which had permitted the use of territorial legislative courts and consular courts to try certain crimes committed overseas, the majority concluded that the jury requirements of Article III of the Constitution and the Sixth Amendment were inapplicable to prosecutions which took place outside the continental limits of the United States. Congress could therefore establish legislative courts in foreign countries to try American citizens for crimes committed there. The use of the existing system of military courts for this purpose was found reasonable and not in violation of due process. Additionally, the majority asserted that utilizing these courts would be better than creating a duplicate legal system or using foreign courts. In both *Reid* and *Kinsella*, Warren, Black, and Douglas dissented; and Frankfurter reserved expression of his views for a later date. The unwillingness of the majority to deny military jurisdiction, as was done in the *Toth* case, was due to the fact that the murdered husbands were in the service while Toth was a civilian.[7]

In conference on both cases, Warren doubted whether the families of servicemen were members of the armed forces for purposes of trial and punishment: "the fact that they may use the post exchange means nothing." In Warren's view, it was not "in keeping with our traditions" to try them in a military court. Black asserted his belief that there was no doubt that soldiers could be subjected to military jurisdiction, but to subject others "stretches the constitution." He added that he felt the situation was not analogous to the use of consular courts since in those cases civilians were trying civilians. At this point, Reed commented that a study of the related legislation left him with the view that "camp followers" were not to be subject to military jurisdiction except in wartime. Although he was unsure about his vote, "he was not ready to say the government was wrong." Frankfurter was troubled because he also did not think the power of military courts extended to civilians. Douglas voted to deny military jurisdiction, while Burton voted to uphold it, without comment. Clark passed, while Minton said he thought drawing an analogy to consular courts was the best approach. Although tentatively agreeing with Minton, Harlan commented that without some judicial vehicle, the government would be powerless to control the civilian dependents of "the entourage," as he called them; but he felt as Minton did that their trials should not be justified by deeming them "military." The vote recorded at that time found Douglas, Black, Frankfurter, and Warren opposed to military jurisdiction; Reed wavering toward them; and Harlan, Minton, Clark, and Burton in favor. The opinion was assigned to Warren but was then transferred to Clark when he reversed his vote. Reed decided to waver in the other direction.[8]

The Court decided few criminal law cases but one, *Griffin* v. *Illinois*, added fuel to the anger of states' righters generated by the *Nelson* and school segregation cases. In *Griffin*, a sharply divided Court held, in a Black opinion, that in criminal trials, states could be required to furnish transcripts for indigent defendants. The majority explained that while a state does not have to provide appellate review, when it does, it cannot "do so in a way that discriminates against some convicted defendants on account of their poverty." However, Burton emphasized that the state procedure did guarantee the right to a free transcript to defendants in capital cases, denying it only to those convicted of noncapital offenses. He cited numerous examples in which the procedural distinction between capital and noncapital cases had been upheld, such as in a greater number of preemptory challenges of jurors. Although it might be "a desirable social policy, the Constitution does not require the states to provide equal financial means for all defendants"; and "a state is not bound to make the defendants economically equal before its bar of justice." To Burton, the majority was interfering "with state power for what may be a desirable result, but which we believe to be within the field of local option."⁹

In preparing for argument in the case, Burton rejected his law clerk's advice that the petitioners ought to prevail on the grounds of equal protection. The clerk told him that the position of the state counsel was "that of the cynic, but fortunately, cynics did not devise the Fourteenth Amendment." Nonetheless, Burton responded that any reform should be left to the state legislature and not the courts.

In conference on the case, Warren voted to reverse, commenting that there could not be "one rule for the rich and one for the poor." He was concerned, however, about the possible "flood" of requests for transcripts and asked if the Court might give the ruling "prospective effect only." Black agreed with Warren on all points except that he was opposed to applying the decision prospectively only; he would vote against any opinion in that regard. Clark and Douglas agreed with Black, and Frankfurter commented that "it would be shabby" to say that defendants who had not raised the issue before had waived their rights. In voting to reverse, Reed stated that he agreed with Black and Warren but doubted that it was necessary to make the decision prospective only. Harlan voted to reverse on equal protection grounds. Only Burton and Minton voted to affirm, with Minton commenting "here we go again," interfering with state criminal procedure. He believed that the issue was "not an inequality of the law but an inequality of riches."¹⁰

After Black's opinion was written and circulated, Burton's clerk again unsuccessfully tried to persuade him not to dissent. He urged "that rules which sharply distinguish between the rich and the poor in an area where individual liberty is at stake can not be tolerated in a democratic community." Burton tried at first to find a basis for joining Harlan's dissent; but after seeing Harlan's draft, he believed that it contained "too many unsupportable premises."¹¹

The Court decided four other state criminal procedure cases, with Burton in the majority each time. In a Georgia case, a semi-literate indigent of low mentality failed to challenge the grand jury composition before his indictment. He was not assigned counsel until after the indictment. The Georgia courts held that a timely failure to challenge the grand jury composition constituted a waiver of the right to challenge. A unanimous Court, speaking through Clark, reversed the lower court decision. The other three petitioners, in a Louisiana case, failed to challenge the composition of the grand jury within three judicial days of the end of the grand jury's term. All three defendants had court-appointed counsel. Again speaking through Clark, six members of the Court, including Burton, affirmed the denial of all three motions, holding that the state practice was reasonable. Apparently, a persuasive oral argument had changed Burton's mind. On his certiorari memo in the case, Burton noted that he did not believe sufficient time had been allowed to the petitioners; and on his bench memo two days before argument, he had noted that he would reverse and remand.[12]

Burton wrote opinions in two criminal law cases. In one, the petitioner was charged with stealing cattle, was convicted in a Florida state court on six counts, and was sentenced to five years of imprisonment on each count, the terms to be served consecutively. He unsuccessfully sought relief by various postconviction remedies, among them a petition for habeas corpus filed in 1952. In an opinion supported by five justices, Burton dismissed the writ of certiorari for lack of jurisdiction, agreeing with the Florida court that the state decision might have been based on an adequate state ground. Burton asserted that even if the alleged facts made for a "shocking case of miscarriage of justice," as Douglas's dissent insisted, the questions of jurisdiction and states' rights had precedence. Burton's opinion in this case was another clear expression of his support of states' rights in criminal cases to the exclusion of acquitting a defendant even when, on the facts, injustice might result. To Burton, upholding state power in most instances was constitutionally required and would benefit the interest of justice in the long run.[13]

In the other criminal case, Burton, speaking for six members of the Court, upheld the conviction for murder and the death sentence of one of four accomplices in a series of armed robberies. The defendant claimed that he did not receive a fair trial since his trial came after that of two of his associates, during which an atmosphere of hysteria and prejudice prevailed. Furthermore, he claimed that he was prejudiced by the presence in the courtroom of another judge of the same court who had presided over the first trial and who had allegedly made hostile statements. Burton was persuaded by the fact that counsel for the petitioner used none of the means available to insulate his client from an unfair trial. For example, there was no motion for a continuance or change of venue. Furthermore, the issue was not raised until three years after the trial. Said Burton, "While this Court stands ready to correct violations of constitutional rights," it also recognized that "it is not asking too much that the burden of showing essential unfairness be sustained by him who claims such injustice and seeks to have the result set aside, and that it be sustained not as a matter of speculation but as a demonstrable reality." Frankfurter and Douglas concurred, while Harlan dissented. Harlan was disturbed by the conduct of the judge who had presided over the first case and had commended the jury for a verdict of guilty in the courtroom during the petitioner's trial. During the second trial, the judge was present on numerous occasions for unexplained reasons. In Harlan's view, the jury might have inferred that he had an unusual interest in the outcome of the case; and this inference might "have tipped the scales with the jury in favor of a death verdict." However, this possibility was not enough to sway Burton.[14]

In the highly significant but less colorful cases during the term, Burton found himself increasingly in dissent. He had over the previous nine years written a number of majority opinions on the issue of the compensation to be paid for the taking of property for power projects and flood control. This time, however, in an opinion by Douglas, five members of the Court decided that the compensation payable under the Fifth Amendment by the United States for the condemnation of land along a navigable river for hydroelectric power operations did not need to include the value for power purposes. The Court distinguished a number of earlier cases without overruling them. Joined by Frankfurter, Minton, and Harlan, Burton dissented, pointing out that the power-site potential of land had always been considered part of its value and should be included in the compensation.

Burton had hoped the vote in the case would narrowly go in favor of his position. After the vote came out 5-4 in favor of the Douglas opinion, Minton consoled him with "if you don't understand this whole business, I don't know who does." Frankfurter asked Burton to write the dissent; and in an effort to obtain a majority for it, Frankfurter lobbied with the other justices, including Reed, whom he thought would be the most likely target of his efforts. Frankfurter encouraged Reed to study the prospective Court's opinion and Burton's dissent contemporaneously, for they agreed about "Harold's habitual care in preparing opinions," and not form even a tentative view of the former "until you have both." Although Burton made the position of the dissenters "luminously clear," he failed to attract the one extra vote needed to obtain a majority.[15]

In a civil procedure case involving the interpretation of the doctrine that a federal court deciding a diversity case should follow the holding, on substantive rather than procedural matters, of the highest state court in the state where the federal court is sitting, Burton again found himself in dissent. The issue was whether the granting of a stay of Court proceedings to permit arbitration was substantive or procedural. The majority, in a Douglas opinion, decided it was substantive; but Burton believed it was procedural. Minton had voted with Burton at first but was persuaded by Douglas's opinion, which left Burton to dissent alone.[16]

In two other procedure cases, Burton wrote majority opinions holding that it was not necessary for all of the claims involved in a case to be decided before an appeal on one or more could be heard.[17] In one of the cases, Frankfurter, who considered himself an expert on questions of procedure, was greatly troubled by Burton's position and dissented. He believed that whether Burton admitted it or not, he was relaxing the final decision requirement and was not giving clear guidance to the lower courts. A relaxed rule would permit too many separate appeals. Frankfurter knew "how hard and conscientiously" Burton had "labored on this opinion." However, this was a subject over which he had "worried long be-

fore and not a little since"; and he wanted to "forestall, if possible," further litigation. In addition, Frankfurter did not like Burton's reference in his opinion to the district courts as "dis-
patchers," for "it is a misleading description of the other aspects of
the problem."[18]

Burton wrote opinions in two statutory liability cases, one involving the respective liabilities of a stevedoring company and shipowner for the injuries of a longshoreman, and the other involving
the validity of an Interstate Commerce Commission order that
dressed chickens were a manufactured commodity. In the longshoreman's case, the Court held (in a 5-4 decision in a Burton opinion) that the shipowner was liable but could be indemnified by the
stevedore company. Even before this case was decided, the weight
of the precedents was that the party primarily at fault was solely liable. When neither party was negligent or where both parties were
equally at fault, the shipowner apparently had to bear the entire
burden. Therefore, Burton's decision that the shipowner had a
right to indemnity from the negligent employer was predictable. In
Burton's view, since the shipowner's negligence lay only in the
failure to discover the employer's improper workmanship, it would
be unreasonable to allow this negligence to be asserted as a defense
by the employer. To Burton, it was not necessary to make such a
simple set of facts more complex by discussing "concepts of primary and secondary or active and passive tortious conduct," as the
circuit court had done.[19]

The chicken case involved an ICC order deeming dressed
chickens a manufactured rather than an agricultural commodity,
with the result that carriers of them had to obtain a certificate of
convenience and necessity. Five justices decided, in a Douglas opinion, that this order was invalid. Joined by Frankfurter, Minton,
and Harlan, Burton dissented, expressing the view that if fresh and
frozen meats were manufactured commodities, "the Commission's
like treatment of poultry is not arbitrary or unreasonable." He
would uphold the power of administrative agencies, "if there is evidence to support them." In Burton's view, a reasonable man might
determine that a dressed chicken was a manufactured commodity.[20]

Burton also wrote opinions in two labor cases during the term. In
one case, a majority of the employees of a sawmill and flooring

plant in Alexandria, Louisiana, chose as their bargaining representative a union which had failed to file required financial and other data with the secretary of labor and the necessary non-Communist affidavits with the National Labor Relations Board. In order to force the employer to recognize the union, the employees struck and established a peaceful picket line. The Louisiana state courts enjoined the picketing. For seven members of the Court, with Harlan not participating, Burton held that the state courts had no power to enjoin the picketing since, under the NLRA, the employer was bound to recognize the union as the bargaining representative of its employees; and the union could, despite its noncompliance with the statute, still take lawful action such as picketing. In the opinion, Burton asserted that congressional policy was "to induce labor organizations to file the described data and affidavits by making various benefits of the Act strictly contingent upon such filing." However, by not filing, the union would not receive NLRA protection; but "the company can, if it so wishes, lawfully recognize the union as the employee's representative. That being so, there is no reason why the employees, and their union under their authorization may not . . . strike . . . and . . . peacefully picket."[21]

Frankfurter dissented on the grounds that the federal act did not contain an implied limitation on the state power to enjoin picketing in this kind of case; therefore, he would leave the states free to use their own devices. It was not necessary for Burton to make changes in his opinion to meet Frankfurter's dissent, for Frankfurter's complaint, that the "reasonable direction of the meaning and purpose" of the non-Communist affidavit and other reporting requirements should be given due weight, was met by Burton's explanation that no consequences other than those indicated could result from noncompliance. Frankfurter's concern that the Court not find "an implied limitation upon power exercised by Louisiana" in the labor statutes was unfounded because the decision was not interfering with a state policy. In Burton's view, Louisiana had, in asserting that the union could not picket, simply misinterpreted the consequences of noncompliance.[22]

In the other labor case, employees were represented by a carpenters' union until a warehouse workers' union began a campaign to become their collective bargaining agent. The employer opposed the warehouse union because he believed it to be Communist controlled. However, since he did not believe the carpenters were strong enough to ward off the alleged Communist threat, he asked the workers to transfer their allegiance to a union of paper mill workers. When they refused to do so, he began proselytizing and assisting designated employees in obtaining signatures on cards for the paper mill union. The two contesting unions filed with the NLRB, both claiming to have replaced the carpenters' union as a representative of the workers. However, the workers continued to adhere to the carpenters. When the president of the company fired an employee of over four years' standing because of his activity in support of the carpenters' union and his opposition to the paper mill union, a strike ensued. The NLRB found that this strike was precipitated by the employer's unfair labor practice. While the strike was in progress, the contract between the union and the corporation expired. The employer refused to negotiate during the statutory sixty-day cooling-off period designated for negotiations. In a hearing before the board, the carpenters' union accused the employer of engaging in unfair labor practices, alleging his support of the paper mill union and his discharge of numerous employees.

In an opinion by Burton, six members of the Court held that the strike waiver provision in the collective bargaining contract barred employees from striking for economic benefits; but it did not deprive them of their right to strike solely against the employer's unfair labor practices. In addition, the Court majority decided that the NLRA was not to be construed as depriving individuals of their status as employees while they engaged in a strike within the "cooling off" period solely as a consequence of their employer's unfair labor practices. Although agreeing with the majority that the strike waiver provision of the collective bargaining agreement did not bar strikes against unfair labor practices, Frankfurter, joined by Minton and Harlan, dissented, for he viewed the NLRA as applicable to all strikes during the cooling off period. The Court had considerable difficulty in arriving at the opinion. Burton apparently had Warren, Reed, and Clark on his side all along, although the other five made up a majority for the Frankfurter position in the first vote. At first, Black adhered to Burton's opinion, shifting the balance the other way; then Douglas and Minton switched, making what had been a 4-5 vote against Burton 7-2 in favor of his position. Again, Minton vacillated and finally ended up with Frankfurter. Harlan thought the sides were very closely balanced; but indicated he would follow "the face of the statute" and not the legislative history and would join Frankfurter's dissent.[23]

Reed and Frankfurter carried on a very lively correspondence as Frankfurter tried to persuade Reed to adhere to his opinion. Frankfurter sent Burton a copy of one of the missives, not to continue "the argument with you but in order to let you know what I say to others about an opinion of yours!" In the same letter, Frankfurter told Reed:

if I did not have as Marion [his wife] insists I have, a cast iron stomach, your attitude toward congressional legislation would give me ulcers. Why don't you face up to the challenge of my dissent that the court is nullifying a provision of Congress? Your compassionate heart says, "The hell with it! We are not going to allow an employee who is guilty of [unfair] labor practices get away with it." . . . Why is it so hard to find a rational purpose in what Congress did? . . . One did not have to be an intimate of Bob Taft [Senator Robert Taft, cosponsor of the Taft-Hartley Act] to appreciate that, if he had spelt out his feelings, it would be most natural for him to feel that discouragement of strikes by way of a cooling period, is the most important thing, and to look to other means to deal with an unfair labor practice.

Apparently, Reed did not mind Frankfurter's characterization of his views or the fact that they might give Frankfurter ulcers, because he adhered to the Burton position.[24]

Burton's other two opinions during the term were in tax cases. In *International Harvester Credit Corporation* v. *Goodrich,* the Court considered a New York statute which granted state highway tax liens priority over the rights of conditional sellers of trucks operated by a motor carrier on New York highways. The sellers challenged the constitutionality of the statute, for they claimed it denied them due process insofar as the liens were made applicable to taxes based upon the carrier's operation of other trucks within the state, whether before or during the time that the carrier had operated the particular trucks within the state. In addition, the vendors complained about the application of the lien priority statute to taxes assessed against the carrier after the vendor had repossessed the particular trucks, such taxes being based upon the carrier's operations on the state's highways before such repossession. The New York courts held the statute valid as applied. Speaking for five members of the Court, Burton affirmed the ruling of the courts below, taking the view that the statute as applied was within the state's discretion in exercising its prerogative to impose a statutory lien for delinquent taxes upon the taxpayer's property. Black concurred in the result but not in the reasoning. Joined by Douglas, Frankfurter dissented, declaring that the due process clause barred the state from according priority to a tax lien based upon taxes arising during the period antedating the conditional sale of the trucks to the carrier. For Burton, it was a case of a state's right to collect revenue as long as the means were reasonable: "refinements of title are without controlling force when a statute, unmistakable in meaning, is assailed by a taxpayer as overpassing the bounds of reason, an exercise by the lawmakers of arbitrary power. . . . The question is whether it is one that an enlightened legislator might act w/o affront to justice." As for the taxes assessed prior to the purchase of the trucks, Burton gave considerable weight to the state's "constitutional right to enforce the collection of all taxes due it from the motor carrier for the latter's use of the highways of New York under a statute giving ample notice of the tax and of the provisions for its collection." Upon reading Frankfurter's dissent, Burton's clerk concluded that he had thought Frankfurter's position was right before oral argument; but he thought Burton's opinion had "done sufficient combat with it."[25]

In the other tax case, *Costello* v. *United States,* the government had indicted a notorious crime figure, Frank Costello, for willful tax evasion. Costello claimed that his conviction should have been dismissed because it was based solely upon the evidence of government witnesses who had no firsthand knowledge of the transactions upon which they based their computations showing that the petitioner and his wife had received far greater income than they had reported. With Clark and Harlan not participating, Black, in an opinion for six members of the Court, upheld the indictments on the grounds that neither the Fifth Amendment, in making a grand jury indictment a prerequisite of a federal trial for a capital or otherwise infamous crime, nor justice and the concept of a fair trial required that indictments be open to challenge on the ground that evidence before the grand jury was inadequate or incompetent. Burton concurred in the result but expressed the view that indictments made without substantial or rationally persuasive evidence should be quashed. However, Black believed that if indictments were open to challenge on the ground that hearsay evidence, for example, had been used, there would be the possibility that before the trial on the merits, a defendant could always insist on a kind of preliminary trial to determine the competence and adequacy of the evidence before the grand jury. The evidence question, he felt, could be considered at trial. Burton thought that even though "the case does not justify the breadth of the declarations made by the court, . . . to hold a person to such an empty indictment for a capital or otherwise infamous federal crime *robs* the Fifth Amendment of much of its protective value to the private citizen." With the strong support of his clerks, Burton adhered to his position, although Frankfurter was opposed to his filing a concurrence. Frankfurter asserted that Burton's language would "encourage" in the federal courts "the vicious state practices of trying indictments on affidavits . . . ,etc." In addition, he found objectionable Burton's quote from Learned Hand that "if it appeared that no evidence had been offered that rationally established the facts, the indictments ought to be quashed." Frankfurter commented: "This is loose talk. I repeat—we ought not to allow heat waves to be fever. Let's wait until we get a case that shocks our conscience."[26]

As the justices finished the 1955 term amid a stir of criticism concerning their civil liberties decisions, a libertarian bloc of justices—including Black, Warren, and Douglas—had emerged. Burton, Minton, and Reed comprised a more anti-civil libertarian conservative bloc. Clark and Frankfurter, and to a lesser extent Harlan, seemed to keep to a center position, with Frankfurter and Clark more often than not providing for a 6-3 libertarian victory. Burton increasingly found himself in dissent. There was tension among the justices, although Burton maintained warm relations with everyone on the Court. For example, Burton was the first to know that Minton was planning to retire. On May 3, 1956, Minton wrote to him confidentially on the bench, noting that "when I leave the bench today it will be my last case as I shall retire this fall." Frankfurter was still very critical of a number of the justices in his discussions with Burton. On December 7, 1955, he shared with Burton, on the bench, a conversation in which Frankfurter had told Black "I'm going to say something that you won't like to hear but it is true even if unpleasant. I've never know anyone who more steadily reads for confirmation of his own views and not for disinterested enlightenment."[27]

Between the terms, Burton reflected with increasing satisfaction upon his own work as a justice. He had continued his rigid work schedule, turning out careful opinions and maintaining his independence and the respect of everyone else on the bench. Even the publication of Fred Rodell's book on the Court, in which he repeated his earlier criticisms concerning the "mediocrity" of Burton and the other Truman justices, did not bother him. Burton thought that while Rodell's book did more harm than good by giving currency to his conception of the Supreme Court's work, nevertheless it was a fair example of the exercise of freedom of speech and opinion. To Burton, it was a warning that there were people who also held similar views, a realization that served to keep the judiciary "on its mettle."[28]

The controversy that stormed about the Court over its civil liberties decisions increased to a roar during the next term. Legislation designed to curb the powers of the Court failed during the 1955 term, but the criticism had not been muted. The changes in Court personnel deeply affected Burton and the pattern of the Court's decisions. When Minton's retirement became effective on October 15, 1956, he was replaced by William J. Brennan, a Democrat and a Catholic from the bench of the New Jersey Supreme Court, who was not approved officially until March 1957. Besides impeding the work of the Court, Minton's absence meant the loss to Burton of one of the Court members with whom he had voted most often over the years. In addition, the other member of the majority bloc during the Vinson years, Justice Reed, retired unexpectedly on February 25, 1957. The possibility that the Court might now become more libertarian was recognized by Eisenhower. That realization led to the appointment of Charles E. Whittaker, a Missourian and a Republican who earlier had been appointed by Eisenhower to the district court and court of appeals. Burton now became an even more frequent dissenter. However, he still found some comfort in the presence of Frankfurter and the views of Harlan, which very often approximated his own.[29]

The Court again ignored Frankfurter's annual memorandum of complaint about the speed of their deliberations. This time he asserted that "I am duly mindful of the wisdom behind the whimsey, 'everybody's out of step but Johnny,' but indifference is not refutation, and neglect of my prior circulations may only mean that the press of other business has derailed their consideration." As before, the Court adhered to its previous practices; and Frankfurter's suggestions, which would have further delayed decisions and decreased the number of cases decided at a time when the Court was still being criticized for delay and for the small number of cases, were again aborted.[30]

Burton wrote opinions in a number of criminal law cases growing out of prosecutional investigations of possible subversive activities. He joined Clark in Reed's dissent to a per curiam which decided that an FBI agent had wrongfully asked three members of a jury, in a labor union official's trial for falsely filing a non-Communist affidavit, whether they had received any union propaganda. However, he wrote libertarian opinions in two other cases. In *Roviaro* v. *United States,* a heroin dealer was convicted of selling to one "John Doe" on the basis of testimony by two government agents who observed the sale. The prosecution's refusal of the defendant's demand that "John Doe" be identified was upheld by the trial court. In a Burton opinion, with Clark dissenting, the Supreme Court held that the refusal was prejudicial error. In his dissent, Clark admitted that past cases had held that when an informer's testimony was the basis of a finding of probable cause for arrests or search, that testimony had to be made; but he thought Roviaro knew who "John Doe" was and could have subpoenaed him and that the government was not actually required to present him in court. However, Burton pointed out that whether an informer must be produced depends on the facts of each case. In the instant case, since the informer, "John Doe," had taken a material part in supplying the evidence on Roviaro's possession of the heroin and was the only other participant in the transaction, he might be a material witness because he was the only person who might contradict the testimony of the government agents. Burton asserted that

we believe that no fixed rule with respect to disclosure is justifiable. The problem is one that calls for balancing the public interest in protecting the flow of information against the individual's right to prepare his defense. Whether a proper balance renders non-disclosure erroneous must depend on the particular circumstances of each case, taking into consideration the crime charged, the possible defenses, the possible significance of the informer's testimony and other relevant factors.

To Burton, the circumstances in this case were such that the government should have disclosed "the identity of its undercover employee in the face of repeated demands by the accused for his disclosure."[31]

Harlan and Brennan, in supporting Burton's opinion, explained that they thought the issues in the case were similar to those involved in the *Jencks* case, which was also under consideration at the time. But as it turned out, Harlan and Brennan parted company in *Jencks*, which was one of the most controversial decisions during Burton's tenure on the Court. The case involved a New Mexico labor leader who was convicted of perjury for falsely taking the Taft-Hartley non-Communist oath. At trial, Jencks's attorney asked two government witnesses if they could recall the information they had given the FBI about Jencks in reports made in 1948 and 1949, about which they were testifying. When neither witness could recall the contents of the reports, the defense attorney asked the court to subpoena the FBI files for examination by the judge in order to ascertain any information which could aid the defendant. If such information was found, they wanted it turned over to the defendant for use in cross-examination. The defendant's request was denied.

In conference, the Court split on the issue of whether only the judge or the defense should have access to the files. Brennan strongly voiced the view that merely allowing the trial judge to see the files was not enough, since only the defense would know whether they were useful. Reluctantly, Clark stated he would be willing to vote for a decision holding that the trial judge could see the reports; but he could not support Brennan's view, which gained a majority.

In a Brennan opinion for Warren, Black, Douglas, and Frankfurter, the Court announced that a prior showing of inconsistency was unnecessary and that the reports must be given directly to the defendant without any prior screening by the judge. Additionally, if the prosecution determined that it was not in the public interest to disclose the reports, then the criminal action based on the reports must be dismissed. Burton and Harlan, in a dissent written by Burton, disagreed with some of the views expressed in the Court's opinion. They held that the documents should be produced for the examination of the judge, who would determine their relevance as well as the applicability of the privilege claimed by the government. However, they concurred in the majority's result, with the agreement of Frankfurter, on the ground that the trial court's instructions were defective on the question of membership in and affiliation with the Communist party. In addition, Clark dissented, asserting that the government could go forward with the prosecution without producing the files; furthermore, he announced that opening files to criminals would impede law enforcement. Burton's concurrence quoted from his opinion in *Roviaro* regarding balancing the public's interest in protecting the flow of information against an accused's right to disclosure of evidence. He asserted that by letting the trial court examine the materials, "the legitimate public interest in safeguarding executive files" and the "interests of justice" could be properly balanced. Additionally, he thought the Court was going too far in its broad disclosure rule by giving the defendant more than he requested, for the "petitioner requested only that the records be produced to the trial court. He is entitled to no more."[32]

Burton's opinion in the end became the rule of law in such cases. The decision was criticized severely by security conscious newspapers and politicians who adhered to Clark's position and led to congressional passage of a statute during the following summer which codified the procedure laid down by Burton for gaining access to FBI files. The trial judge would screen files when the prosecution claimed a privilege and would balance the claims of liberty and authority in ruling upon admissibility.[33]

The Court's rulings in four cases in addition to *Jencks* generated fresh congressional attempts to limit its power. In the decisions, which generally supported claims of individuals in opposition to governmental authority, Burton again found himself on the side of the dissenters. In *Watkins* v. *United States*, the Court limited, in a Warren opinion, the investigative powers of the House Un-American Activities Committee. Burton did not participate because his nephew, William Hitz, assistant United States attorney, was the government's chief trial counsel. During an appearance before HUAC in 1954, Watkins, a UAW organizer, confessed his own past participation in the Communist party; but he refused to give the committee names of reformed party members. When he claimed that such questions went beyond the scope of the investigator's authority, he was convicted of contempt of Congress. Warren ruled, with Frankfurter concurring and Clark dissenting, that in order to support a conviction under the statute, a congressional investigating committee must, upon the objection of a witness, state for the record the subject under inquiry at that time and the manner in which the propounded questions are pertinent. In the instant case, the evidence failed to show that the question at issue was ever made known to the witness. If the makeup of the Court during the previous term had stood, the case would have gone the other way or at the very least been a 5-4 decision. Minton and Reed had voted to deny certiorari, and Burton agreed with the government's position. Clark, Minton, Reed, and Burton might have been able to persuade Frankfurter to join them.[34]

When a state university professor's contempt conviction for refusing to answer questions relating to an investigation of possible subversive activities within the state was appealed to the Court in *Sweezy* v. *New Hampshire,* lines were drawn in the same manner as in the *Watkins* case. In conference, Warren pointed out that even though there was no preemption by federal law of the area covered by the state's actions—and it was within the state's rights to investigate security, sabotage, and state employees—he thought that there was "no question" as to Sweezy's right to believe what he chose, "except as to Communism." He would reverse and decide in favor of Sweezy, using the same reasoning they had used in the *Watkins* case. After Black agreed with Warren, Frankfurter stated that he would also reverse but that his "chief concern" was the special position of teachers and educational institutions. However, he did not mean to imply that they had a "preferred position." He would begin to analyze and "stay with" the issues within the First Amendment and would disregard the due process clause. Additionally, Douglas believed that the First Amendment could be a ground for the decision. However, Burton asserted that Sweezy's conviction should be affirmed and that the opinion should support the powers of the states in security matters "with limitation." In agreement with Burton, Clark added that he was aware of a number of precedents for New Hampshire's action. At this point, Harlan asserted that the questions put to Sweezy seemed acceptable, and the state clearly had legislative interest in the investigation; yet, the state could not put a "block on teaching," for the teaching profession should be the last one investigated. He believed the states should restrict themselves in these matters. But to Brennan, the investigation was "all bad"; the "classroom is a sanctuary," and there should be no questions about teaching activities. When Warren, with Douglas and Black, reversed Sweezy's conviction and Frankfurter, joined by Harlan, concurred, Burton joined Clark's dissent on the ground that the investigation was state business designed to protect state interests and should be of no concern to the Court.[35]

When the Court considered appeals concerning two decisions by state courts that applicants for the bar had failed to establish the good moral character necessary for admission, based on the Fourteenth Amendment, Burton had great difficulty in reaching a decision. He was very deeply interested in and concerned about the potential effects of the decision on the petitioners and upon the unfettered right of lawyers to regulate their profession. Both petitioners were men in their forties and recent law school graduates; and both had been accorded hearings before the state boards of bar examiners, at which they were questioned and permitted to present witnesses and other evidence to establish their good character and to overcome the examiners' doubts as to their qualifications. One,

Schware, acknowledged that he had been a Communist party member until 1940, while the other, Konigsberg, who had allegedly been a Communist in 1941, declared that he was not a "philosophical communist" and that he had never advocated the violent overthrow of the government. Relying on the First Amendment and asserting that the "informer" testimony presented would be believed in contradiction to his testimony if he answered, Konigsberg refused to answer any other questions about his political beliefs and associations. While Schware's rejection was based upon his past membership in the Communist party, his use of aliases, and his record of arrest in the past, Konigsberg's was based upon his previous Communist party membership, his public criticism of American foreign policy, and his refusal to answer certain questions.

In conference, Warren opened by explaining that Konigsberg had been a Communist when it was legal to be such and, indeed, when the party was on the ballot. Furthermore, both petitioners had served in the army and in public service. According to Warren, Schware's army record was good, and his arrests meant nothing. Black agreed with Warren, but Reed announced he would decide against Konigsberg because of his refusal to answer questions. Frankfurter asserted that Konigsberg's case was not ripe for review because the basis of California's denial was not clear, but the *Schware* case was a clear case of denial of due process. Douglas, Brennan, and Burton voted to reverse in both cases, while Clark thought he would affirm both. Harlan agreed with Frankfurter and Reed that the state had a right to ask Konigsberg questions but that Schware's due process rights had been violated.[36]

With Reed included, the votes at that juncture would have stood at 5-4 for *Konigsberg* and 8-1 for *Schware*; but Reed retired in February before the decisions were handed down. Although Burton had voted to reverse, great pressure was exerted on him in order to change his mind. Frankfurter simply could not understand, philosophically, how Burton could uncharacteristically vote to override state control where there might be an adequate state ground for the decision. In addition, Burton's clerk advised him to reject the petitioner's view as espoused by Black because "Black . . . read the record with rose colored glasses" in

*Konigsberg*. The clerk believed that Konigsberg had evaded "perfectly reasonable questions and given misleading (and I think probably untrue) answers." However, Black exerted a counter-vailing force. He held frequent discussions with Burton concerning the cases and made several changes to meet Burton's objections to the language of the opinion. Burton held firm against all impor-tunities and went with Black's majority opinions. His concern over the defendants' exclusion from their chosen occupation overrode his usual support of states' rights and judicial self-restraint.[37]

Burton supported two Harlan opinions providing further protec-tion for individuals from overweening government authority. In the first case, *Yates* v. *United States*, the Court, in a brilliantly technical Harlan opinion, interpreted the Smith Act narrowly in finding innocent fourteen Communists who were charged with ad-vocating and teaching the forcible overthrow of the government and with organizing as the Communist party, a society of persons who advocated forcible overthrow of the government. Burton con-curred in the result and in Harlan's opinion, except for Harlan's nine-page discussion of the term *organize*. The Court opinion in *Yates* was a clear departure from the hostile characterization of the "clandestine" nature of Communist party activity under which the Court had justified making no distinction between advocacy of ac-tion and advocacy of belief when its activities were involved, as ex-pressed in the opinions of Vinson and especially Jackson in the *Dennis* case during the 1950 term. The result reached in *Yates* would clearly make convictions under the act difficult and almost impossible.

At best, it first appeared that *Yates* would be a close 5-4 decision in favor of the position finally taken by Harlan, with the possibility of some wavering toward the other side. In the first conference, Reed, Minton, Clark, and Burton voted to affirm the convictions; Warren, Black, and Douglas voted to reverse; and Frankfurter and Harlan passed because they were not ready to vote. Burton and Reed expressed some doubts about the sufficiency of the evidence but thought that "violent overt acts" were not required for convic-tion. In the second conference, which was held after Minton retired and in which Brennan took no part, the vote was Reed, Burton, and Clark to affirm and Frankfurter, Harlan, Black, Douglas, and

Warren to reverse. After having had time to read more of the record, Frankfurter and Harlan now thought the instructions given by the trial judge to the jury were confusing and inadequate. Burton did not part company with Clark until after Reed's retirement and the circulation of Harlan's opinion. He was also influenced by his clerk's advice that the opinion would not destroy the effectiveness of the Smith Act.[38]

The other case in which Burton supported a Harlan opinion was *Service v. Dulles*, in which John S. Service was discharged by Secretary of State Dean Acheson as a foreign service officer after sixteen years of experience in China even after seven loyalty hearings found no basis for his discharge. In a final audit, the Loyalty Review Board declared him a possible risk and advised the secretary of state to fire him, which he did as a matter of his own discretion and not as a result of the board's finding. In a Harlan opinion, with Clark not participating, a unanimous Court increased the anger of those who thought it soft on communism by deciding that his discharge was in violation of the Loyalty and Security Regulations of the Department of State and that while the secretary of state could use his discretion, he was bound by the department's regulations. Only Whittaker, Brennan, Douglas, Black, and Warren had voted to grant certiorari. Burton's clerk had told him that certiorari should not be granted because the case was not likely to arise again, even though the "petitioner may have been wronged and his dismissal may be invalid." In conference, after Warren stated that Service's dismissal had been on "shoddy grounds," only Burton and Whittaker voted to affirm; and Clark asserted he would stay out of the case "unless it was 4-4." But upon seeing Harlan's opinion, Clark and Burton agreed with it; and the newly appointed Whittaker followed their lead.[39]

Among the criminal cases during the 1956 term, Burton supported Frankfurter's majority opinion upholding the indictment of a labor union for violating the Federal Corrupt Practices Act by spending money for a television broadcast endorsing candidates for Congress. In conference on the case, Burton was not persuaded by Warren's comment that if the Court forbade expenditures of this type for unions, they must do the same for corporations, for there were "so many ways that corporations do influence [the] public and so few [ways] that workmen can." The government "can't keep Reuther [President Walter Reuther of the UAW] off the air." At this point, Reed commented that he was troubled because he would like to uphold the indictment, but it was difficult to "slip past the constitutional questions." Burton believed that not only was there no need to discuss freedom of speech in the case, but that Congress could "prevent unions from using other people's money" to support candidates for election.[40]

In another criminal case, which upheld the conviction of a petitioner who conspired with others to possess and transport alcohol in unstamped containers and to evade payment of federal taxes on the alcohol, Burton wrote for the majority in a 5-4 decision. Frankfurter dissented, with the concurrence of Black, Douglas, and Brennan. The petitioner claimed that when the trial court admitted in evidence a confession by a codefendant made after the termination of the alleged conspiracy and containing a clear statement that the confession was to be considered only in determining the guilt of the confessor and not that of other defendants, reversible error was committed. Burton upheld the conviction because the trial judge had given clearly limiting instructions, which properly insulated the confession and rendered it admissible. According to Burton, "unless we proceed on the basis that the jury will follow the court's instructions where those instructions are clear and the circumstances are such that the jury can reasonably be expected to follow them, the jury system makes little sense." Since the judge's choice was the holding of either separate trials or a joint trial under appropriate instructions, the trial judge had acted within his discretion. While Burton was preparing his opinion, he and Harlan, who was competing with Frankfurter as his supporter and confidant, consulted at great length; and finally Harlan was satisfied with the opinion which, he commented, reflected Burton's "usual clarity of style." After the decision was handed down in January, Harlan told Burton that Learned Hand had told him at a state bar dinner in New York that he was glad that the case had been decided the way it was. Harlan, an admirer of Hand, previously thought that he "would have been on the other side"; but if Hand agreed, "we of the majority must have been right!" However, Burton did not always agree with Harlan. He filed a brief dissent from Harlan's ma-

jority opinion in *Chessman* v. *Teets,* which involved the famed
Birdman of Alcatraz, who had been petitioning unsuccessfully
since 1948 to have his death sentence for murder reversed on various grounds. This time, Chessman successfully challenged the use
of a record on his appeal which was partially transcribed after the
court reporter's death by another reporter, the prosecutor, and
police officers without Chessman's participation or the participation of counsel to represent him.[41]

Finally, in *United States* v. *Turley,* Burton's majority opinion reversed the lower court's dismissal of charges that a defendant had
violated the National Motor Vehicle Theft Act. After having lawfully obtained possession of an automobile from its owner for the
purpose of driving some of their friends to their homes in South
Carolina, the defendant unlawfully transported it to Maryland,
where he sold it without the owner's permission. The lower court
had dismissed the charges on the ground that the word *stolen,* as
used in the act, did not cover the activities which took place. In his
opinion for the majority, Burton concluded "that the Act requires
an interpretation of 'stolen' which does not limit it to situations
which at common law would be considered larceny." To Burton,
the act included "all felonious takings of another vehicle with intent to deprive the owner of the rights and benefits of ownership,
regardless of whether or not the theft constitutes common law
larceny." His opinion drew even Brennan, who "was originally
along the lines of Felix's [Frankfurter's] dissent." Joined by Black
and Douglas, Frankfurter dissented, preferring to construe the
statute strictly to exclude the activities engaged in by Turley.[42]

Burton also wrote opinions in three cases involving the introduction of evidence at trial. In *Nilva* v. *United States,* with Black,
Douglas, Warren, and Brennan dissenting, he characteristically affirmed the conviction of a petitioner for failing to produce certain
corporate records against his claim that due process had been violated. In *Kremen* v. *United States,* Burton, joined by Clark, dissented from a per curiam decision reversing for a new trial the convictions of three petitioners on charges of assisting and harboring a
fugitive from justice. The per curiam announced that evidence introduced by the prosecution had been unlawfully seized because all
contents of a cabin in which the defendants were found were con-

fiscated without a search warrant. Burton and Clark asserted that the "validity of a seizure is not to be tested by the quantity of items seized" and that if any items were illegally seized, their use was "harmless error" since there was sufficient additional evidence of guilt. This restrictive view of the Fourth Amendment protection was consistent with Burton's previously announced views. In *Curcio* v. *United States*, however, Burton decided, for a unanimous Court, that a union officer who refused, on the ground of self-incrimination, to answer questions concerning the whereabouts of union books and records which he had failed to produce was not guilty of criminal contempt. Curcio was successful in his petition because Burton held that a custodian of corporate or association books, by accepting his custodianship voluntarily, assumes a duty which overrides his claim of privilege with respect to the production of the records themselves; but he does not waive his privilege against self-incrimination in oral testimony. The lower court had cited him for contempt for refusing to give oral testimony and not for a failure to produce the records.[43]

On the same day that the bar admission cases were decided, the Court alarmed many business and corporation lawyers when Brennan, for a four-judge majority—with Clark, Harlan, and Whittaker not participating—ruled in *United States* v. *DuPont* that Section 7 of the Clayton Act had been aimed at vertical as well as horizontal mergers of businesses that resulted in the monopolization of the market. This decision held illegal DuPont's acquisition of General Motors stock because it gave DuPont a competitive advantage in the sale of paint and fabrics to that automobile giant and, in the view of many businessmen, opened the doors for widespread ex post facto government action against firms which had purchased stock in customer corporations. Burton dissented, joined by Frankfurter; and both justices emphasized that the language of the act could be interpreted to preclude its application to vertical acquisitions. In addition, the dissenters accepted DuPont's argument that even if the Clayton Act applied, it must be shown that a probability of monopoly existed at the time of acquisition in order to later compel disgorgement of stocks. According to Burton and Frankfurter, the majority position that an acquisition, even though valid when made, can become illegal could create great uncertainty in corporate planning. Burton's dissent made a wide-ranging analysis of relevant market and competitive effects in the products involved and concluded that the act

did not apply to vertical acquisitions; that the Government failed to prove that there was a reasonable probability (1917-1919) of a restraint of commerce or a tendency toward monopoly; and that, in any event, the District Court was not clearly in error in concluding that the Government failed to prove that DuPont's competitors have been or may be foreclosed from a substantial share of the relevant market.

Additionally, the dissent cited several instances in which Brennan had miscited or quoted the evidence out of context.[44]

Burton, as had been his pattern in the past, wrote opinions in a number of labor cases during the term. In each case, he supported states' rights and voted against the union involved. In *Textile Workers Union* v. *Lincoln Mills*, and in the companion cases, *General Electric Co.* v. *Local 205* and *Goodall San Ford, Inc.* v. *United Textile Workers of America*, the Court considered the question of what law could be applied in a suit brought under the Taft-Hartley Act, Section 301, by a union specifically to enforce an agreement to arbitrate. Section 301 was designed to meet one of the principal objectives of the act, to facilitate the enforcement of collective bargaining agreements by making it easy to sue unions. However, the problem remaining unresolved was which law, state or federal, would apply. In addition, the American Arbitration Act of 1952 empowered federal courts to enforce specifically arbitration provisions in contracts; and the Norris LaGuardia Act required that certain procedures, which could be interpreted to include arbitration, be followed before an "injunction" could be issued in a labor dispute. In *Lincoln Mills*, a labor union sought to enforce in federal court an arbitration provision in a contract. For five members of the Court, Douglas held that Section 301 permitted federal courts to entertain such suits and to fashion a body of federal law for such purposes, including the arbitration provisions in the contract. The Court did not mention the arbitration act but held that jurisdiction to entertain such suits was not affected by the Norris LaGuardia Act. Joined by Harlan, Burton concurred in the jurisdictional result but disagreed with the conclusion that the substantive law to be applied was federal law. The decision of the Court raised the new issue of whether the federal law to be applied must be uniform throughout the country, while Burton's opinion would have left the way clear for varying rules in different states.[45]

In *Guss* v. *Utah Labor Relations Board,* a labor preemption case, Burton filed a dissent which also applied to the companion cases, *Amalgamated Meat Cutters* v. *Fairlawn Meats, Inc.* and *San Diego Building Trades Council* v. *Garmon.* In all three cases, the Court considered state court efforts to control a labor dispute after the National Labor Relations Board had declined its jurisdiction. In the majority opinion for all three cases, Warren indicated, for six members, that the NLRA precluded state jurisdiction over any matter entrusted to the board unless the board had formally ceded jurisdiction to the state, as provided by Section 10 (a) of the act. In his dissent, which Black joined, Burton expressed the view that the Court was creating "an extensive no-man's land within which no federal or state agency is empowered to deal with labor controversies." According to Burton, Section 10 (a) should be interpreted to mean that the board could cede jurisdiction; otherwise, the states could not act in areas of "pre-existing power to deal with labor matters." Although the Court knew it was creating a "no-man's land," the decision in the case seemed to be the only way in which a possible conflict between state and federal policy could be prevented. Burton held fast to his views even though his clerks disagreed with him and wanted him to support Warren's result in the cases.[46]

Among the other statutory cases, Burton wrote a dissent to a Douglas majority opinion upholding the authority of the Interstate Commerce Commission to issue successive temporary licenses to a steamship corporation until the application for a permanent license was processed. Harlan and Whittaker joined in his dissent. Burton believed that the majority approach would provide easy access by transportation companies to the industry for an indefinite period and would possibly result in over-competition, in violation of the purpose of the Interstate Commerce Act.[47]

Burton also filed opinions in four tax cases, dissenting in three and writing the majority opinion in one. He dissented from Harlan's majority opinion that a numbers pickup man was not receiving wages and therefore did not have to pay an occupational tax required by the Internal Revenue Code in *United States* v. *Calamaro;* and he dissented, with Harlan, from Black's opinion that sickness benefits collected from a health plan paid for by an employer were not taxable to the employee in *Haynes* v. *United States.* In these cases, both of which were leading tax decisions, Burton's vote reflected his position in favor of revenue collection. He believed that in the *Calamaro* case, the pickup man was "accepting wages" even though he was not a bookmaker; and in the *Haynes* case, he felt that health insurance proceeds were intended to be exempt from taxation only if the employee paid the premiums. In *Automobile Club of Michigan* v. *C.I.R.,* he dissented in part, joined by Clark, from Brennan's opinion that the Internal Revenue commissioner was within his powers in revoking retroactively a ruling of tax exemption for the automobile club and a determination that prepaid membership dues should be treated as income in the year rather than, as the club was doing, in the year to which they applied. Burton concurred in support of the commissioner's retroactive determination but opposed the commissioner's rejection of the club's accounting method.[48]

In another tax case, *Libson Shops* v. *Kohler,* a corporation resulting from the merger of sixteen separate incorporated businesses sought, in its income tax return for the first year after the merger, to deduct net operating losses sustained by three of the constituent corporations prior to the merger, asserting that it was entitled to the benefit of the net operating loss carry-over provisions of the Internal Revenue Code. The commissioner of Internal Revenue disallowed the deduction; and the corporation, having paid the tax, brought suit for a refund and lost. For seven of the justices, with Douglas dissenting without opinion, Burton affirmed the decision below, stating that the net operating loss carry-over provisions of the code reflected congressional concern with the fluctuating income of a single business and were not designed to permit the averaging of the premerger losses of one business with the postmerger income of other businesses which had been operated and taxed separately before their merger. Burton's view that only a "continuity of business enterprise" could sustain the deduction was important for businesses covered under the 1929 code; but the

1954 IRC contained specific sections, 381 and 382, outlining requirements relating to loss carry-over deductions which could be applied in this case.[49]

Burton wrote opinions in four other statutory interpretation cases during the term. In *United States* v. *Bergh,* he dissented, with the concurrence of Black and Frankfurter, from Clark's decision that certain government employees had a right to holiday pay for nonwork days. In *Baltimore and Ohio Railway Co.* v. *Jackson,* he again dissented—along with Frankfurter, Harlan, and Whittaker—from Clark's decision that a railroad employee could obtain a judgment for injuries sustained in the derailment of a four-wheel motor tract car because the car was not properly equipped, as required under the Safety Appliance Act. In *United States for the Benefit of Sherman* v. *Carter,* for eight members of the Court and with Whittaker not participating, Burton held that a government contractor and his surety were liable by statute for health and welfare fund contributions which had not been paid and which could be recovered by employees when they were not paid. Additionally, in *Morey* v. *Doud,* he decided for six members—with Black, Frankfurter, and Harlan dissenting—that it was invidious discrimination for Illinois to require firms selling money orders, except American Express, to secure a license and to submit to state regulation. The freshman Whittaker had voted the other way in conference, but Burton's opinion persuaded him to change his mind.[50]

As the Court arrived at the end of the term, Burton was satisifed with his own careful role in the Court's deliberations. He had filed more opinions than ever before, all of which were carefully done and most of which were on important issues. Although he and Frankfurter were often on different sides of the issues, he had drawn close to Black during that year and remained close to Harlan. The three of them often lunched together with their clerks on Saturdays after a morning of work. Warren had become decidedly libertarian during the year, which may have been due in part to his discontent with Frankfurter, with whom there were often personality conflicts, and to his friendly relations with Black. Although Frankfurter voted consistently with the chief justice and the activist wing of the Court in several key cases, he would often concur instead of joining in the majority opinions; and Warren assigned him few civil liberties opinions to write. Warren's clerks often believed they served only to restrain him from what they regarded as a headlong plunge toward the ideological left. Concerning Burton, Frankfurter often said that if he were on trial for his life, of all the justices he might have as judge, he would prefer Burton for his open- and fair-mindedness. Burton had begun to show signs of Parkinson's disease toward the end of the term, but his afternoon naps refreshed him, and he continued to bear up well under a heavy load. He was still regarded as unspectacular and methodical in his opinion writing by those who did not see the necessity for such care, but he had clearly carved out a niche of respect among the members of the Court. Complimentary as always, Frankfurter told Burton, "you are so . . . courteous—an old-fashioned quality that for me can never be outmoded."[51]

# 7

## Burton's Last Term: A Minority Justice on the Warren Court

I N T H E fall of 1957, Burton began his last term on the bench. It was his second term as a minority justice after the years of always being among the majority. He generally found himself voting with Harlan and Whittaker and sometimes with Clark in the civil liberties cases that gained the greatest public notice. As the swing man on the Court, Clark voted about half the time with the civil libertarians and half the time against them. Although Clark and Warren had had a close relationship since their days of working together to evacuate the Japanese during World War II, that fact did not seem to influence his vote. Chief Justice Warren increasingly joined with the civil libertarian bloc of Brennan, Black, Frankfurter, Douglas, and sometimes Clark. Although Warren had developed into a strong chief justice who was often able to harmonize the personalities on the Court by using common sense and a magnetic personality, his efforts were not completely successful. The more libertarian justices still found Frankfurter more abrasive than not, and Warren preferred Black's ingratiating personal style to that of Frankfurter.[1]

As a result of the five big internal security decisions of the 1956 term—*Watkins, Sweezy, Yates, Service,* and *Jencks*—and the continued furor over segregation, the Court was still under attack from its large number of critics. A conservative coalition, which denounced the Court for everything from lack of clarity in its writing to the content of its opinions, continued the attack all during the 1957 term. Aside from the Jencks bill, other legislation introduced in Congress, including the proposal by Senator Wil-

1957—The Warren Court (from left to right): Douglas, Brennan, Black, Clark, Warren, Harlan, Frankfurter, Whittaker, and Burton

liam Jenner of Indiana for limiting the Court's jurisdiction in internal security cases, was unsuccessful. The Court survived the attacks and was staunchly defended by such traditional civil liberties supporters as the American Civil Liberties Union, the NAACP, the American Jewish Congress, and the ADA, which had been the most energetic critics of the earlier anti-civil libertarian decisions of the Vinson period.[2]

Burton and the other justices, of course, were aware of reports of the controversy about their work in the newspapers and on television and the radio. They were aware of the "Impeach Earl Warren" billboards which were beginning to appear across the country and that the conference of chief justices of the states and a special committee on Communist tactics, strategy, and objectives of the American Bar Association had denounced their lack of judicial self-restraint. The hostility was not directed at Burton, who in dissent most often adopted the positions which the conservatives supported. Frankfurter's annual repetition of his strictures about the procedure by which cases were decided was a minor irritant amid these larger concerns. This time, Frankfurter "reformulated" his ideas and "added new matter," especially concerning the "procedure of the massing of far-reaching adjudications" toward the end of the term, which he thought was one of the reasons for so much criticism of the Court in the 1956 term; the highly significant internal security cases had all been handed down in June. To Frankfurter, massing cases toward the end of the term not only hampered the internal judicial process but made for "public indigestion, with consequent misinformation and mischievous reaction to decisions." Additionally, he asserted that announcing a large number of decisions at one time "overtaxes the already meager ability of the press to report our decisions with a fair degree of accuracy. Greater sensationalizing, because of the restricted space for reporting, normally follows a 'big day' at the court, and Congressional response—not merely talk but legislative proposals—is apt to be based on distorted and inadequate reporting of opinions." He suggested that one solution might be to have enough case records printed before January so that instead of taking long recesses in both December and February, two weeks of argument from the end of the term could be moved into earlier weeks, and only one recess would be taken. The remainder of his suggestions merely repeated his long-standing belief that there should be longer consideration of cases before discussion at conference and before the opinions were approved. This plan included per curiams in which certiorari would be granted and a decision announced all in a matter of days.[3]

This time, Frankfurter's comments generated a somewhat more heated reaction from the other justices. Burton agreed with the need for some changes; but Warren, in accepting Harlan's suggestion that the memo be discussed at conference during the first weeks, bristled at any suggestion that "the controversy which the Court found itself in at the conclusion of last term or any recent term was due to 'massing' of important cases at the conclusion of the term." To underscore his hostility toward what he regarded as Frankfurter's criticism of his administration as chief, Warren circulated a list of "most controversial" cases decided in June. This list included dates of argument, first circulation of the opinion, and when it was handed down, along with a similar list of cases to be argued during the 1957 term. Warren commented that it was clear from these materials that any "massing of cases" resulted from the length of time it took to write and get approval of an opinion. The problem, in his opinion, lay in the rate of writing, circulating, and approval among the justices, a matter personal to each one and not a matter of administrative procedure. Additionally, Warren indicated that he was opposed to any rule which would defer action on important argued cases to a date later than the first conference or would delay the handing down of per curiams for a week after the decision was made. In neither of these situations was a rule necessary, for any justice could have decisions delayed in any case merely by requesting it. Furthermore, it was "better to make our tentative decision while the arguments of counsel are fresh in all our minds." He thought Frankfurter's suggestion that cases be assigned to two or more justices before conference would delay the deliberative process; "and at the time of voting, the issues would be vivid only in the minds of the researchers." Warren offered his views only as a basis for discussion on the theory that "no matter how thin you make a pancake, there are always two sides to it."[4]

Clark, who thought circumstances might preclude his being present when the memo was discussed, expressed views similar to those of Warren. He was not opposed to setting cases for December and February since he was there anyway, "usually working on opinions"; but he felt the extra time was needed to "catch up." In his view, what was most necessary was a deadline for writing opinions and dissents, which sometimes held up opinions for months. He also agreed with Warren that the procedure whereby any justice could request a delay on the vote or the handing down of a decision was more effective than making a rule on the subject. His suggestion for solving the "press problem" was that decisions should be handed down on any day rather than only on Monday, for there was nothing "sacred" about Monday. Furthermore, he stated that oral arguments, "like Mr. Toots, are dull and of no help to us; some are a Babel of words bringing more confusion than clarity; and at times repartee takes the place of advocacy with the result that the points in issue are deferred, often never reached or receive only summary treatment." To Clark, the time in oral argument was spent "chasing rainbows." He suggested that before going on the bench, they should each indicate what issues they needed to have discussed so that the chief justice could keep counsel from straying from the matter at hand and could thereby ensure that argument would be helpful. In a second memo, Frankfurter defended himself by pointing out that he did not mean that anyone was purposely massing cases; but in practice, that was what had happened. However, he had failed again to reconstruct the process of decision.[5]

The tensions within and outside the Court had some demonstrable effect. Although the docket was slightly reduced, the number of cases reviewed increased again for the seventh year in succession. This increase resulted from a sharp rise in the number of cases disposed of on the merits by memorandum without argument, a practice which brought forth a great deal of criticism by law professors and students who believed that summary disposition indicated inadequate consideration or a fear of announcing the reasons for the decisions.[6]

The first months of the term were spent on the ordinary grist of authoritative decisions in major areas of the law. Burton managed to discharge his duties, although he was increasingly weakened by Parkinson's disease; his hands shook so that his writing sometimes became almost impossible to decipher, and his afternoon naps became longer and longer. The views he expressed continued to follow the pattern he had previously established. Continuing his hostility toward tax avoidance mechanisms, he dissented from the Court decision in an important estate tax case in which the decedent in 1934, at age seventy-six, purchased a series of annuity-life insurance policies, with her children as primary beneficiaries, under a trust established to protect the interests of any of the children who predeceased her. The decedent assigned all rights and benefits under two of the life insurance policies to the children and the other to the trust company as trustee, paid a gift tax on the transfer in 1935, and in 1938 amended the trust agreement to make it irrevocable. When the insured died in 1946, the proceeds of the insurance policies were not included in her estate in the estate tax return. The issue was whether they should be included as income from property transferred to the children through the use of life insurance policies. Speaking for the Court majority, Warren held that the proceeds were not includable because the two kinds of policies were separate transactions, the use of the annuity being entirely independent of the life insurance policies. Joined by Black and Clark, Burton dissented because he thought the case indistinguishable from one in which a settlor places a sum in trust and receives the income for life, with the principal going to beneficiaries at this death. In effect, he believed that Warren's opinion left the way open for taxpayers to avoid paying estate taxes by extruding principal from their estates through the use of insurance policies which had no real purpose except tax avoidance. He wanted to interpret the statute in such a way as to permit the government to capture the revenue involved.[7]

When the Court reacted to its state court critics by retreating from their position of restricting state control of labor unions in deference to the NLRB, Burton found himself in the majority, announcing a position he had previously espoused in dissent. In fact, he wrote three important labor opinions for the majority during the term—*International Union Automobile Workers* v. *Russell, NLRB* v. *Wooster Division of Borg-Warner Corp.,* and *Youngdahl* v.

*Rainfair.* In *Youngdahl,* strikers at an Arkansas plant made offensive remarks to the employees who worked despite a strike. Upon the employer's complaint, an Arkansas court enjoined the strikers and union representatives from threatening violence and similar actions and from all picketing or patrolling of the premises. In an opinion for six members of the Court, Burton expressed the view that the state court was within its discretionary power in enjoining the strikers' conduct, except insofar as it enjoined peaceful picketing, which was in the domain preempted by the National Labor Relations Board. According to Burton, the plant involved was in a small community where, when "more than 30 people get together and act as they did here, and heap abuse on their neighbors and former friends, a court is justified in finding that violence is imminent. . . .The picketing proper, as contrasted with the activities around the headquarters, was peaceful." Warren, Black, and Douglas dissented, holding to their former views on the ground that all of the activities involved were under the exclusive jurisdiction of the National Labor Relations Board, and the state courts therefore had no jurisdiction.[8]

While drafting the opinion, Burton had the greatest difficulty with Harlan and Frankfurter, who were willing to join in the retreat but were anxious that strikers be permitted the use of language unrelated to violence and that the states not enter the domain of the NLRB in all instances. In response to Burton's statement that the state court was correct in finding "that the conduct and massed name-calling by petitioners were calculated to provoke violence and were likely to do so unless promptly restrained," Harlan suggested that such a statement "might make one believe that the language of the strikers by itself was sufficient to warrant the injunction." He thought the statement was "going unreasonably far" and suggested "that it be made clear that we are not viewing the language in isolation from its context of violence." To Burton's statement that the state court "entered the preempted domain of the National Labor Relations Board insofar as it enjoined peaceful picketing by petitioners," Frankfurter wanted to add the following: "which in no wise offended any policy of the state." Burton rejected both suggestions but placated Frankfurter by citing another case which discussed the state policy considerations which worried him; and he skillfully explained away Harlan's fears, even though he thought any supposed ambiguity in his opinion had "to be dug to be discovered."[9]

In *Borg-Warner,* Frankfurter and Harlan partially disagreed with the decision for a five-member majority in which Burton held that an employer had committed an unfair labor practice under the NLRA when he insisted that the union agree to a "recognition" clause, which excluded the certified international union of the employees, and also to a "ballot" clause calling for a prestrike vote by employees, both union and nonunion, on the employer's last offer. In his opinion, Burton upheld the board and the union's contention that the two clauses were not subjects of mandatory collective bargaining under the act, which provided that each party had to bargain in good faith with respect to wages, hours, and other terms and conditions of employment. Therefore, when the employer insisted that he would not bargain at all unless the union accepted nonmandatory items of disagreement, he was guilty of a refusal to bargain. Joined by Clark and Whittaker, Harlan concurred on the recognition clause issue but disagreed on the characterization of the ballot clause, as did Frankfurter. Upon circulation of Burton's opinion in late March, after the case was argued in late November, Harlan first agreed with his "excellent analysis of the problem"; however, he then became concerned about the ballot clause and prepared a dissent. When the dissent was circulated, not only Whittaker and Frankfurter, who were with Burton at first, but even his law clerk, changed their minds. Frankfurter and Whittaker expressed their regret but joined Harlan's dissent.[10]

The Court further cut away at the doctrine that when the NLRB had jurisdiction over an unfair labor practice, state jurisdiction was preempted in *International Union, UAW* v. *Russell* and *International Association of Machinists* v. *Gonzalez.* In the *Gonzalez* case, Burton supported a Frankfurter opinion which gave jurisdiction to a state court to award damages for breach of contract against a union for expelling a member contrary to the union's constitution. *Russell,* the last labor opinion written by Burton, was a common law tort action by an employee against the union for preventing him from entering the factory in which he worked by mass picketing and threats of bodily harm. For the Supreme Court majority,

Burton held that state court jurisdiction to award compensatory and punitive damages against a union for malicious interference with an employee's lawful occupation was not preempted by the NLRA. The two decisions gave additional pleasure to critics of the Court's interference with state rights in labor as well as internal security matters during the previous term. In both *Gonzalez* and *Russell,* Warren and Douglas dissented, holding to their support of a broad interpretation of preemption by the NLRB. Despite Burton's attempt to limit his holding permitting damages in *Russell* to cases in which violent action occurred, the fact that the case was decided at the same time as *Gonzalez* and on the same preemption issue raised a presumption that states could award damages in any kind of tort or contract case, as the dissent warned, because *Gonzalez* involved no use of violence. However, Burton did not adjust his opinion to meet Warren's dissent because he believed that Warren's objections to state power in the allowance of punitive damages in such cases was overdone and "unanswerable." Burton and his clerk agreed that they had said all they could, in a legal way, on the subject; and it was now merely a matter of "choosing sides" on the issue.[11]

Burton's other opinions during his last term on the Court came in a compensation case, four criminal cases, and three civil liberties cases in which he expressed his long held views on the appropriate balance between the claims of liberty and authority. In *United States* v. *Central Eureka Mining Corp.,* Burton held that the claims of gold mine owners involving compensation for the governmental closure of their mines in order to relieve the workers and equipment for use in mining metals related to war production during World War II, had appropriately been heard by the court of claims but that it was not necessary that compensation actually be paid. Furthermore, he found that the closing was not "a taking of private property for public use within the meaning of the Fifth Amendment." Burton, whose two sons had served in the war and who had himself been heavily involved in Senate committee work relating to defense supplies, was out of sympathy with the mining companies' claims. He asserted that "war, particularly in modern times, demands the strict regulation of nearly all resources. It makes demands which otherwise would be insufferable. But wartime economic restrictions, temporary in character, are insignificant when compared to the widespread uncompensated loss of life and freedom of action which war traditionally demands." Although Brennan thought that Burton had "spelled this out so that I doubt even the mining companies can still feel they are right," Harlan and Frankfurter dissented on the grounds that there had been a taking, for which the claims court should determine compensation. Burton and his clerk agreed that despite Frankfurter's plea, "it would be a complete waste of time" to send the case back to the court of claims.[12]

In the criminal cases, Burton wrote two majority opinions upholding the defendants' convictions and two dissents in opposition to the majority's opinions in favor of the defendants. In *United States* v. *Sharpnack,* he decided that a Texas defendant could be convicted of a sexual crime which was perpetrated on federal property, even though it was not explicit in federal law that a crime defined only in state law was punishable if it took place on federal property. He preferred to interpret broadly general federal authority over the property of the United States in order to permit state enforcement of criminal law on federal reservations within any particular state so as not to permit the defendant to escape punishment.[13]

The other criminal cases in which Burton wrote opinions involved the right to counsel and the use of confessions by the prosecution. The Court's decisions on such issues still showed a rather mixed pattern, although the decision in *Mallory* v. *United States* in the 1956 term, which voided the conviction of an alleged rapist because he was held too long in custody without benefit of counsel, led critics to accuse them of being soft on criminals.

In *Moore* v. *Michigan,* Burton, joined by Frankfurter, Clark, and Harlan, dissented from Brennan's reversal of the conviction of a black male, who had been convicted of murder eighteen years before, on the ground that the defendant had not intelligently waived his right to counsel. He believed that there was no finding that Moore was "so alarmed that he was not able freely, intelligently and understandably to plead guilty and to waive his right to counsel." The majority, according to Warren in the conference, agreed that it was the kind of case to which one could apply Frankfurter's expression that "it shocks the conscience." But Frankfurter disagreed, pointing out that the trial judge had attempted to protect Moore's interest. Burton's clerk disagreed with him completely and urged him to join Brennan's opinion, but Burton refused and held fast to his original point of view.[14]

For the Court majority in *Ashdown* v. *Utah,* Burton upheld the use of an oral confession in a murder case in which the defendant admitted poisoning her husband during five and one-half hours of interrogation with no counsel present. Frankfurter regarded Burton's opinion as a perfect model of their shared view that each case turned on its facts and that as long as the record indicated nothing "shocking," the states were free to fashion their own criminal procedures. Burton cited no cases and indulged in "no rhetoric" in finding that "the record as a whole convinces us that the interview with petitioner was temperate and courteous."[15]

In *Payne* v. *Arkansas,* Burton dissented from Whittaker's opinion reversing the murder conviction of a nineteen-year-old black male because the undisputed evidence showed a course of conduct on the part of the law enforcement officers which, viewed in its totality and in light of the culminating threat of mob violence, resulted in a coerced confession. Payne was arrested for the murder of an elderly lumber dealer in Pine Bluff and was held incommunicado for three days. During this time and shortly before he confessed, the chief of police threatened that a mob outside the jail would take him unless he told the truth. Burton, who had been the only justice to vote to deny certiorari, was more firmly wedded to the view that state court conclusions concerning voluntariness should stand than any other members of the Court.[16]

In three civil liberties cases, Burton wrote opinions in which he exhibited his characteristic belief in the primacy of order and governmental power. He dissented, joined by Clark and Whittaker, from Harlan's reversal of a denaturalization order directed at two persons who answered in the negative a question on the naturalization forms concerning whether they were not associated with any organization which taught or advocated the overthrow of the government. Burton believed that they were members of the Communist party at the time and should have answered the question in the affirmative. He believed that although the question was somewhat ambiguous, both petitioners knew what the question meant and had not behaved as persons who were attached to the principles of the Constitution.

In two cases involving the firing of public employees, Burton again indicated his disposition toward giving the government the benefit of the doubt on civil liberties questions in decisions which gave additional comfort to anti-civil libertarian critics of the Court. In *Lerner* v. *Casey,* Burton joined with the five-member majority in Harlan's opinion that the firing of a subway conductor in New York, after he claimed the Fifth Amendment privilege against self-incrimination when asked about membership in the Communist party, was not a violation of due process. To the majority, the discharge was reasonable and was based on the doubt created as to his reliability by his refusal to answer a relevant question asked by his employer rather than on any inference of Communist party membership drawn from the exercise of the Fifth Amendment privilege. In *Beilan* v. *Board of Public Education,* Burton wrote the majority opinion for five members approving the discharge of a Philadelphia school teacher for incompetence after he refused to answer a question asked by his superintendent concerning his membership in a Communist political association. Burton emphasized that no due process violation was involved because the teacher had not discharged his "obligations of frankness, candor and cooperation in answering inquiries made of him by his employing board examining into his fitness to serve as a public school teacher." To Burton, classroom conduct was not the only permissible basis for determining a teacher's fitness. The Court majority in both cases clearly wanted to leave the states free to ask employees questions related to fitness for a job since there was no right to public employment. In both cases, the court distinguished the earlier decision in *Slochower* v. *Board of Higher Education* on the ground that in *Slochower,* impermissible questions were asked during a federal inquiry that had nothing to do with job fitness. However, five days before his dismissal, Beilan had pleaded the Fifth Amendment during a congressional committee hearing. In *Beilan* and *Casey,* Clark and Frankfurter switched from their position in *Slochower* to vote against the employees because the dismissals were related to fitness for the job and not to an invocation of the privilege alone. Black,

Douglas, Warren, and Brennan dissented in both cases. Frankfurter, who as senior justice assigned the cases to Burton and Harlan, was "so stirred up by Bill Brennan's dissent" that he "was moved to underscore what you [Burton] and John [Harlan] have written with a few lines [of his own]."[17]

*Beilan* and *Ashdown,* both handed down on June 30, 1958, were Burton's last Supreme Court opinions. During the term, as he became increasingly ill with Parkinson's disease, he had to reconsider his earlier decision to attempt to serve one more term on the Court and now planned to retire soon after his seventieth birthday on June 22, when he would be eligible for a pension. When his physician advised him in June that he should definitely retire, Burton informed Warren, who expressed his regrets and the hope that Burton could wait at least until September 30. Attorney General William Rogers came to see him and urged him to stay on; but when Burton fully explained his physical disabilities, they agreed he would see the president to resign formally. Various crises kept intervening so that it was not until July 17, 1958, that the conversation actually took place. Only Rogers, the president, and Burton were present during the discussion, which centered on the choice of a successor. Eisenhower, in expressing dissatisfaction with "the decisions of the Chief Justice and Justice Brennan," asked the attorney general to be "most careful" in the selection of Burton's successor. Potter Stewart, a Republican from Ohio and a member of the Court of Appeals for the Sixth Circuit, was the only possibility discussed; but the president asked Rogers "to be especially careful" in making sure Stewart's views were acceptable because "Stewart's age is 43 and therefore he would have very long service." Still mindful of his own experience in the legislative branch, Burton told Eisenhower that Chief Justice Stone had said that "the Court needed someone from Congress because ⅔[rds] of the Court's litigation involved interpretation of the Acts of Congress and the Constitution." The president said that he was aware of the usefulness of nonjudicial experience and that his appointment of Warren as chief justice was based primarily upon Warren's years of legal practice as well as his governorship. However, he added that he was deeply interested in ensuring "a conservative attitude" in Burton's successor.[18]

With his retirement arranged for October 13, the Burtons left a still deeply divided court for a European vacation. However, the vacation was interrupted in August by the continued controversy over school segregation. Southern states enacted pupil assignment, freedom of choice plans, and other stratagems designed to avoid the effect of the *Brown* decision. Since the *Brown* decision, the Court had struck down a wide range of segregation laws relating to such tax-supported facilities as swimming pools, golf courses, public housing, and the like. However, the controversy between the Court and Congress had been more open and heated than disputes over the Court's race relations decisions. But opposition to school desegregation persisted and now began to overshadow the unsuccessful attack on the Court for its civil liberties decisions. In June, at the end of the term, the Court, in a per curiam opinion, had refused to review a federal district court decision suspending an integration plan in Little Rock, Arkansas, where intermittent violence had been occurring at Central High School since September 1957, when a handful of black students had been admitted, until after the court of appeals had fully reviewed the order. When the court of appeals reviewed the case, reversed the stay, and ordered integration to proceed, the Court was hastily reconvened to hear an appeal from a decision of the court of appeals in time for the school term, which began on September 15. Once the Court affirmed, in a unanimous Warren opinion, the exercise of federal authority and the duty of states to abide by federal court orders, Burton's work on the Court had come to an end. Rogers came to see him on September 19 to ask if he could delay his retirement to a later time, for the president wanted to make the announcement in order to avoid complications over the approval of his replacement in view of the possible effect on the segregation cases and the Little Rock problem. When Burton insisted that he must not attempt to carry on through another term, Rogers agreed that the announcement would be made the next week and added that Herbert Brownell, the former attorney general, and Potter Stewart were the two leading contenders for the appointment. In Rogers's opinion, however, an effort to confirm Brownell would stir up political controversy over Justice Department prosecution in civil liberties cases while he was attorney general. Burton agreed with Rogers that Stewart should be the choice.[19]

While Burton was awaiting the public announcement of his retirement, he was awarded the Bowdoin Prize from his former college "in recognition of his distinctive contributions through his outstanding service to his nation and his fellow men." The prize was established in 1928 to be awarded once every five years to a graduate or former member of the college or faculty who had made a distinctive contribution. In his speech upon accepting the prize, Burton praised public service as a satisfying career for young persons and explains his view of the Supreme Court as similar to that of an "umpire" in a baseball game, "the keystone that holds in place the members of the governmental arch that our Constitution has designed to sustain a representative Federal Government dedicated to the preservation for the individual of the greatest freedom consistent with like freedom for all."[20]

When his retirement was announced on October 6, photographers and radio and television reporters came to record the event. Newspaper editors commented on his hard work, courteousness, and methodical habits; but there was no consensus about his ideological bent. The *Washington Daily News* of October 8 stated that he was a "judge of sturdy legal competence," about whom there was nothing "ornate," and described his opinions as "among the most lucid in recent years." And on the same day, the *New York Times* noted that he had "won universal regard for his untiring diligence, unswerving fairness and deep sense of moderation" and was "a conservative of sometimes liberal and quite independent cast of mind." In addition, the *Washington Post* of that day described him as an example of "the tradition of judicial independence" and as a justice who had "grown in stature during each year of service." The article continued that his "openmindedness has given a good deal of trouble to those who like to classify all judges in either 'liberal' or 'conservative' columns, although his tendency in the present court has been to keep somewhat right of center." On October 20, 1958, the *New Republic* commented that Burton was "honest, open-minded, conscientious, selfless and humble in his performance of judicial duties"; but a statement in the article that those were more or less common characteristics brought a retort from Alexander Bickel, who had been Frankfurter's clerk. Bickel pointed out that he was sure no "belittling" reference was intended; but Burton "had these virtues to an uncommon degree. In him they were talents of a high order; they made him an ornament of the institution that he served with unsurpassed fidelity."[21]

Aside from the Court's usual letter of farewell, in which the justices expressed the belief that "of all the justices who have sat on this Bench, not one has adhered more closely than you to the ideal for which we all strive—'Equal Justice under Law,'" Burton received a number of individual letters from his colleagues, friends, and politicians. Frankfurter told him that "awareness that you were around the hall, your presence in conferences, the considerations that lay behind your expressed views, in short your discharge of the judicial function, have served as a deep source of comfort to me and have helped to fortify the spirit of my own endeavors." Brennan wrote that "none has so deservedly earned the high respect and very deep personal affections in which we all hold you."[22]

On October 13, his last day on the bench, Burton's retirement was announced as he sat through the entire hearings but asked no questions. Thereafter, as he settled into retirement, Burton remarked that after almost forty years of public service and attention to duty, "for the first time that I can recall in my life, I found myself not caught up with my immediate duties and free to read and do what I pleased for about an hour." As a retired but not resigned justice, he still maintained an office at the Court. In January, after consulting with retired Justice Reed, he followed the usual practice of making himself available to the chief judge of the United States Court of Appeals for the District of Columbia, which meant that he could sit in on cases at any time during the term upon assignment by the chief and with the consent of Warren.[23]

Burton's Parkinson's disease was apparently under reasonable control during the next two years. He sat in on eighteen cases in the court of appeals and wrote three opinions in 1958-59, twenty-one cases with four opinions in 1959-60, eighteen cases with two opinions in 1960-61, and nine cases with one opinion in 1961-62. His condition worsened considerably in early 1962, and he did not participate thereafter. However, Burton was not forgotten by the members of the Supreme Court, who visited with him from time to time and sent him notes on holidays and his birthday. On his

seventy-fifth birthday, Harlan wrote to him that his "shining example of what it takes to be a judge remains a daily source of
inspiration." Arthur Goldberg, who replaced Frankfurter on the
court, wrote to him that his "serenity" despite a trying affliction
and "in face of all that must be endured because of it—is an example to everyone of character, an affirmation of life and a really no-
ble spirit and mind." During this time, his deteriorating physical
condition was indeed difficult for Burton, who had always drunk
and smoked in moderation, taken regular exercise, and paid particular attention to his physical well-being. His death on October
28, 1964, in George Washington University Hospital brought an
end to a trying final phase of his illness and an end to the judicial
career of a typical justice.[24]

# 8

## Summary and Conclusions

H A R O L D  H. Burton retired from the Court at a time when it was under attack from critics for its libertarian segregation and internal security decisions.[1] He was more favorably disposed toward governmental authority than individual freedom in freedom of expression cases, a stance which put him out of step with the libertarians—Black, Douglas, and Warren—and more in sympathy with the views of Clark, Frankfurter, and Harlan.[2] However, on race relations questions he had usually been more willing than anyone else on the Vinson Court to construe broadly the Constitution's protection for blacks; and in this area, he was entirely comfortable with the libertarians in the Warren Court.[3]

He left a Court still torn by internal conflict, which made ignoring the critics' barbs more difficult. For example, Frankfurter and Warren suffered each other's presence; but Warren, unlike Vinson earlier, was not at all intimidated by Frankfurter's professional attainments and obvious knowledge of the technical aspects of law. Burton, however, remained a center of serenity, appearing unruffled in his open-mindedness and evenhandedness throughout his long career on the Court and even as he watched tensions from within and attacks from without grow in intensity during the final stages of his illness.

Burton effectively added his voice to those of the other justices, whose votes and powers of persuasion were as important as the opinions they wrote. He believed that the opinions were a joint product decided upon in the give-and-take of the conferences and the private lobbying they did with each other. Within the framework of each justice's value system, he thought that the decision reached was molded by several factors: (1) the justice's conception of the legal process; (2) the justice's beliefs about the role of law in preserving the society; (3) the justice's view of the image of the Court in the minds of the legal fraternity and the public; and (4) the personal relations among the justices themselves. He personally regarded the maintenance of the court as a respected institution of authority as the most important aspect of his duty.[4]

Burton's entire judicial career as a "lawyer's judge" was an example of a justice who believed and took seriously the view that he could decide most cases without any attention to personal philosophy or practical circumstances. He took this approach despite the fact that his family background and education at Bowdoin and Harvard, his experiences in corporate law practice and in politics as mayor of Cleveland and as senator from Ohio, and his espousal of Republican political principles molded him into a generally conservative mind-set, which he bought to the Court and which persistently guided him in deciding cases. Burton would have described his judicial attitude as resulting in spite of the factors which molded him rather than as because of those factors. For him, there were certain givens in the constitutional system: states' rights should not be invaded by federal power; criminals should not be acquitted because of procedural niceties; contracts should be interpreted in such a way as to protect free enterprise; labor unions should not be more powerful than employers; congressional statutes should be interpreted in such a way as to maximize congressional authority; the president should not be permitted to run roughshod over Congress but should have freedom to act, particularly when it came to making war; the Supreme Court should only decide those cases which were necessary; and a justice should not write unnecessary dissenting or concurring opinions, for the former created uncertainty in the public mind and the latter were a vain show of erudition.[5]

A vote taken by the Court's clerks in the 1954 term offered perhaps the best tribute to this very practical man. The clerks voted for the one justice they would choose if there had to be nine of any one justice on the Court as the total membership of the tribunal. Burton was the overwhelming choice of the clerks. Their decision was for a "professional" justice who would interpret the Constitution and laws in such a way as to promote unquestioningly the status quo of the American economic and social system, weighing and balancing the interests involved within that framework and reaching a lawyerlike result; and Burton was, for them, that ideal justice.[6]

The high regard in which Burton was held by the other justices and the clerks was generally not shared by law school critics and the elites of the practicing bar. He came to the Court criticized as another crony of Harry Truman and left with that lingering reputation. The assessment endured despite the fact that some of his labor opinions remain leading interpretations of the Taft-Hartley Act, while others are models of clarity on difficult and intricate issues.

How did these criticisms become the rule? It is true that Burton was Truman's friend, and they had served together on the Special Committee to Investigate the National Defense. But Burton was appointed to the Court instead of some other Truman friend because he was a Republican, as was the retiring Justice Roberts, because Stone approved of him beforehand, because of his legislative and executive experience, because Truman believed that Burton was an open-minded and honest representative of proper judicial temperament, because there was no one from Ohio on the bench, because he had been a faithful supporter of internationalist Democratic foreign policy, and because his Senate seat would be filled by Ohio Governor Frank Lausche, a Democrat. There was no reason for Truman not to appoint him.

The assessment as mediocre followed him throughout his career because he was average, like most of the justices who had served on the Court. His opinions were written directly and simply, to the great approbation of practicing lawyers and law students. His opinion output was low compared to others, but he was a junior justice voting with the chief for most of his tenure. Also, it was a time when the Court docket was low and therefore did not produce more assignments. However, he admitted working long and hard on his final products. Burton knew he was not a brilliant jurist like Frankfurter; but conscious of his place in history, he sought to write in a fashion which could be understood by ordinary lawyers like himself. Even aware of the Court's history, he realistically regarded himself as most like the majority of competent justices who had served on the Court since its beginning.[7]

Unlike most justices, great and not so great, he did not rely on his clerks in the drafting of opinions. He relied more heavily on his experienced clerk during his freshman term but not thereafter. Even in the first term, he drafted every opinion over and over in his own handwriting, learning as he proceeded; and he never hesitated to reject his clerks' views concerning the outcome of a case. His vote was always his own, and his clerks never knew how he stood until after the conference in a case. The exception came in his last two terms. During those years, his clerks persuaded him to write and file more dissents; and he let his clerk draft the opinion in the highly praised *DuPont* case.[8]

Many of Burton's critics quite simply disapproved of the decisions of the Vinson Court in the highly visible civil liberties cases and found it easier to attack the Truman bloc for incompetence rather than for substantive disagreement. Practically none of the criticisms were directed at the tax cases, full faith and credit cases, and other grist of the Court's normal mill. Additionally, since Burton's opinions contained few rhetorical flourishes that could be highlighted and quoted, even the opinions which libertarian critics would have approved were often overlooked. His concurring opinion in the *Jencks* case, in which he announced that governmental prosecutors must make evidence available at least to the judge for screening to see if it should be made accessible to the defense, was enacted into federal law and was a model of advanced libertarian thinking. His opinion in *Joint Anti-Fascist Refugee* that the attorney general's practice of listing and specifically classifying an organization as Communist was "patently arbitrary" and a violation of due process as guaranteed by the Fifth Amendment, did not overcome the view that he was an anti-civil libertarian, barely competent justice.[9]

Criticized as a lackadaisical party-goer, Burton was actually the epitome of the hard-working, disciplined WASP with a quiet sense of humor. In fact, he lived simply in the Dodge Hotel with Selma throughout his Washington career, went to parties because Selma liked them and because meals had to be eaten somewhere, and seldom drank or smoked. His life was orderly but admittedly not arduous. His pleasures were bird watching, daily exercise, the work of the Court, and researching the history of the Court and its per-

sonnel, as is reflected in a number of articles he wrote on the subject. The articles were all done with the careful attention to historical detail that he exhibited in his opinions.[10]

In the history of the Supreme Court, Burton should properly be
noted as the quiet, unassuming model of the competent justice. His
career is a classic example of the Court as a day-to-day institution
rather than in the rare instances when a case of monumental significance was decided or when some particularly flamboyant or
outstanding justice focused upon some innovation in the law. For
that reason, his career informs us more, rather than less, about the
Court as an institution within the American system of government.
Burton wanted to be remembered as a justice who had discharged
seriously the responsibilities of judging without diminishing the
Court as an institution. In all fairness, that is how he should be
remembered.

# Appendix: Law Clerks of Mr. Justice Burton

*1945 Term:*
Howard Mann
Professor of Law
State University of New York
Buffalo, New York

*1946 Term:*
Harris K. Weston
Dinsmore, Shohl, Coates, Dupree
Cincinnati, Ohio

*1947-48 Terms:*
James Lake
Professor of Law
University of Nebraska
Lincoln, Nebraska

H. Bruce Griswold
Calfee, Fogg, McChord & Halter
Cleveland, Ohio

*1949 Term:*
Harvey Levin

Norman W. Colquhoun
Cleveland, Ohio

*1950 Term:*
Marvin Schwartz
Sullivan and Cromwell
New York, New York

Ray Simmons
Fremont, Nebraska

*1951 Term:*
John W. Douglas
Covington & Burling
Washington, D.C.

Charles C. Hileman, III
Schnader, Harrison, Segal and
    Lewis
Philadelphia, Pennsylvania

*1952-53 Terms:*
James Ryan
Connon, Winters, Randolph, Barry
    and McGowen
Tulsa, Oklahoma

*1952 Term:*
John M. Leahy
Appliance and Television Receiver
    Division
General Electric Co.
Louisville, Kentucky

*1953 Term:*
Raymond S. Troubh
Lazard Freres and Co.
New York, New York

*1954 Term:*
William B. Matteson
Debevoise, Plimpton, Lyons and
Gates
New York, New York

Thomas N. O'Neill, Jr.
Montgomery, McCracken, Walker
and Rhoades
Philadelphia, Pennsylvania

*1955 Term:*
P. J. DiQuinzio
Dechert, Price and Rhoades
Philadelphia, Pennsylvania

*1956 Term:*
David E. Wagoner

Roger C. Cramton
Dean, Cornell School of Law
Ithaca, New York

*1957 Term:*
Carl Schneider
Wolf, Block, Schorr and Solis-Cohen
Philadelphia, Pennsylvania

Preble Stolz
Professor of Law
University of California
Berkeley, California

*1958 Term:*
Goncer, M. Krestal
Blank, Rome, Klaus and Comisky
Philadelphia, Pennsylvania

Terrance Sandalow
Professor of Law
University of Michigan
Ann Arbor, Michigan

# Notes

## CHAPTER 1

1. Donald Matthews, *U. S. Senators and Their World* (Chapel Hill, 1960), chap. 2; and John Schmidhauser, "The Justices of the Supreme Court: A Collective Portrait," *Midwest Journal of Political Science,* vol. 1 (1959), 1-57.

2. Cushing's Indexed Geneological Register, Burton Family History; Harold Burton (HHB) to J. Edgar Hoover, Box 70, Burton Papers, Manuscript Division, Library of Congress, Washington, D.C. (Unless otherwise indicated, all Burton MSS are contained in this collection); HHB to Alfred Bertholdi, October 8, 1945, Box 38.

3. *Occasional Proceedings of the Bar and Officers of the Supreme Court, May 24, 1965, in Memory of Harold H. Burton* (Washington, D.C., 1965), 26-27, 39; Bowdoin Prize Proceedings, *Bowdoin College Bulletin,* no. 332, March, 1959, 26-27; HHB to Bertholdi, October 8, 1945, Box 38.

4. Chronological Service Record of HHB, April 6, 1919, to June 1920, vol. 1, Cheatham Collection (a collection of data and MSS on HHB's life compiled by his secretary Tess Cheatham, a copy of which is in the author's possession). HHB prepared the official regimental history of his World War I division, *600 Days of Service* (Portland, Ore., 1921); *Proceedings,* 43.

5. Thomas F. Campbell, *Daniel E. Morgan, 1877-1949: The Good Citizen in Politics* (Cleveland, 1966), 83 n. 5; see letters collected in Box 446, especially HHB to Newton D. Baker, December 6, 1928; Baker to HHB, December 10, 1928; HHB to William Hitz, September 4, 1928.

6. Campbell, *Daniel E. Morgan,* 148.

7. *Cleveland News,* February 5, 1944.

8. Author's personal interviews with William and Robert Burton, Deborah Adler, and Barbara Weidner.

9. *Cleveland Plain Dealer,* March 10, 1948.

10. HHB to Charles P. Conners, December 28, 1940, Box 8; Robert S.

Burton, personal interview with author, June 14, 1972; HHB to Floyd Downs, March 29, 1945, Box 28.

11. Roland Young, *Congressional Politics in the Second World War* (New York, 1956), 5.

12. HHB's Fourth Semi-Annual Report, January 15, 1943, Box 31; HHB's Diary, January 17, 1944, Box 1 (hereafter HHB's diaries will be cited as "Diary").

13. Young, *Congressional Politics,* 26-28; David J. Danielski, "Legislative and Judicial Decision-Making: The Case of Harold H. Burton," in S. Sidney Ulmer, ed., *Political Decision-Making* (New York, 1970), 121-46. HHB's First Semi-Annual Report, August 11, 1941, Box 30; Diary, March 1, 1945, Box 1; see also HHB's address on "Town Meeting of the Air," September 13, 1945, Box 367; HHB to Mr. and Mrs. Franklin Baker, November 7, 1945, Box 38. For a discussion of the impact of the Hill-Burton Act (U.S.C. 1958 Title 42, Sec. 291 et seq. August 13, 1946, C 958, 60 Stat. 1040), see Walter J. McNerney et al., *Hospital and Medical Economics,* 2 vols. (Chicago, 1962), 24, and passim.

14. Cabell Phillips, *The Truman Presidency: A History of Triumphant Succession* (New York, 1966) 33-37; see also Donald H. Riddle, *The Truman Committee: A Study in Congressional Responsibility* (New Brunswick, N.J., 1964).

15. HHB to Hawley L. Lodge, March, 1948; HHB to Wilber Edel, July 7, 1950, Box 367.

16. Diary, March 4 and 6, 1943, Box 1; *Newsweek,* March 22, 1943, 26; *Time,* March 22, 1943, 11; *New Republic,* March 29, 1943, 399-400, vol. 108.

17. Compare S. Res. 114 ($B_2H_2$) to S. Res. 192 (the Connally Resolution), 78 Cong., 1st sess., 1943.

18. HHB's statement of November 30, 1943, Box 387.

19. Diary, November 21, 1944, Box 1; HHB to Wallace White, November 24, 1944, Box 36.

20. HHB to Justice Rollman, September 26, 1943, Box 33; HHB to E. L. Dakar, April 21, 1944, Box 19; HHB to Rollman, March 4, 1942, Box 33; Joel Seidman, *American Labor from Defense to Reconversion* (Chicago, 1953), chaps. 8 and 10; William Jameson to HHB, March 5, 1942, and HHB to Jameson, March 7, 1942, Box 25.

21. Seidman, *American Labor,* 188-89; Young, *Congressional Politics,* 63-65.

22. Seidman, *American Labor,* 244, 255.

23. HHB to Harry L. Lodge, March 24, 1948, Box 363; *Congressional Record,* June 20, 1945, 6323-30.

24. *Newsweek,* July 2, 1945, 57; *Union Leader,* Toledo, Ohio, June 29, 1945; *Union Leader,* Cleveland, Ohio, clipping, n.d., Box 420.

25. *Cleveland Press,* August 11, 1945; *Cleveland Plain Dealer,* September 4, 1945; Diary, July 2 and 3, 1945, Box 1; *Public Papers of the Presidents of the United States: Harry S. Truman, 1945* (Washington, D.C., 1961), 399.

26. James Dyer to HHB, April 16, 1940, Box 126; William Rose, *Cleveland: The Making of a City* (Cleveland, 1950), 943; HHB to J. Wilson Ramey, January 18, 1941, Box 37.

27. *Ohio Republican News,* clipping, n.d., Box 28; press release of Ball and HHB, August 7, 1945, Box 440; HHB to Thomassina Johnson, August 13, 1945, Box 28; HHB to F.O. Patterson, February 19, 1944, Box 35; Walter White to HHB, December 29, 1941; HHB to White, January 2, 1942; petition to HHB, September, 1943, Box 28.

28. Diary, July 7, 1941, Box 1; Eugene C. Gerhart, *America's Advocate: Robert H. Jackson* (Indianapolis, 1958), 231-32.

29. HHB to Raymond Jeffreys, March 28, 1943, Box 25; Diary, November 1, 1943, August 22, 1943, Box 1.

30. *Cleveland News,* February 5, 1944; *Boston Herald,* February 22, 1944; Diary, February 5, 1944, Box 1.

31. Diary, September 19, 1943, e.g., records a gift of one thousand dollars to Earl Hart for HHB's political future; Diary, February 18, 1944; June 23 and 25, 1944, Box 1.

32. Earl Hart to Byron Wade, February 14, 1945, and Wade to Hart, February 19, 1945, Box 36; HHB to Carl D. Fribolin, July 9, 1945, Box 19; also HHB to Paul Bellamy, July 15, 1945; HHB to A.M. Piper, July 16, 1945, Box 17; HHB to Wilbur Astwer, July 9, 1945; HHB to Henry T. Bombardt, July 1, 1945, Box 16; Diary, July 11, July 12, and July 24, 1945, Box 1.

33. HHB to Carter, August 13, 1945, Box 17; Earl Hart to Ruth Neff, July 14, 1945, Box 28; Diary, August 3, 1945, Box 1; Hart to Fred Cornell, August 10, 1945, Box 18.

34. See, for example, Diary, May 18, 1945, Box 1.

35. Diary, September 17, 1945, Box 1; *Public Papers of the Presidents,* 326; *Congressional Record,* September 19, 1945, 5.

36. See *Washington Post,* Drew Pearson's column, September 25, 1945; see letters of congratulation, Boxes 38, 40, 431; see also nos. 13-16, vol. 2, and nos. 72-74, vol. 5, Cheatham Collection; *Washington Post,* September 19, 1945.

37. Black to Burton, September 18, 1945, Box 431; Alpheus T. Mason, *Harlan Fiske Stone: Pillar of the Law* (New York, 1956), 801; Fred Rodell,

"An Open Letter to Mr. Justice Brown," *Progressive,* clipping, October 1, 1945, p. 5, Box 420.

## CHAPTER 2

1. Hubert Holloway, "Notes and Quotes," clipping, n.p., n.d., Box 27.

2. Mason, *Harlan Fiske Stone,* 640-45, 670; *Jewel Ridge Coal Corp.* v. *Local No. 6167,* 325 U.S. 161 (1945). For a discussion of the differences between judicial self-restraint and activism, see Martin Shapiro, "Judicial Modesty: Down with the Old!—Up with the New?" *UCLA Law Review,* vol. 10 (1963), 533-60.

3. W. Howard Mann, personal interview with the author, July 19, 1972; Eloise Synder, "The Supreme Court as a Small Group," *Social Forces,* vol. 36 (1958), 236-38; Walter F. Murphy, *Elements of Judicial Strategy* (Chicago, 1964), esp. chap. 3; J. Woodford Howard, "On the Fluidity of Judicial Choice," *American Political Science Review,* vol. 62 (1968), 43-56; Walter F. Murphy, "Courts as Small Groups," *Harvard Law Review,* vol. 79 (1966), 1565-72; S. Sidney Ulmer, *Courts as Small and Not So Small Groups* (New York, 1971).

4. Diary, October 5, 15, 16, and 23, 1945, Box 1; HHB to the Reverend Benjamin H. Clark, November 11, 1945, Box 45. In his diary, Burton noted that "P.H. Harris, representing a colored church [19th Street Baptist Church], came in to ask me to speak at his church. I declined as I have in all cases." Diary, December 7, 1945, Box 1. For other instances in which HHB declined invitations to speak publicly or to accept a public role outside the Court, see HHB to J. Edgar Hoover, February 13, 1946, Box 44; and Stone to Truman, February 13, 1946, Box 49; HHB to Frederick M. Elliot, February 27, 1946, Box 38.

5. Mann, personal interview; Henry J. Abraham, *The Judicial Process* (New York, 1962), 202-06 and notes there cited; Richard J. Richardson and Kenneth N. Vines, "Review, Dissent, and the Appellate Process: A Political Interpretation," *Journal of Politics,* vol. 29 (1967), 597-616; S. Sidney Ulmer, "Dissent Behavior and the Social Background of Supreme Court Justices," *Journal of Politics,* vol. 32 (1970), 580-98.

6. 326 U.S. 657; HHB to Harry L. Lodge, March 24, 1948, Box 367; Douglas's comments on HHB's draft opinion, n.d., no. 45, Box 148; see Rutledge's comments on HHB's draft opinion, n.d., no. 45, Box 148; E. Merrick Dodd, "The Supreme Court and Fair Labor Standards, 1941-1945," *Harvard Law Review,* vol. 59 (1946), 321-73. A concurrence to a decision interpreting the Trading with the Enemy Act in *Markham* v. *Cabell,* 325 U.S. 404, was Burton's first opinion.

7. See Frankfurter's underlining and comments on HHB's draft opinion, January 17, 1946, no. 45, Box 148; Frankfurter to HHB, n.d., Box 148.

8. Rutledge to HHB, February 22, 1946, no. 73, Box 150; *Boutell* v. *Walling*, 327 U.S. 463; *Martino* v. *Michigan Window Cleaning Co.,* 327 U.S. 173.

9. Mann, personal interview with author; Frankfurter to HHB, April 26, 1946, no. 603, Box 143; HHB to Douglas and Douglas to HHB, October 26, 1945, no. 22, Box 148; *First Iowa Hydro-Electric* v. *FPC,* 328 U.S. 152; *United States* v. *Detroit and Cleveland Navigation Co.,* 326 U.S. 238.

10. HHB to Murphy, November 2, 1945, no. 31, Box 148; *Chatwin* v. *United States,* 326 U.S. 455; J. Woodford Howard, Jr., *Mr. Justice Murphy: A Political Biography* (Princeton, 1968), 341.

11. *Hawk* v. *Olson,* 326 U.S. 272; Mann to HHB, n.d., no. 17, Box 146; John P. Frank, "The United States Supreme Court: 1946-47 Term," *University of Chicago Law Review,* vol. 15 (1947-48), 27, n. 119.

12. *Marsh* v. *Alabama,* 326 U.S. 501; *Tucker* v. *Texas,* 326 U.S. 517; Henry W. Barber, "Religious Liberty v. Police Power—Jehovah's Witnesses," *American Political Science Review,* vol. 41 (1947), 226-47; Richard Lee Haugh, "The Jehovah's Witnesses Cases in Retrospect," *Western Political Quarterly,* vol. 6 (1953), 78-92; Conference Notes, December 10, 1945, nos. 87 and 114, Box 144.

13. Mann to HHB, December 29, 1945, nos. 87 and 114, Box 144.

14. *State of New York and Saratoga Spring Commission and Saratoga Authority* v. *United States,* 326 U.S. 572; Carter Glass, III "Intergovernmental Immunities from Taxation," *Washington and Lee Law Review,* vol. 4 (1946) 48-68; 325 U.S. 572, 590; Conference Notes, December 8, 1945; Mann to Burton, n.d., no. 5, Box 144; Stone to Conference, January, 1946, no. 5, Box 146.

15. Frankfurter to "Brethren," December 29, 1945, Box 146; Frankfurter to "Brethren," December 12, 1945, no. 5, Box 146; HHB to George Morris, February 13, 1946, Box 46.

16. *Mabee* v. *White Plains Publishing Co.,* 327 U.S. 177, deciding that the small volume of interstate newspaper circulation did not exclude the publishers of a daily newspaper with a circulation of about .50 percent outside the state in which it is published from the operations of the Fair Labor Standards Act; and *Oklahoma Press Publishing Co.* v. *Walling,* 327 U.S. 186, deciding that the FLSA applied to workers in the business of publishing and distributing newspapers and validating the enforcement of a subpoena duces tecum to determine whether the FLSA had been violated; Conference Notes, December 10, 1945; Mann to HHB, n.d., no. 57, Box 149; Mann to HHB, January 29, 1946; HHB to Mann, January 30, 1946, no. 61, Box 144.

17. 327 U.S. 304, Conference Notes, December 15, 1945, no. 4, Box 144;

Frankfurter to HHB, February 9, 1946, no. 14, Box 146; see 327 U.S. 304, 357, and drafts of dissents in no. 14, Box 146; Frankfurter to HHB, February 14, 1946, Box 146; compare Frankfurter to HHB, February 12 and 15, 1946, to 327 U.S. 304 and 343 and drafts of the dissent, no. 14, Box 146.

18. 327 U.S. 357.

19. Howard, *Justice Murphy,* 378; HHB to Truman, February 25, 1946, Box 49; Truman to HHB, February 26, 1946, Box 431; Michaud to HHB, February 26, 1946, and HHB to Michaud, March 11, 1946, Box 46; Diary, February 27, 1946, Box 1.

20. *In re Yamashita,* 327 U.S. 1; *In re Homma,* 327 U.S. 759, and 327 U.S. 304; Mann to HHB, n.d., nos. 61 and misc. 672, Box 149; 327 U.S. 1, 8, and 9; Adolf F. Reel, *The Case of General Yamashita* (Chicago, 1949); Howard, *Justice Murphy,* 375, believes this was one of the opinions that established Murphy's immortality.

21. Mann to HHB, n.d., no. 163, Box 151; Mann to HHB, August 23, 1946, Box 46; *Commissioner of Internal Revenue* v. *Wilcox,* 327 U.S. 404; *James* v. *United States,* 366 U.S. 213 (1961); Clarence Opper to HHB, May 19, 1961, vol. 4, no. 45, Cheatham Collection.

22. *Nippert* v. *Richmond,* 327 U.S. 416; *United States* v. *Carbone,* 327 U.S. 633; *Williams* v. *United States,* 327 U.S. 723; Mann to HHB, December 24, 1945, Frankfurter to HHB, n.d., HHB's note, January 29, 1946, no. 72, Box 150; Howard, *Justice Murphy,* 379; HHB to Frankfurter, March 11, 1946, no. 474, Box 152; Reed to HHB, March 21, 1946; Frankfurter to HHB; Rutledge to HHB, March 21, 1946, no. 123, Box 151.

23. 328 U.S. 61, 69; *Girouard* v. *United States,* 328 U.S. 61; *Schwimmer* v. *United States,* 274 U.S. 644 (1929); Frankfurter to HHB, two letters, March 20, 1946, no. 572, Box 153. On stare decisis see Martin Shapiro, "Toward A Theory of Stare Decisis," *Journal of Legal Studies* vol. 1 (1972), 125-34.

24. Frankfurter to HHB, March 21, 1946, no. 572, Box 153; 328 U.S. 65, 59; *Helvering* v. *Halleck,* 309 U.S. 106 (1940); Albert P. Blaustein and Andrew H. Field, "Overruling Opinions in the Supreme Court," *Michigan Law Review* vol. 57 (1958), 151-94.

25. *Pennekamp et al* v. *Florida,* 328 U.S. 331, 369, 370, 372; Conference Notes, February 11, 1946, no. 473, Box 145; *Bridges* v. *California,* 314 U.S. 352 (1941); Mann to HHB, n.d.; Mann to HHB, May 21, 1946, no. 473, Box 152.

26. *Colegrove* v. *Green,* 328 U.S. 549, 556, cf. Howard, *Justice Murphy;* 328 U.S. 568; Conference Notes, March 11, 1946, no. 806, Box 145; Frank-

furter to Conference, February 7, 1946, no. 489, Box 145; Frankfurter to Conference, February 27, 1946, no. 404, Box 152.

27. Howard, *Justice Murphy,* 402, 404; Docket Book, no. 342, Box 143; 328 U.S. 680, 696, et. seq.; *Anderson* v. *Mt. Clements Pottery,* 328 U.S. 680; *Tennessee Coal, Iron and Railroad Co.* v. *Muscoda Local,* 321 U.S. 590 (1944).

28. *Morgan* v. *Virginia,* 328 U.S. 373, 394; draft dissent, no. 704, Box 154.

29. Conference Notes, n.d., no. 704, Box 145; HHB's memo to Conference, n.d., no. 704, Box 154; Diary, May 20, 1946, and June 3, 1946, Box 1; no. 704, Box 154.

30. Charles P. Lucas to HHB, June 10, 1946, Box 45; John O. Holly to HHB, June 5, 1946, Box 44; Ada Murry Clark to HHB, Box 39; M.C. Busic to HHB, June 4, 1946, Box 38; Robert M. Chafee to HHB, June 5, 1946, Box 39; Mann to HHB, August 23, 1946, Box 46; and HHB's replies.

31. *Davis* v. *United States,* 328 U.S. 582; *Zap* v. *United States,* 328 U.S. 624; *American Tobacco Co.* v. *United States,* 328 U.S. 782; Rutledge to HHB, June 9, 1946, nos. 18-20, Box 147; law clerk's memo to Stone, n.d., nos. 18-20; Conference Notes, November 15, 1945, Box 144.

32. Howard, *Justice Murphy,* 268-70; interviews with Howard Mann and other Burton clerks, June 1972.

33. Diary, April 22, 23, 27, and 30, and June 6, 1946, Box 1; HHB to Earl Hart, April 27, 1946, Box 44.

34. Diary, February 19 and May 8, 1946, Box 1.

35. HHB to M. A. Cowderly, March 14, 1946, and June 11, 1947, Box 52.

## CHAPTER 3

1. Diary, October 7 and 10, 1946, Box 1; Howard, *Justice Murphy,* 405-08.

2. John P. Frank, "Court and Constitution: The Passive Period," *Vanderbilt Law Review,* vol. 4 (1951), 400-26.

3. Diary, October 12 and 13, 1946, Box 1.

4. John P. Frank, "The United States Supreme Court 1946-47," *University of Chicago Law Review,* vol. 15 (1947-48), 39.

5. *Cleveland* v. *United States,* 329 U.S. 14 (1946); the earlier case was *Caminetti* v. *United States,* 242 U.S. 470 (1917); Conference Notes, October 19, 1946, nos. 12-19, Box 157. Often-used reasons for opinion assignment are to hold the vote of a wavering justice and to make the opinion more palatable to the dissenters. See Abraham, *The Judicial Process,* 470 (1962), 211-13 and notes there cited.

6. *Everson* v. *Board of Education,* 330 U.S. 1; *Ballard* v. *United States,* 329 U.S. 187 (1946); *Cox* v. *United States,* 332 U.S. 442 (1947); *McCollum* v. *Board of Education,* 333 U.S. 203.

7. Diary, October 22, 1946, Box 1; Frankfurter to HHB, November 13, 1946, no. 37, Box 167; Frankfurter to HHB, December 5, 1946, Frankfurter Papers, Manuscript Division, Library of Congress, Washington, D.C.; 329 U.S. 187, 205, 193; Conference Notes, October 19, 1946, no. 37, Box 157; Howard, *Justice Murphy,* 446-47.

8. *Cox* v. *United States,* 332 U.S. 442 (1947); Docket Book nos. 66-68, Box 173; Conference Notes, October 24, 1947, nos. 66-68, Box 173.

9. *Everson* v. *United States,* 330 U.S. 1 (1947); *McCollum* v. *Board of Education,* 333 U.S. 203; Conference Notes, November 23, 1946, nos. 52 and 911, Box 157; Conference Notes, n.d., no. 90, Box 174; Howard, *Justice Murphy,* 447-51, and Fowler V. Harper, *Justice Rutledge and the Bright Constellation* (Indianapolis, 1965), 348-51, do not emphasize Burton's role; in *Engel* v. *Vitale,* the New York prayer case, 370 U.S. 421 (1962), 443. Douglas asserted that, based on his crucial fifth vote, *Everson* was wrongly decided.

10. HHB's comment on note from Rutledge, March 6, 1948, Box 336.

11. Lake to HHB, n.d., and HHB's handwritten comment thereon, n.d., no. 90, Box 174; HHB to Black, January 4, 1948, and draft letter; Black to HHB, January 6, 1948, no. 90, Box 186.

12. Frankfurter to Jackson, Rutledge, and HHB, January 6, 1948, Frankfurter Papers, Box 19; Howard, *Justice Murphy,* 450-52; Frankfurter to HHB, January 28, 1948; Frankfurter to HHB, January 30, 1948; Reed to Frankfurter, January 28, 1948, no. 90, Box 186. See Frankfurter's dissent in *Zorach* v. *Clauson,* 343 U.S. 306, 320 (1952).

13. Black to HHB, January 6, 1948, no. 90, Box 186; HHB to Black, and HHB to Frankfurter, February 9, 1948; see also draft letters, February 6, 1948, no. 90, Box 186; Diary, February 7 and 11, 1948, Box 2; correspondence file on *Everson,* Box 52. On Burton's concern with the Court as an institution, see David N. Atkinson and Dale A. Newman, "Toward A Cost Theory of Judicial Alignments: The Case of the Truman Bloc," *Midwest Journal of Political Science,* vol. 13 (1969), 271-83.

14. Frankfurter to Conference, February 11, 1948; Black to Conference, February 11, 1948, no. 90, Box 186.

15. Frankfurter to HHB, February 11, 1948; Black to Rutledge and HHB, February 12, 1948; Rutledge to HHB, n.d., no. 90, Box 186.

16. HHB to Rutledge, March 2, 1948, no. 90, Box 186; Frankfurter to HHB, March 13, 1948, Box 186; Rutledge to HHB, n.d., Box 336; on the general issues, see Phillip B. Kurland, *Religion and the Law* (Chicago,

1962), 80-85; Paul G. Kauper, "Church and State: Cooperative Separation," *Michigan Law Review,* vol. 60 (1961), 35; Note, "The Released Time Cases Revisited: A Study of Group Decisionmaking by the Supreme Court," *Yale Law Journal,* vol. 83 (1974), 202-360.

17. *Adamson* v. *California,* 332 U.S. 46 (1947); *Barnes* v. *New York,* 329 U.S. 719; memo on cert., n.d., no. 152, Box 160.

18. Frankfurter to HHB, March 25, 1948, and April 16, 1948, no. 398, Box 186.

19. *Wade* v. *Mayo,* 334 U.S. 672; *Townsend* v. *Burke,* 334 U.S. 376; *Uveges* v. *Pennsylvania,* 335 U.S. 437; *Turner* v. *Pennsylvania,* 338 U.S. 562; Conference Notes, October 18, 1947, no. 40, Box 174.

20. 332 U.S. 596, 620-21; 335 U.S. 252.

21. Docket Book, no. 51, Box 173; law clerk's memo, n.d., and HHB to law clerk, n.d., no. 51, Box 183.

22. 332 U.S. 742; 335 U.S. 252; Frankfurter to Conference, November 7, 1947; Douglas to Conference, November 17, 1947, no. 91, Box 183; Conference Notes, November 24, 1947, no. 91, Box 174; HHB's comments, n.d., on cert. memo no. 91, Box 183; Docket Book, nos. 91 and 721, Box 173; 335 U.S. 410.

23. 333 U.S. 257; Docket Book, no. 215, Box 173; Conference Notes, December 20, 1947, no. 215, Box 174.

24. Mann to HHB, February 5, 1948, Box 61. *Harris* v. *United States,* 331 U.S. 145; *Trupiano* v. *United States,* 334 U.S. 699; overruled in *United States* v. *Rabinowitz,* 339 U.S. 56, 67 (1950).

25. 338 U.S. 25, 31; Docket Book, nos. 17 and 18, Box 188; Conference Notes, October 23, 1948, nos. 17 and 18, Box 189.

26. *Carroll* v. *United States,* 267 U.S. 132 (1925); *Brinegar* v. *United States,* 338 U.S. 160; *McDonald* v. *United States,* 335 U.S. 451; HHB's note on bench memo, n.d., no. 36, Box 189; HHB's note on cert. memo, n.d., no. 75, Box 189; Conference Notes, November 20, 1948, no. 107, Box 189.

27. 336 U.S. 440, 459.

28. 329 U.S. 459, 471.

29. 329 U.S. 459, 179, 481.

30. Frankfurter to HHB, December 13, 1946, Box 171; Frankfurter to Lemonn, February 3, 1947, Box 336; Frankfurter to HHB, December 31, 1946, no. 142, Box 171; Liva Baker, *Felix Frankfurter* (New York, 1969), 282-83; Conference Notes, November 23, 1946, no. 142, Box 171; Howard, *Justice Murphy,* 438; see also HHB to Frankfurter, December 26, 1946, Box 38, Frankfurter Papers.

31. William S. Burton, personal interview with author, June 6, 1972;

HHB to Austin H. MacCormick, January 24, 1947, Box 53; Harris Weston, personal interview with author, July 2, 1972.

32. *Craig* v. *Harney,* 329 U.S. 696; Conference Notes, January 11, 1947, no. 241, Box 158; law clerk to HHB, May 16, 1947; HKW to Burton, May 16, no. 241, Box 158.

33. 335 U.S. 106; Conference Notes, May 1, 1948, no. 695, Box 175.

34. Docket Book, no. 3, Box 173; 337 U.S. 507; see also *Lanzetta* v. *New Jersey,* 306 U.S. 451 (1939), Conference Notes, March 27, 1946, no. 3, Box 174.

35. 338 U.S. 25, 31; Docket Book, nos. 17 and 18, Box 188; Conference Notes, October 23, 1948, nos. 17 and 18, Box 189.

36. Conference Notes, February 5, 1949, no. 272, Box 188; *Terminello* v. *Chicago,* 337 U.S. 1 (1948); *Kovacs* v. *Cooper,* 336 U.S. 717; *Saia* v. *New York,* 334 U.S. 558.

37. HHB's handwritten note on bench memo, n.d., no. 11, Box 188.

38. See C. Herman Pritchett's *Civil Liberties and the Vinson Court,* (Chicago, 1954).

39. *Shelly* v. *Kramer,* 345 U.S. 1; *Sipuel* v. *Board of Regents,* 332 U.S. 631; *Bob Lo Excursion* v. *Michigan,* 333 U.S. 28; *Bronson* v. *North Carolina,* 333 U.S. 581; *Patton* v. *Mississippi,* 332 U.S. 463. See *Missouri ex rel. Gaines* v. *Canada,* 305 U.S. 337 (1938), in which it was held that a state must provide professional education for black students within the state if it does so for white students, regardless of the limited demand; Conference Notes, January 10, 1948, no. 369, Box 175; Conference Notes, February 9, 1948, nos. 292-96, Box 175.

40. Lake to Burton, n.d.; HHB's handwritten note on cert. memo, n.d., no. 122, Box 174.

41. *Buchanan* v. *Warley,* 245 U.S. 60 (1917); Docket Book, nos. 72, 87, 290, 291, Box 173; Conference Notes, January 17, 1948, nos. 72, 87, 290, 291, Box 174; for a discussion of the restrictive convenant cases see Clement Vose, *For Caucasians Only: The Supreme Court, the NAACP, and the Restrictive Covenant Cases* (Berkeley, 1959); see case letter file, Box 59.

42. HHB's note on JS's memo, n.d.; Conference Notes, October 25, 1947, no. 44, Box 174; Frank, "The United States Supreme Court," 28; *Oyama* v. *California,* 332 U.S. 633; 334 U.S. 410, 422; Conference Notes, n.d., no. 53, Box 175.

43. *United States* v. *United Mine Workers,* 330 U.S. 258; Conference Notes, January 20, 1947, no. 759, Box 159; Howard, *Justice Murphy,* 413-14; Frankfurter to HHB, February 3, 1947, Box 53.

44. *United Brotherhood* v. *United States,* 330 U.S. 345; *Packard Car Co.* v. *National Labor Relations Board,* 330 U.S. 485; *Levinson* v. *Spector Mo-*

*tor Co.,* 330 U.S. 649; *Pyramid Motor Corp.* v. *Ispass,* 330 U.S. 695; *Morris* v. *McComb,* 332 U.S. 472; *United States* v. *Petrillo,* 332 U.S. 1; Conference Notes, September 5, 1946, nos. 9-13, Box 157.

45. Conference Notes, January 8, 1949, no. 182, Box 189.

46. 337 U.S. 217; see *Thornhill* v. *Alabama,* 310 U.S. 88 (1940); Howard, *Justice Murphy,* 251-83.

47. Jackson to HHB, May 27, 1949; Murphy to HHB, May 27, 1949, no. 197, Box 220.

48. *United States* v. *National Lead,* 332 U.S. 319.

49. Washington to HHB, July 17, 1947, Box 57.

50. Note on Washington's letter to HHB, July 17, 1947; law clerk to HHB, August 28, 1947; HHB to Conference, September 25, 1947, Box 57; L.S. Mercer to HHB, July 21, 1947; law clerk to HHB, n.d.; HHB to Mercer, September 5, 1947, Box 57.

51. Frank, "The United States Supreme Court," 3, n. 11; 333 U.S. 364; 333 U.S. 287; HHB to Harry L. Lodge, March 24, 1948, Box 60. On price-restricted licenses, see Gerald R. Gibbons, "Price Fixing in Patent Licenses and the Antitrust Laws," *Virginia Law Review,* vol. 5 (1965), 273-304.

52. Frankfurter to Reed, March 1, 1948; Frankfurter to HHB, n.d., no. 8, Box 181.

53. *United States* v. *Paramount Pictures,* 334 U.S. 131; *United States* v. *Columbia Steel,* 334 U.S. 495; *Mandeville Island Farms* v. *American Crystal Sugar Co.,* 334 U.S. 219; Conference Notes, November 24, 1947, no. 75, Box 174.

54. 334 U.S. 37; 333 U.S. 683; see clipping dated April 29, 1948, nos. 23 and 24, Box 182; Conference Notes, n.d., nos. 23 and 24, Box 174.

55. 337 U.S. 293, 314; 337 U.S. 78.

56. Revised judicial code, 28 USCA 1404 (a) (1948); Frank, "The United States Supreme Court," 10.

57. 331 U.S. 477; 331 U.S. 586; Frankfurter to HHB, n.d., Box 172.

58. 333 U.S. 178; Docket Book, no. 50, Box 173. Interestingly, Burton, Reed, and Jackson had voted against the granting of certiorari.

59. See Frank, "The United States Supreme Court," 15, no. 58; 334 U.S. 742, 758-760; *United States* v. *Bethlehem Steel,* 315 U.S. 289 (1942).

60. *New York ex rel. Halvey* v. *Halvey,* 330 U.S. 610; *Williams* v. *Williams,* 317 U.S. 287 (1942); *Williams* v. *North Carolina,* 325 U.S. 226 (1945); *Sherrer* v. *Sherrer,* 334 U.S. 343; Howard, *Justice Murphy,* 323-24, for Catholic Justice Murphy's opposition to "quickie divorces,"

61. 334 U.S. 541; 334 U.S. 554; HHB's handwritten note, n.d., no. 36, Box 174; Conference Notes, October 18, 1947, no. 36, Box 174. On migratory divorce, see Thomas Reed Powell, "And Repent at Leisure: An

Inquiry Into the Unhappy Lot of Those Whom Nevada Hath Joined Together and North Carolina Hath Rent Asunder" *Harvard Law Review,* vol. 58 (1945), 930-1017; David Currie, "Suitcase Divorce in the Conflict of Laws," *University of Chicago Law Review,* vol. 34 (1966), 26-77.

62. *Funk Brothers Seed Company* v. *Kalo Inoculant,* 333 U.S. 127; *United States* v. *Baltimore and Ohio Railroad Co.,* 333 U.S. 169.

63. 335 U.S. 632, 696; 335 U.S. 701, 721, 726; see also Frankfurter to HHB, January 8, 1949, Box 336.

64. 336 U.S. 28; the earlier case was *Helvering* v. *American Dental Co.,* 318 U.S. 322 (1943); 337 U.S. 369; 337 U.S. 733; Watson Washburn to Vinson, April 7, 1949, no. 84, Box 199.

65. 336 U.S. 118; law clerk to HHB, n.d., no. 35, Box 198; Frankfurter to HHB, n.d., no. 35, Box 198.

66. 336 U.S. 725, 738.

67. Conference Notes, February 11, 1949, no. 35, Box 198; Diary, March 7, 1949; Rutledge to HHB, March 9, 1949; Frankfurter to HHB, n.d., Reed to Frankfurter, March 28, 1949, no. 355, Box 201.

68. 337 U.S. 662; Reed to HHB, March 30, 1949; Frankfurter to HHB, April 21, 1949; HHB to Frankfurter, April 30, 1949; Frankfurter to HHB, n.d., no. 287, Box 201.

69. 337 U.S. 198; Frankfurter to HHB, June 6, 1949, no. 253, Box 200; HHB to law clerks, February 3, 1949; Reed to HHB, May 6, 1949; HHB to Conference, May 6, 1949; Jackson to HHB, May 7, 1949; Black to HHB, May 10, 1949; HHB to Conference, May 17, 1949; Douglas to Burton, May 17, 1949; Reed to HHB, May 25, 1949, no. 253, Box 200; 335 U.S. 359; 336 U.S. 931; Jackson to HHB, November 17, 1948, no. 6, Box 196.

70. HHB to Harry L. Lodge, March 24, 1948, Box 66.

71. Douglas to HHB, June 23, 1947; Frankfurter to HHB, June 23, 1947, vol. 1, no. 45, Cheatham Collection; Vinson to HHB, June 23, 1947, vol. 5, no. 48, Cheatham Collection; Diary, June 23, 1947, Box 2; Harris Weston, personal interview with author, August 1, 1972.

72. HHB to Harry Barnwell, December 21, 1947, Box 58.

73. Diary, November 2, 1947, Box 2.

## CHAPTER 4

1. Pritchett, *Civil Liberties and the Vinson Court.*

2. Irving Dillard, "Truman Reshapes the Supreme Court," *Atlantic Monthly,* vol. 184 (1949), 30-33; C. B. Dutton, "Mr. Justice Tom C. Clark," *Indiana Law Journal,* vol. 26 (1951), 169; Henry L. Wallace, "Mr. Justice Minton: Hoosier Justice on the Supreme Court," *Indiana Law Journal,* vol. 34 (1959), 145.

3. 339 U.S. 382.

4. Conference Notes, October 17, 1949, no. 10, Box 204; 339 U.S. 323; 339 U.S. 349; 339 U.S. 162.

5. 341 U.S. 494. On this case and others related to the Communist subversion issue, see Harold W. Chase, *Security and Liberty: The Problem of the Native Communists, 1947-1955* (New York, 1955); see also John A. Gorfinkel and Julian W. Mack, II, "Dennis v. United States and the Clear and Present Danger Rule," *California Law Review,* vol. 39 (1951), 475. For the Smith Act, see 54 Stat: 671 (1940), 18 USCA (1950); HHB's note on bench memo, n.d., no. 336, Box 217; Docket Book, no. 336, Box 216; Conference Notes, December 9, 1950, no. 336, Box 217.

6. 341 U.S. 494.

7. *Sacher* v. *U.S.,* 182 F. 2d; George Marion, *The Communist Trial: An American Cross Roads* (New York, 1950), 416; 341 U.S. 952 (1951); Frankfurter to Conference, February 27, 1951, Box 221; Nathaniel L. Nathanson, "The Communist Trial and the Clear-and-Present Danger Test," *Harvard Law Review,* vol. 63 (1950), 1167-75.

8. *Sacher* v. *United States,* 343 U.S. 1.

9. Frankfurter to HHB, October 15, 1951, Box 81; HHB's note on Frankfurter's letter of October 15, 1951, Box 81.

10. Conference Notes, November 11, 1950, no. 93, Box 217. Clark, Burton, Jackson, Douglas, and Black all voted to grant certiorari. The balance of the Court voted to deny. Docket Book, no. 93, Box 216.

11. Law clerk to HHB, n.d., and HHB's note thereon, n.d., no. 93, Box 217.

12. 343 U.S. 250; Docket Book, no. 118, Box 230; David Riesman, "Democracy and Defamation: Control of Group Libel," *Columbia Law Review,* vol. 42 (1942), 727-80; Loren P. Beth, "Group Libel and Free Speech," *Minnesota Law Review,* vol. 39 (1955), 167. Conference Notes, December 1, 1951; HHB's bench memo and handwritten notes thereon, November 26, 1951, no. 118, Box 231.

13. 341 U.S. 56; 341 U.S. 716.

14. 341 U.S. 716, 722; 341 U.S. 716, 729. The earlier cases were *Cummings* v. *Missouri,* 4 Wall 277 (1867); *Ex Parte Garland,* 4 Wall 383 (1967); *United States* v. *Lovett,* 328 U.S. 303 (1906).

15. HHB to Douglas, May 17, 1951; Douglas to HHB, May 18, 1951; HHB to Frankfurter, May 21, 1951, no. 453, Box 229.

16. 344 U.S. 183, 194; HHB's notes on law clerk's memo, no. 14, Box 244.

17. *Joint Anti-Fascist Refugee Committee* v. *McGrath,* 341 U.S. 123; Eleanor Bontecou, *The Federal Loyalty-Security Program* (Ithaca, 1953), 202-04; Seth Richardson, "The Federal Employee Loyalty Program," *Columbia Law Review,* vol. 51 (1951), 546-63.

18. *Bailey* v. *Richardson,* 341 U.S. 918; Frankfurter to Conference, November 22, 1950; law clerk's memo to HHB, discussing Frankfurter's point of view, no. 49, Box 225.

19. Conference Notes, October 14, 1950; HHB's notes on his bench memo, n.d., no. 49, Box 217.

20. Black to HHB, April 25, 1951, and HHB's note thereon, Box 336; - *Feiner* v. *New York,* 340 U.S. 315.

21. 341 U.S. 123, 136, 202; 341 U.S. 918.

22. 342 U.S. 485; Conference Notes, January 5, 1952, no. 8, Box 231; Morris Arval, "Academic Freedom and Loyalty Oaths," *Law and Contemporary Problems,* vol. 28 (1963), 487-524.

23. 343 U.S. 306; Conference Notes, February 21, 1952; HHB's bench memo, no. 431, Box 231. See also *Doremus* v. *Board of Education,* 343 U.S. 429.

24. Frankfurter to HHB; Burton to Frankfurter and Frankfurter's note thereon, February 18, 1952, Box 81. Commentators usually regard the Court as having given way in *Zorach* to public pressure generated by *McCollum.* See Frank J. Sorauf, "Zorach v. Clauson; The Impact of a Supreme Court Decision," *American Political Science Review,* vol. 53 (1959), 777-91; Donald E. Boles, *The Bible, Religion and the Public Schools* (Ames, Iowa, 1965).

25. *Savorgnan* v. *United States,* 338 U.S. 491, 500.

26. *Harisiades* v. *Shaughnessy,* 342 U.S. 580; Alien Registration Act, 342 U.S. 580, 601; cert. memo, n.d., and HHB's comments thereon, n.d., no. 43, Box 231.

27. *Carlson* v. *Landon,* 342 U.S. 524.

28. *United States* v. *Grainger,* 346 U.S. 235; see Sen. Rep. no. 1544, 77th Cong. 2d sess. (1942), for Burton's committee report while in the Senate on the 1942 Wartime Suspension of Limitations Bill; *Bridges* v. *Wixon,* 144 F. 2nd 927 (1944); *Ex parte Bridges,* 49 F. Supp. 292 (1943).

29. *Shaughnessy* v. *United States ex rel. Mezei,* 345 U.S. 206, 214, quoting from *Kwong Hai Chew* v. *Colding,* 344 U.S. 590, 599 (1953); Docket Book, no. 139, Box 243.

30. Conference Notes, October 1, 1952; HHB's handwritten note on bench memo, n.d., no. 139, Box 244.

31. For a discussion of American immigration policy of the period, see "Developments in the Law—Immigration and Nationality," *Harvard Law Review,* vol. 66 (1952-53), 643-745.

32. See votes recorded in Docket Book in Box 207: no. 44, *Holt* v. *California;* no. 202, *Crombie* v. *Ragen;* no. 422, misc., *Arrington* v. *Alabama;* no. 324, *Patton* v. *Mississippi;* nos. 190-95, misc., *Melanson et al.* v. *Massachusetts.*

33. *United States* v. *Rabinowitz,* 339 U.S. 356; *Harris* v. *United States,* 331 U.S. 451 (1947); *Trupiano* v. *United States,* 334 U.S. 699 (1948); Conference Notes, January 14, 1950, no. 293, Box 204; *Rabinowitz* was overruled by the Warren Court in *Chimel* v. *California,* 395 U.S. 752 (1969).

34. *District of Columbia* v. *Little,* 339 U.S. 1, 8.

35. 339 U.S. 200, 217; *Wade* v. *Mayo,* 334 U.S. 672; *Darr* v. *Buford,* 339 U.S. 200.

36. Reed to HHB, n.d., no. 51, Box 212; law clerk to HHB, Frankfurter to HHB, n.d., no. 51, Box 212; Frankfurter to HHB, April 1, 1950, Box 330.

37. *Darr* v. *Buford,* 339 U.S. 200 (1950); *Brown, Speller, Daniels* v. *Allen,* 344 U.S. 443; 344 U.S. 443, 487; also see HHB's note on a memo from Reed and Frankfurter, October 27, 1952, no. 32, Box 250; Frankfurter to Conference, June 3, 1952, no. 32, Box 250.

38. Frankfurter to Conference, October, 1952; HHB to Frankfurter, December 22, 1952, no. 32, Box 250.

39. Frankfurter to Conference, December 31, 1952, no. 32, Box 250.

40. 343 U.S. 747, 766; 277 U.S. 438 (1928); 316 U.S. 129 (1942); Docket Book, no. 543, Box 230; Conference Notes, April 26, 1952, no. 543, Box 231; Jacob W. Landynski, *Search and Seizure and the Supreme Court* (Baltimore, 1966).

41. *Rochin* v. *California,* 342 U.S. 165 (1952); Glendon A. Schubert, *Constitutional Politics: The Political Behavior of Supreme Court Justices and the Constitutional Policies That They Make* (New York, 1960), 610-11; Glendon Schubert, *The Judicial Mind* (Evanston, 1965).

42. *Madsen* v. *Kinsella,* 343 U.S. 341, 372; William G. McLaren, "Constitutional Law: Military Trials of Civilians," *American Bar Association Journal,* vol. 45 (1959), 1255.

43. Conference Notes, June 13, 18, and 19, 1953, Box 257; Diary, June 19, 1953, Box 3; Samuel Fineberg, *The Rosenberg Case: Fact and Fiction* (New York, 1953).

44. Jackson relied mainly on *United States* v. *Harris,* 106 U.S. 629 (1883).

45. 341 U.S. 651, 657, 3, 664.

46. Conference Notes, April 8, 1950; law clerks to HHB, n.d., HHB's note on cert. memo, n.d., nos. 34 and 44, Box 204; *Sweatt* v. *Painter,* 339 U.S. 629; *McLaurin* v. *Oklahoma State Regents,* 339 U.S. 637; *Henderson* v. *United States,* 339 U.S. 816.

47. Conference Notes, March 8, 1948, no. 25, Box 205; John P. Frank, "The United States Supreme Court: 1949-50," *University of Chicago Law Review,* vol. 18 (1950-51), 35-36.

48. Frankfurter to HHB, May 26, 1950, no. 25, Box 210.

49. Douglas to Conference, June 19, 1950, no. 25, Box 208; Diary, October 8, 1952, Box 3; Black to Conference, November 28, 1952; Frankfurter to Conference, November 28, 1952, Box 337.

50. Law clerk to HHB, n.d., Box 337.

51. 345 U.S. 972-73; S. Sidney Ulmer, "Bricolage and Assorted Thoughts on Working in the Papers of Supreme Court Justices," *Journal of Politics,* vol. 35 (1973), 286; Richard Kluger, *Simple Justice: The History of Brown* v. *Board of Education and Black America's Struggle for Equality* (New York, 1976), ch. 23.

52. Black to Conference, June 13, 1953, Box 337.

53. Docket Book, no. 52, Box 243; *Terry* v. *Adams,* 345 U. S. 461; *Nixon* v. *Herndon,* 273 U. S. 536 (1927); *Nixon* v. *Condon,* 286 U. S. 73 (1932); *Smith* v. *Allwright,* 321 U. S. 649 (1944); see Clay P. Malick, "Terry v. Adams: Governmental Responsibility for the Protection of Civil Rights," *Western Political Quarterly,* vol. 7 (1954), 51-64.

54. Conference Notes, January 17, 1953, no. 52, Box 244; Diary, March 18 and 20, 1953, Box 3.

55. *Barrows* v. *Jackson,* 346 U. S. 249; *Shelly* v. *Kraemer,* 334 U. S. (1948); *District of Columbia* v. *John R. Thompson Co.,* 346 U. S. 100; Conference Notes, May 2, 1953, no. 517, Box 244.

56. See Alan F. Westin, *The Anatomy of a Constitutional Law Case: Youngstown Sheet and Tube Co. v. Sawyer: The Steel Seizure Decision* (New York, 1958), for a broad documentary survey; Edward S. Corwin, "The Steel Seizure Case—A Judicial Brick Without Straw," *Columbia Law Review,* vol. 53 (1953), 53-56; Harry S Truman, *Memoirs: Years of Trial and Hope* (Garden City, N.Y., 1955), vol. 2, 466-71.

57. Edward S. Corwin, *The President, Office and Powers* (New York, 1940); Diary, April 11, 1952, Box 3; Conference Notes, May 3, 1951, no. 744, Box 231.

58. Diary, May 1, 1952, Box 3.

59. Conference Notes, May 16, 1952, no. 744, Box 231.

60. 343 U. S. 579, 657, 658, and notes cited therein, 659.

61. Diary, May 10 and June 2, 1952, Box 3.

62. *Thornhill* v. *Alabama,* 310 U. S. 88 (1940); *Senn* v. *Tile Layers Union,* 301 U. S. 468 (1937); *Manufacturers Trust Co.* v. *Becker,* 338 U. S. 304; *International Union UAW, CIO* v. *O'Brien,* 339 U. S. 454; *Building Services Employees* v. *Gazzam,* 339 U. S. 532; Joseph Tanenhaus, "Picketing as Free Speech: The Growth of the New Law of Picketing from 1940 to 1952," *Cornell Law Quarterly,* vol. 38 (1952), 1-50.

63. Taft-Hartley Act, 61 Stat. 141 (1947), 29 USCA sec. 141 (1964), 341 U. S. 675, 692. Douglas was quoting Judge Rifkind in *Dowds* v. *Metropolitan Federation,* 75 F. Supp. 672, 677 (1948).

64. 341 U. S. 675; 341 U. S. 694; 341 U. S. 707; and 341 U. S. 665, 671.

65. Local Union No. 10, *American Federation of Labor* v. *Graham*, 345 U. S. 192.

66. 338 U. S. 278; 339 U. S. 497.

67. 345 U. S. 100; 345 U.S. 117; Conference Notes, November 21, 1952, nos. 53 and 238, Box 244; Black to HHB, February 23, 1953, no. 53, Box 251.

68. Douglas to HHB, December 7, 1949, Box 70.

69. *United States* v. *Kansas City Life Insurance Co.,* 339 U. S. 799.

70. Conference Notes, April 1, 1950, no. 12, Box 333; 5 Stat. 797, 798 (1845); *United States* v. *California*, 332 U. S. 19 (1947).

71. *McGrath* v. *Manufacturers Trust Co.*, 338 U. S. 241; *Mullane* v. *Central Hanover Bank and Trust Co.*, 339 U. S. 306, 320.

72. *Hiatt* v. *Brown*, 339 U. S. 103; *Railway Labor Executive Association* v. *United States*, 339 U. S. 142; *King* v. *United States*, 344 U. S. 254.

73. *Schwegman Brothers* v. *Calvert Distillers, Inc.*, 341 U. S. 384; Miller-Tydings Act, 50 Stat. 693 (1927), 15 USCA sec. 1 (1951); Frankfurter to HHB, May 16, 1951, and HHB's appended note, n.d., Box 336.

74. *Standard Oil Co.* v. *FIC*, 340 U. S. 231; Robinson Patman Act, 49 Stat. 1526 (1936), 15 USCA sec. 15 (b) (1951), 340 U. S. 231, 250; Frankfurter to HHB, n.d., no. 1. Box 217.

75. 340 U. S. 602, 614; Frankfurter to HHB, December 3, 1950, Box 336.

76. *United States* v. *Yellow Cab Co.*, and *Capital Transit Co.* v. *United States*, 340 U. S. 543; Conference Notes, February 9, 1951; HHB to Conference, n.d., Black to HHB, February 16, 1951; Douglas to HHB, February 15, 1951; Frankfurter to HHB, February 8, 1951, nos. 204 and 218, Box 228.

77. 342 U. S. 143; Conference Notes, October 22, 1951, no. 26, Box 231; *Times Picayune Publishing Co.* v. *U.S.*, 345 U. S. 594.

78. *Lilly* v. *Commissioner*, 343 U.S. 90; *Lykes* v. *United States*, 343 U.S. 118; *Watson* v. *Commissioner*, 345 U.S. 544; 343 U.S. 90, 97; Frankfurter to HHB, March 1, 1952, no. 158, Box 238, compare to 343 U.S. 90, 97; 343 U.S. 118, 125; Minton to HHB, March 17, 1952, no. 173, Box 238.

79. 343 U.S. 130; *Commissioner* v. *Wilcox*, 327 U.S. 404 (1945); Minton to HHB, December 21, 1951, Vinson to HHB, December 21, 1951; HHB to Conference, December 19, 1951, no. 175, Box 238.

80. Frankfurter to Conference, December 20, 1951, recirculated and dated January 1952, no. 195, Box 238.

81. Frankfurter to HHB, January 7, 1952, Box 81.

82. Clark to HHB, January 9, 1952, Box 336; Diary, February 4, 1952, Box 3; Jackson to HHB, March 14, 1952, Box 336; *Rutkin* was overruled in *James* v. *U. S.*, 366 U.S. 213 (1961).

83. 342 U. S. 437; *Isbrandtsen Co.* v. *Johnson*, 343 U.S. 779; *Pillsbury* v. *United Engineering Co.*, 342 U.S. 197.

84. 345 U. S. 528, 533; Black to HHB, May 9, 1953, no. 244, Box 253; Leonard G. Ratner, "Child Custody in a Federal System," *Michigan Law Review*, vol. 62 (1964), 795-846.

85. 345 U.S. 653; *United States* v. *Henning*, 344 U.S. 66, 78; for the text of the act, see 38 USC 801 et seq; Vinson to HHB, November 4, 1952, no. 10, Box 249.

86. *Polizzi* v. *Cowles Magazine Co.*, 345 U.S. 663, 669, 672.

87. See, for example: Fowler V. Harper and Alan S. Rosenthal, "What the Supreme Court Did Not Do in the 1949 Term—An Appraisal of Certiorari," *University of Pennsylvania Law Review*, vol. 99 (1950-51), 293. Fowler V. Harper and Edwin D. Etherington, "What the Supreme Court Did Not Do in the 1950 Term," *University of Pennsylvania Law Review*, vol. 100 (1951-52), 354; but c.f. Paul A. Freund," The Supreme Court, 1951 Term Foreword: The Year of the Steel Case," *Harvard Law Review*, vol. 66 (1952), 89.

88. See Frankfurter to Conference, June 1, 1951, and October 10, 1951. Also see Vinson to Frankfurter, October 11, 1951, Box 80, about Frankfurter's efforts to institutionalize a procedure to slow down the decision-making process; 1925 Judiciary Act 43 Stat. 938 (1925), 28 USCA 38 (1950). In *United States* v. *Shannon*, 342 U.S. 288 (1952), and *United States* v. *Jordan*, 342 U. S. 911 (1952), Frankfurter refused to vote at all. The decisions below were affirmed by an equally divided Court.

89. Fred Rodell, "The Supreme Court is Standing Pat," *New Republic*, December 10, 1949; Fred Rodell, "Our Not So Supreme Court," *Look*, July 31, 1951, 60-63.

90. Diary, June 2, 1951, Box 2; *American Bar Association Journal*, vol. 38 (1951), 735, 785-88; Fred Rodell, "Our Not So Supreme Court," 64.

91. Mann to HHB, September 3, 1951; Cheatham to Mann, September 6, 1951, Box 82.

92. Burton to William S. Voorsinger, April 12, 1950, Box 74; A. Powell Davies to HHB, June 6, 1950, Box 70.

## CHAPTER 5

1. Leo Katcher, *Earl Warren: A Political Biography* (New York, 1957), 295, 300-02, 307; see also John D. Weaver, *Warren: The Man, the Court, the Era* (Boston, 1967).

2. Clyde E. Jacobs, "The Warren Court After Three Terms," *Western Political Quarterly*, vol. 9 (1956), 938, 942-45.

3. *Brown* v. *Board of Education*, 347 U.S. 483; *Bolling* v. *Sharpe*, 347

U.S. 497; *Briggs* v. *Elliott, Davis* v. *County Board of Prince Edward,* *Gebhart* v. *Belton,* 347 U. S. 483 (1954), Box 264; Alfred H. Kelly, "The School Desegregation Cases," in John A. Garraty, ed., *Quarrels That Have Shaped the Constitution* (New York, 1964), 243-68; Leon Friedman, ed., *Argument* (New York, 1969); Daniel M. Berman, *It Is So Ordered: The Supreme Court Rules on School Segregation* (New York, 1966), 92ff.

4. Frankfurter to Conference, December 3, 1953, no. 1, Box 263.

5. Conference Notes, December 12, 1953, Box 337.

6. Law clerk to HHB, n.d.; HHB's handwritten sample decree, Box 263.

7. Frankfurter to Conference, January 15, 1954, no. 1, Box 263; c.f. S. Sidney Ulmer, "Earl Warren and the Brown Decision," *Journal of Politics,* vol. 33 (1971), 691-97; see also 697-99 for Ulmer's belief that Frankfurter was opposed to the Warren opinion until the end. However, Frankfurter characteristically would not have bothered to write a memo on how to form a decree in conformity with a decision in which he intended to dissent until after he had written his dissent; Kluger, *Simple Justice,* 685-88.

8. Diary, December 17, 1953, and May 8, 12, and 15, 1954, Box 3; Ulmer, "Earl Warren and the Brown Decision," 699.

9. Law Clerks' Guidelines for Segregation Decree, Box 337. On Harlan, see Edward L. Friedman, Jr. "Mr. Justice Harlan," *Notre Dame Lawyer* vol. 30 (1955), 349-59.

10. Law Clerks' Guidelines for Segregation Decree.

11. Conference Notes, April 16, 1955; HHB's handwritten memo; Frankfurter to Brethren, January 15, 1959, Box 337; Diary, May 25 and 27, 1955, Box 3; Brown case file, 349 U.S. 70, 72, 74, 80. The case was *Virginia* v. *West Virginia,* 222 U.S. 17 (1911); Ulmer, "Bricolage and Assorted Thoughts on Working in the Papers of Supreme Court Justices," 286. The language from the case is "But a state cannot be expected to move with the celerity of a private businessman; it is enough if it proceeds in the language of the English chancery with all deliberate speed," 19-20.

12. Federal Regulation of Lobbying Act, 2 USC Sec. 261-70 (1952). *United States* v. *Harriss,* 347 U. S. 612. *Superior Films, Inc.* v. *Department of Education* and *Commercial Pictures Corp.* v. *Regents of University of State of New York,* 346 U.S. 587; *Irvine* v. *California,* 347 U.S. 128; 346 U.S. 545, 553-54.

13. HHB to Warren, December 31, 1953, no. 38, Box 264; Frankfurter to HHB, February 4, 1954, Box 336. Schubert, *Constitutional Politics,* 610-11; on search and seizure generally, see Landynski, *Search and Seizure and the Supreme Court.*

14. 347 U.S. 442.

15. Barsky was convicted of violating 2 USC 102; *Joint Anti-Fascist Refugee Committee* v. *McGrath*, 341 U.S. 123 (1951); C. Herman Pritchett, *The Political Offender and the Warren Court* (Boston, 1958), 9-11, 62.

16. McKinney's *N. Y. Laws*, Education Law, sects. 6515 and 6516.

17. Law clerk's comments on Frankfurter's dissent, n.d., no. 69, Box 264.

18. *Delta Airlines* v. *Summerfield*, 347 U.S. 574; law clerk to HHB, n.d., no. 223, Box 259.

19. Diary, February 25, 1954, Box 3; Frankfurter to HHB, n.d., no. 28, Box 264. The earlier cases were *United States* v. *Gerlach*, 339 U.S. 725 (1944); *First Iowa Hydroelectric Corp.* v. *Federal Power Commission*, 328 U.S. 152; and *Grand River Dam Authority* v. *Grand Hydro*, 335 U.S. 354 (1948).

20. *Alaska Steamship Co.* v. *Patterson*, 347 U.S. 596, 402.

21. Defense Production Act of 1950, 50 USC 2101-10; general saving statute, 1 USC 109; Douglas to HHB, May 19, 1954; Frankfurter to HHB, n.d., no. 450, Box 267; Diary, May 18, 1954, Box. 3. *Avondale Marine Ways, Inc.* v. *Henderson*, 346 U.S. 366; *Allen* v. *Grand Aircraft*, 347 U. S. 535.

22. *National Labor Relations Board* v. *Local Union No. 1229, International Brotherhood of Electrical Workers*, 346 U.S. 464, 468, 472.

23. *United Construction Workers* v. *Laburnum Construction Corp.*, 347 U.S. 656, 663-64, 671; Maxwell Brandwen, "Punitive-Exemplary Damages in Labor Relations Litigation," *University of Chicago Law Review*, vol. 29 (1963), 460-82.

24. 346 U.S. 356, 364-65. *Federal Baseball Club of Baltimore* v. *National League of Professional Baseball Clubs*, 259 U.S. 200.

25. *Hart* v. *B. F. Keith Vaudeville Exchange*, 262 U.S. 271, 274 (1923), quoted at 346 U.S. 356, 361; Reed to HHB, October 26, 1953; also see Reed's comment on HHB's first draft dissent, Diary, November 12, 1953, no. 18, Box 264.

26. *United States* v. *Schubert*, 348 U.S. 222; *United States* v. *International Boxing Club*, 348 U.S. 236; Conference Notes, November 13, 1954, nos. 36 and 53, Box 269.

27. *United States* v. *California*, 332 U.S. 19 (1947); Executive Order 10426 (1953).

28. *Alabama* v. *Texas et al.*, 347 U.S. 272 (1954); *United States* v. *California*, 381 U.S. 139 (1965).

29. *Rice* v. *Sioux City Memorial Park Cemetery*, 349 U.S. 70.

30. HHB's notes on his bench memo, n.d., no. 28, Box 269; Conference Notes, April 10, 1954, no. 28, Box 269; Docket Book, no. 28, Box 268.

31. *Peters* v. *Hobby*, 349 U.S. 331, 352; Conference Notes, April 23, 1955, no. 376, Box 270; Docket Book, no. 376, Box 268. Raph S. Brown, *Loyalty and Security: Employment Tests in the United States* (New Haven, 1958), 46-47, 408-10.

32. Jacobs, "The Warren Court," 944-45.

33. 349 U.S. 190, 195.

34. Conference Notes, April 9, 1955, nos. 8, 9, and 117, Box 269. The vote to grant certiorari in *Quinn* and *Bart* was unanimous; but only Jackson, Frankfurter, Douglas, and Black voted to grant in *Emspak*; Docket Book, nos. 8, 9, and 117, Box 268.

35. 348 U.S. 407, 417, 419.

36. 348 U.S. 385; 348 U.S. 397; law clerk's memo on Clark's opinion, n.d.; HHB's draft dissent; Reed's draft dissent; Reed to HHB, n.d.; law clerk to HHB, n.d., no. 69, Box 277.

37. 349 U.S. 58, 62.

38. Conference Notes, n.d., no. 412, Box 270; 349 U.S. 375; *Avery* v. *Georgia*, 345 U.S. 559 (1953); David Fellman, *The Defendant's Rights* (New York, 1958), 103.

39. *Williams* v. *State,* 88 S.E. 2nd, 376 (1954).

40. *Commissioner* v. *Estate of Sternberger,* 348 U.S. 1811.

41.Docket Book, no. 24, Box 268; Black to HHB, n.d., no. 24, Box 275; Thomas O'Neill, interview with author, June 20, 1972.

42. Frankfurter to HHB, and Frankfurter to Reed, December 3, 1954, no. 24, Box 275.

43. 348 U.S. 296, 304; *United States* v. *Capps,* 348 U.S. 296.

44. *Federal Power Commission* v. *Colorado Interstate Gas Co.*, 348 U.S. 492, 501-02.

45. Reed to HHB, June 1, 1955; Frankfurter to HHB; O'Neill to HHB, n.d., no. 367, Box 278; *Federal Power Commission* v. *Oregon,* 349 U.S. 435, 457.

46. *National Union of Marine Cooks and Stewards* v. *Arnold*, 348 U.S. 37, 41; 349 U.S. 254.

47. 349 U.S. 254, 273.

48. *Bisso* v. *Inland Waterways Corporation,* 349 U.S. 85; *Boston Metals* v. *Winding Gulf,* 349 U.S. 122; *United States* v. *Nielson,* 349 U.S. 129.

49. Thomas O'Neill and William Matteson, interviews with author, June 20, 1972, and July 2, 1972; HHB to Truman, July 20, 1955; Truman to HHB, July 23, 1955, Box 99.

## CHAPTER 6

1.Clifford E. Lytle, *The Warren Court and Its Critics* (Tucson, 1968); Frankfurter to HHB, October 1, 1955, vol 5, no. 41, Cheatham Collection; Diary, October 1, 1955, Box 3; Robert McKay, "With All Deliberate Speed: Legislative Reaction and Judicial Development, 1956-1957," *Virginia Law Review,* vol. 44 (1958), 1205-45.

2. Frankfurter to Conference, September 15, 1955, Box 286.

3. Conference Notes, November 18, 1955, no. 50, Box 280; Docket Book, no. 50, Box 279; Steve Nelson, *The 13th Juror: The Inside Story of My Trial* (New York, 1955); Roger C. Cramton, "The Supreme Court and State Power to Deal with Subversion and Loyalty," *Minnesota Law Review,* vol. 43 (1959), 1025-82.

4. Conference Notes, October 21, 1955, no. 23, Box 280; Docket Book, no. 23, Box 279; law clerk to HHB, n.d., no. 23, Box 280. The 1892 case was *McAuliffe* v. *Mayor,* 155 Mass. 216 (1892).

5. *Cole* v. *Young,* 351 U.S. 536; Charles Fairman, "The Supreme Court, 1955 Term, Foreword: The Attack on the Segregation Cases," *Harvard Law Review,* vol. 70 (1956), 165; Leon H. Salomon, ed., *The Supreme Court* (New York, 1961), 112ff; *Ullman* v. *United States* 350 U.S. 422.

6. Conference Notes, n.d., no. 3, Box 288; law clerk to HHB, n.d.; Conference notes, October 15, 1955, no. 3, Box 280; *United States ex rel. Toth* v. *Quarles,* 350 U.S. 11; 64 Stat. 107 (1950) UCMJ.

7. Clark cited *Balzac* v. *Puerto Rico,* 258 U.S. 298 (1922); *Hawaii* v. *Mankichi,* 190 U.S. 197 (1903); *Kinsella* v. *Krueger,* 351 U.S. 470; *Reed* v. *Covert,* 351 U.S. 487; Federick B. Wiener, "Court Martial and the Bill of Rights: The Original Practice," *Harvard Law Review,* vol. 72 (1958), 1-49, 266-301; William G. McLaren, "Constitutional Law: Military Trials of Civilians," *American Bar Association Journal,* vol. 45 (1954), 1255ff.; 50 USC Sec. 639 (1952).

8. Conference Notes, May 4, 1956, nos. 701 and 713, Box 281; Docket Book, nos. 701 and 713, Box 278. Two years later (after a change in personnel), the Court, in a Black plurality opinion for four members, reversed its rulings in both cases. *Reid* v. *Covert,* 354 U.S. 1 (1957); see also *Kinsella* v. *U.S. ex rel. Singleton,* 361 U.S. 234 (1960).

9. *Griffin* v. *Illinois,* 351 U.S. 12, 18, 28-29.

10. Law clerk to HHB, n.d., and HHB's notes thereon, no. 95, Box 290; Conference Notes, December 9, 1955, no. 95, Box 290.

11. Law clerk to HHB, March 6, 1956, and HHB's note thereon; 351 U.S. 13, 34; law clerk to HHB, two memos, n.ds., no. 95, Box 290.

12. *Reece* v. *Georgia,* 350 U.S. 85; *Michel* v. *Louisiana,* 350 U.S. 91; Conference Notes, February 5, 1956, no. 32, Box 280; Docket Book, no. 32, Box 278; HHB's notes on certiorari and bench memos, no. 32, Box 280;

John M. Harlan, "What Role Does Oral Argument Play in the Conduct of An Appeal?" *Cornell Law Quarterly,* vol. 41 (1955), 6-11.

13. Frankfurter to HHB, n.d., no. 489, Box 291; *Durley* v. *Mayo*, 351 U.S. 277, 285.

14. *Darcy* v. *Handy*, 351 U.S. 454, 462, 463-64, 469.

15. *United States* v. *Twin Cities Power Co.,* 350 U.S. 222, 239, 242-43; Minton to HHB, October 21, 1955, Box 336; Diary, October 26, 1955, Box 3; Frankfurter to Reed, October 27, 1955, no. 21, Box 288.

16. *Erie* v. *Tompkins*, 304 U.S. 64 (1938) established the doctrine; *Bernhardt* v. *Polygraphics*, 350 U.S. 198, 212; Minton to HHB, December 29, 1955, no. 49, Box 289.

17. *Sears Roebuck and Co.* v. *Mackey*, 351 U.S. 427 (1956); *Cold Metal Process* v. *United Engineering and Foundry Co.,* 351 U.S. 445 (1956).

18. Frankfurter to HHB, May 23, 1956, no. 34, Box 288.

19. *Ryan Stevedoring Co.* v. *Pan-Atlantic S.S. Corporation,* 350 U.S. 124.

20. *East Texas Lines* v. *Frozen Food Express,* 351 U.S. 49.

21. *United Mine Workers* v. *Arkansas Oak Flooring Co.,* 351 U.S. 62; Paul R. Hays, "State Courts and Federal Preemption," *Missouri Law Review,* vol. 23 (1958), 373.

22. Law clerk to HHB, n.d., no. 227, Box 290.

23. *Mastro Plastics Corporation* v. *NLRB*, 350 U.S. 270; 350 U.S. 270, 284, 288; Diary, February 23, 1956, Box 3; Archibald Cox, "The Legal Nature of Collective Bargaining Agreements," *Michigan Law Review*, vol. 57 (1958), 1-18, criticized the decision.

24. Frankfurter to Reed, February 14, 1956, the HHB's note thereon, no. 19, Box 287.

25. *International Harvester Credit Corporation* v. *Goodrich*, 350 U.S. 537, 547; HHB was quoting from Cardozo's opinion in *Burnet* v. *Wells*, 289 U.S. 670, 677, 678 (1933); law clerk to HHB, n.d., no. 82, Box 289.

26. 350 U.S. 359, 364; HHB to law clerks, n.d.; Frankfurter to HHB, December 7, 1955, no. 72, Box 289.

27. Minton to HHB, May 3, 1956; Frankfurter to HHB, and HHB's note thereon, December 7, 1955, Box 336.

28. Fred Rodell, *Nine Men: A Political History of the Supreme Court from 1900-1950* (New York, 1955), see especially 309-10 for his treatment of HHB; HHB to John Murphy, April 10, 1956, Box 102.

29. Leo Katcher, *Earl Warren: A Political Biography* (New York, 1967), 354-55; Walter Murphy, *Congress and the Court: A Case Study in the American Political Process* (Chicago, 1962), 86-96; Francis P. McQuade and Alexander T. Kardos, "Mr. Justice Brennan and His Legal Philosophy," *Notre Dame Lawyer,* vol. 32 (1958), 321-49; Daniel M. Berman,

"Mr. Justice Whittaker: A Preliminary Appraisal," *Missouri Law Review,* vol. 24 (1959), 1-15.

30. Frankfurter to Conference, September 5, 1956, Box 302.

31. *Gold* v. *United States,* 352 U.S. 985; *Roviaro* v. *United States,* 353 U.S. 53, 62, 65; Docket Book, no. 137, Box 292, everyone voted to grant certiorari; Conference Notes, January 25, 1957, no. 137, Box 295; Frankfurter to HHB, January 25, 1957, Box 336.

32. Brennan to HHB, March 7, 1957; Harlan to HHB, March 7, 1957, no. 58, Box 305. *Jencks* v. *United States,* 353 U.S. 657, 676-78; critics of the decision noted Brennan's misuse of a John Marshall quote from the Burr trial and his failure to say whether the decision was based on a statute of the Constitution; L. Brent Bozell, "Blueprint for Judicial Chaos," *National Review,* vol. 4 (July 20, 1957), 80-85; Murphy, *Congress and the Court,* 121.

33. Conference Notes, October 19, 1956, and March 22, 1957, no. 23, Box 298; 71 Stat. 595 (1957). Note, "The Jencks Legislation: Problems in Prospect," *Yale Law Journal,* vol. 67 (1958), 674-99; see also *Rosenberg* v. *U.S.,* 360 U.S. 367 (1959).

34. Murphy, *Congress and the Court,* 100-102; 354 U.S. 178; Alan L. Bioff, "*Watkins* v. *United States* as a Limitation on the Power of Congressional Investigating Committees," *Michigan Law Review,* vol. 56 (1957), 272-84.

35. 354 U.S. 254; Conference Notes, March 8, 1951, no. 175, Box 295; Clark and Reed were the only ones who did not vote to grant certiorari, Docket Book, no. 175, Box 292.

36. *Schware* v. *Board of Bar Examiners,* 353 U.S. 232; *Konigsberg* v. *State Bar,* 353 U.S. 252; Conference Notes, January 18, 1957, nos. 5 and 92, Box 297.

37. Law clerk to HHB, no. 5, Box 297, Roger Cramton, HHB's law clerk, personal interview with author, July 6, 1972. The state bar committee refused to certify Konigsberg a second time on the ground that he had obstructed an investigation into his qualifications to practice law. The Supreme Court upheld this second exclusion; *Konigsberg* v. *California,* 336 U.S. 36 (1961); Warren, Black, Douglas, and Brennan dissented. William H. Rehnquist, "The Bar Admission Cases: A Strange Judicial Aberration," *American Bar Association Journal,* vol. 44 (1958), 229ff.

38. Conference Notes, October 12, 1956, and November 2, 1956; law clerk to HHB, two memos, n.ds., nos. 6-8, Box 293; Harlan to HHB, June 4, 1957, Box 336. Robert Mollan, "Smith Act Prosecutions: The Effect of the Dennis and Yates Decisions, *University of Pittsburgh Law Review,* vol. 26 (1965), 705-48; Murphy, *Congress and the Court,* 22.

39. 354 U.S. 363; Docket Book, no. 407, Box 292; law clerk to HHB, n.d.; Conference Notes, April 5, 1957, no. 407, Box 296.

40. *United States* v. *International Union United Automobile Workers*, 352 U.S. 567, 589; Conference Notes, December 7, 1956, no. 44, Box 293. The Court voted unanimously to grant probable jurisdiction. Docket Book, no. 44, Box 292.

41. *Paoli* v. *United States,* 352 U.S. 232, 242; Conference Notes, October 22, 1956, no. 33, Box 293; Harlan to HHB, January 8, 1957, no. 33, Box 304; Harlan to HHB, January 28, 1957, Box 336; *Chessman* v. *Teets,* 354 U.S. 156.

42. 352 U.S. 407, 417; Diary, February 19, 1957, Box 3; Brennan to HHB, February 19, 1957, no. 289, Box 307.

43. 352 U.S. 385; 353 U.S. 346; 354 U.S. 118; also, in *Walker* v. *City of Hutchinson,* 352 U.S. 112, Burton dissented from Black's opinion that newspaper publication alone was inadequate notice of a condemnation proceeding to a home owner.

44. 353 U.S. 586, 654; law clerk to HHB, n.d., no. 3, Box 293; Cramton, personal interview, July 6, 1972; Bruce Bromley, "Business's Views of the DuPont-General Motors Decision," *Georgetown Law Journal,* vol. 46 (1958), 646-54; William L. McGovern, "The Power and the Glory: The DuPont-GM Decision," *Georgetown Law Journal,* vol. 46, 655-71.

45. 353 U.S. 448; 353 U.S. 547; 353 U.S. 550.

46. 353 U.S. 1; 353 U.S. 20; 353 U.S. 26.

47. *Pan-Atlantic Steamship Corporation* v. *Atlantic Coast Line Railroad Company,* 353 U.S. 436.

48. 354 U.S. 351; 353 U.S. 81; 353 U.S. 180; HHB's dissents were actually filed largely because his clerks persuaded him to do so. Cramton note; also see law clerk to HHB, n.d., no. 89, Box 306; Harlan to HHB, March 28, 1957, no. 257, Box 306.

49. 353 U.S. 382.

50. 353 U.S. 325; 353 U.S. 210; 354 U.S. 457.

51. S. Sidney Ulmer, "Supreme Court Behavior and Civil Rights," *Western Political Quarterly,* vol. 13 (1960), 293; Cramton, personal interview, July 1972; Frankfurter to HHB, June 12, 1957, Box 306; E. W. Kelly and M. Leiserson, "The Use of Power in the Supreme Court: The Opinion Assignments of Earl Warren, 1953-1960," *Journal of Public Law,* vol. 19 (1970), 49-68.

## CHAPTER 7

1. Harold Spaeth, "The Judicial Restraint of Mr. Justice Frankfurter: Myth or Reality, *"Midwest Journal of Politics,* vol. 8 (1964), 22-38; S. Sidney Ulmer, "An Analysis of Behavior Patterns on the United States

Supreme Court," *Journal of Politics,* vol. 22 (1960), 629-53; S. Sidney Ulmer, "Supreme Court Behavior and Civil Rights," *Western Political Quarterly,* vol. 13 (1960), 293; Roger Cramton, interview with author, July 1972.

2. Murphy, *Congress and the Court,* 120-22; in Chaps. 9 and 10, Murphy states that the Court backed down because of legislative attempts to curb its power by the 1958 term—in such cases as *Barenblatt* v. *United States,* 360 U.S. 104 (1959), and *Uphaus* v. *Wyman,* 360 U.S. 72 (1959)—when it was not really necessary. This backing away, he believes, might have begun surfacing during the 1957 term. See also John R. Schmidhauser, Larry L. Berg and Albert Melon, "Dimensions in Supreme Court-Congressional Relations, 1945-1968, "*Washington University Law Quarterly* (1971), 209-51.

3. Katcher, *Earl Warren,* 342; Murphy, *Congress and the Court,* 226-27; C. Herman Pritchett, *Congress versus the Supreme Court* (Minneapolis, 1961), 89-95. Frankfurter to Conference, September 30, 1957, Box 320.

4. Warren to Conference, October 7, 1958, Box 320.

5. Clark to Conference; Frankfurter to Conference, October 7, 1957, Box 320.

6. "Supreme Court Per Curiam Practice: A Critique," *Harvard Law Review,* vol. 69 (1955-56), 707; Ernest J. Brown, "The Supreme Court—1957 Term, Foreword: Process of Law," *Harvard Law Review,* vol. 72 (1958-59), 77. There were 235 opinions, including 15 per curiams and 119 opinions of the Court.

7. *Fidelity Philadelphia Trust Co.* v. *Smith,* 356 U.S. 274, 281.

8. 356 U.S. 634; 356 U.S. 342; 355 U.S. 131.

9. Harlan to HHB, December 4, 1957; Frankfurter to HHB, two memos; law clerks to HHB, no. 11, Box 321.

10. Frankfurter to HHB; Harlan to HHB, March 26, 1958; Whittaker to HHB, May 2, 1958; law clerk to HHB, no. 53, Box 323.

11. Law clerk to HHB, no. 21, Box 32; Brown, "The Supreme Court—1957 Term," 145; law clerk to HHB, n.d., no. 21, Box 321.

12. 357 U.S. 155, 168; Brennan to HHB, April 21, 1958; law clerk to HHB, no. 29, Box 322.

13. 355 U.S. 286.

14. 355 U.S. 155, 164; Docket Book, no. 42, Box 309; Burton, Harlan, Reed, and Clark had voted to deny certiorari. Conference Notes, October 21, 1957; law clerk to HHB, November 15, 1957, no. 42, Box 322; Joseph M. Sneed, "The McNabb-Mallory Rule: Its Rise, Rationale and Rescue," *Georgetown Law Journal,* vol. 47 (1958), 1-44.

15. 357 U.S. 426, 430; Frankfurter to HHB, no. 158, Box 324.

16. 346 U.S. 560; Docket Book, no. 99, Box 309; HHB's notes on certiorari and bench memos, no. 99, Box 311.

17. 357 U.S. 399, 405; Frankfurter to HHB, n.d., no. 63, Box 324; *Slow-chower* v. *Board of Higher Education,* 350 U.S. 551 (1956); *Nowak* v. *United States,* 356 U.S. 370.

18. Diary, April 2 and 30, May 7 and 24, June 7 and 13, and July 1, 9, 14, 16, and 17, 1958, Box 4. Burton was the last justice to be appointed from the Congress; Daniel M. Berman, "Mr. Justice Stewart: A Preliminary Appraisal," *University of Cincinnati Law Review,* vol. 28 (1959), 401-21.

19. Diary, September 19, and October 6, 1958, Box 5; *Cooper* v. *Aaron,* 358 U.S. 1, 18 (1958); *Faubus* v. *Aaron,* 361 U.S. 197 (1959); *New York Times,* August 31, 1958, sect. 4, 1.

20. *Bowdoin College Bulletin,* no. 322 (March 1959), 12, 18.

21. Diary, October 6, 1958, Box 4; *New Republic,* October 20, 1958, vol. 139, 6, editorials and clippings in Box 427; vol. 5 of the Cheatham Collection contains copies of letters, newspapers articles, and clippings dealing with HHB's retirement.

22. Court to HHB, October 13, 1958; Frankfurter to HHB, October 7, 1958; Brennan to HHB, n.d., Box 432.

23. Dairy, October 13, and December 9, 1958, January 11 and 19, 1959, Box 4; David Danielski, "A Supreme Court Justice Steps Down," *Yale Review,* vol. 54 (1965), 411-25.

24. Court of appeals material, Boxes 344-60, Harlan to HHB, June 29, 1963; Goldberg to HHB, May 2, 1963, Box 432; *New York Times,* October 29, 1964, 35.

## CHAPTER 8

1. John R. Schmidhauser, "The Justices of the Supreme Court: A Collective Portrait," *Midwest Journal of Political Science,* vol. 1 (1959), 1-57; Stuart Nagel, "Characteristics of Supreme Court Greatness," *American Bar Association Journal,* vol. 56 (1970), 957-59. Most justices have been white Anglo-Saxon Protestants of high social status who have been reared in urban environments by civic-minded, politically active, economically comfortable families. They tend to be holders of B.A. and L.L.B. degrees, to have held public office, and to be generally well educated. Harold Burton fit the pattern almost perfectly.

2. Glendon A. Schubert, *The Judicial Mind: The Attitudes and Ideologies of Supreme Court Justices, 1946-1963* (Evanston, 1965), describes the activities and ideologies of Supreme Court justices between 1946 and 1963 by using scalogram analysis and factor analysis. His conclusion that Burton was a conservative, based upon the voting patterns in the cases alone, was well founded. The results of his scalogram analysis are confirmed by the traditional approach of judicial biography used herein. Where significant differences in coefficients occurred (a coefficient of less

than 0.900 in my replication of Schubert's work using his method), the errors were in Schubert's characterizations of the cases. Civil liberties cases, deciding between governmental authority and the claims of private citizens, were easy to characterize. Economic $E$ scale cases involving a choice between the "economically affluent and the economically underprivileged" were more difficult. The method is explained by Schubert in Chap. 3, and the coefficients are in the Appendix. A good, recent bibliographical essay on the development of behavioral methods in the historical context is Glendon Schubert, "Judicial Process and Behavior, 1963-71," in James A. Robinson, ed., *Political Science Annual in International Review III,* 1972, 73-280.

3. More recent work has demonstrated that analysis of subscales within Schubert's broad Economic and Civil Liberties categories may indicate more or less libertarian characteristics in the voting pattern of a justice. For example, Burton's race relations decisions, which were extremely liberal, except in his first opinion, when aggregated with all of his civil liberties opinions did not relieve him from the anti-civil libertarian appearance of Schubert's $C$ scale. See, for example, Harold J. Spaeth, "An Analysis of Judicial Attitudes in the Labor Relations Decisions of the Warren Court," *Journal of Politics,* vol. 25 (1963), 290-311; and Harold J. Spaeth, "Race Relations and the Warren Court," *University of Detroit Law Journal,* vol. 43 (1965), 255-72.

4. David J. Danielski, "Legislative and Judicial Decision Making: The Case of Harold H. Burton," in S. Sidney Ulmer, ed., *Political Decision Making* (New York, 1970), 121-46; David N. Atkinson and Dale A. Neuman, "Toward a Cost Theory of Judicial Alignments: The Case of the Truman Bloc," *Midwest Journal of Political Science,* 13 (1969), 271-83.

5. Abraham, *The Judicial Process,* 355ff., on adherence to the sixteen great maxims of judicial self-restraint. Burton would have achieved a perfect positive score.

6. Interview with Burton's clerks, July 1972.

7. Glendon A. Schubert, *Constitutional Politics,* New York, 1960, 573.

8. On the role of clerks, see William H. Rehnquist, "Who Writes Decisions of the Supreme Court?" *U.S. News and World Report,* December 13, 1957. The conclusions concerning Burton's relationship with his clerks are based upon interviews with at least one clerk from each term of his service on the Court.

9. *Jencks* v. *U.S.,* 353 U.S. 657 (1957). See *Rosenberg* v. *United States,* 360 U.S. 367 (1959); *Palermo* v. *United States,* 360 U.S. 343 (1959); *Joint Anti-Fascist Refugee Committee* v. *McGarth,* 341 U.S. 123 (1951).

10. All by Harold H. Burton: "The Cornerstone of Constitutional Law: The Extraordinary Case of Marbury v. Madison," *American Bar Association Journal* (hereafter cited as *ABA Journal*), vol 36 (1950), 805-08, 881-83; "Two Significant Decisions: Ex Parte Milligan and Ex Parte McCardle," *ABA Journal,* vol. 41 (1955), 121-24, 176-77; "The Legal Tender Cases: A Celebrated Supreme Court Reversal, *ABA Journal,* vol. 42 (1956), 231-34; "Justice the Guardian of Liberty: John Marshall at the Trial of Aaron Burr," *ABA Journal,* vol. 37 (1951), 735-38, 785-88; "John Marshall, the Man," *University of Pennsylvania Law Review,* vol. 104 (1955), 3-8; "The Dartmouth College Case: A Dramatization," *ABA Journal,* vol. 38 (1952), 991-94, 1055-57. His clerks took no part in the research or writing. For his efforts, Warren dubbed him "Court Historian."

# Bibliography

## I. Primary Sources

### A. UNPRINTED

Harold H. Burton Papers, Manuscript Division, Library of Congress, Washington, D.C.

Felix Frankfurter Papers, Manuscript Division, Library of Congress, Washington, D.C.

Harold H. Burton Photographic Collection, Photographic and Film Division, Library of Congress, Washington, D.C.

Felix Frankfurter Papers, Treasure Room, Harvard Law Library, Cambridge, Massachusetts

Transcripts of Oral Arguments before the Supreme Court, National Archives, Washington, D.C.

Frank Murphy Papers, Michigan Historical Collection, University of Michigan, Ann Arbor, Michigan

Sherman Minton Papers, Truman Library, Independence, Missouri

NAACP Papers, Manuscript Division, Library of Congress, Washington, D.C.

Tess Cheatham Collection, in possession of William S. Burton, Cleveland, Ohio

Interviews with Burton clerks

Interviews with William S. Burton, Robert S. Burton, Deborah Adler, and Barbara Weidner

### B. PRINTED

*Atlantic Monthly,* Boston, Massachusetts.
*Bowdoin College Bulletin* #332, Brunswick, Maine.
*Boston Herald,* Boston, Massachusetts.
*Cleveland News,* Cleveland, Ohio.

*Cleveland Plain Dealer,* Cleveland, Ohio.
*Cleveland Press,* Cleveland, Ohio.
*Cleveland Union Leader,* Cleveland, Ohio.
*Congressional Record,* Government Printing Office, Washington, D.C.
*New Republic,* Washington, D.C.
*Newsweek,* New York, New York.
*New York Times,* New York, New York.
*Public Papers of the Presidents of the United States.*
*Occasional Proceedings of the Bar and Officers of the Supreme Court in Memory of Harold H. Burton, May 24, 1965,* 381 U.S. v. (1964).
*Time,* Chicago, Illinois.
*Toledo Union Leader,* Toledo, Ohio.
*United States Reports,* Government Printing Office, Washington, D.C.
*United States Statutes At Large,* Government Printing Office, Washington, D.C.
*Washington Post,* Washington, D.C.

## II. Secondary Sources

### A. BOOKS

Abraham, Henry J. *The Judicial Process.* New York, 1962.
Atkinson, David. "Justice Sherman Minton and the Supreme Court." Ph.D. dissertation, University of Iowa, 1969.
Baker, Liva. *Felix Frankfurter.* New York, 1969.
Berman, Daniel. *It Is So Ordered: The Supreme Court Rules on School Segregation.* New York, 1966.
Boles, Donald E. *The Bible, Religion and the Public Schools.* Ames, Iowa, 1965.
Bontecor, Eleanor. *The Federal Loyalty Security Program.* Ithaca, 1953.
Burton, Harold H. *600 Days of Service.* Portland, Oregon, 1921.
Campbell, Thomas F. *Daniel E. Morgan, 1877-1949: The Good Citizen in Politics.* Cleveland, 1966.
Chase, Harold W. *Security and Liberty: The Problem of the Native Communists, 1947-1955.* New York, 1955.
Corwin, Edward S. *The President, Office and Powers.* New York, 1940.
Fellman, David, *The Defendant's Rights.* New York, 1958.
Friedman, Samuel. *The Rosenberg Case: Fact and Fiction.* New York, 1953.
Friedman, Leon, ed. *Argument.* New York, 1969.
Garraty, John A., ed. *Quarrels That Have Shaped the Constitution.* New York, 1964.

Gerhart, Eugene C. *America's Advocate: Robert H. Jackson.* Indianapolis, 1958.

Harbaugh, William. *Lawyer's Lawyer: The Life of John W. Davis.* New York, 1973.

Harper, Fowler V. *Justice Rutledge and the Bright Constellation.* Indianapolis, 1965.

Howard, J. Woodford, Jr. *Mr. Justice Murphy: A Political Biography.* Princeton, 1968.

Katcher, Leo, *Earl Warren: A Political Biography.* New York, 1967.

Kluger, Richard. *Simple Justice: The History of Brown v. Board of Education and Black America's Struggle for Equality.* New York, 1976.

Kurland, Phillip B. *Religion and the Law.* Chicago, 1962.

Landynski, Jacob W. *Search and Seizure and the Supreme Court.* Baltimore, 1966.

Lytle, Clifford E., *The Warren Court and Its Critics.* Tucson, 1968.

McNerney, Walter J., et al. *Hospital and Medical Economics.* 2 vols. Chicago, 1962.

Marion, George. *The Communist Trial: An American Cross Roads.* New York, 1950.

Mason, Alpheus T. *Harlan Fiske Stone: Pillar of the Law.* New York, 1956.

Matthews, Donald. *U.S. Senators and Their World.* Chapel Hill, 1960.

Morgan, Richard E. *The Supreme Court and Religion.* New York, 1972.

Murphy, Paul L. *The Constitution in Crisis Times, 1918-1969.* New York, 1972.

Murphy, Walter F. *Congress and the Court: A Case Study in the American Political Process.* Chicago, 1962.

———. *Elements of Judicial Strategy.* Chicago, 1964.

Nelson, Steve, *The 13th Juror: The Inside Story of My Trial.* New York, 1955.

Patterson, James T. *Mr. Republican: A Biography of Robert A. Taft.* Boston, 1972.

Phillips, Cabell. *The Truman Presidency: A History of Triumphant Succession.* New York, 1966.

Pritchett, C. Herman. *Civil Liberties and the Vinson Court.* Chicago, 1954.

———. *Congress versus the Supreme Court.* Minneapolis, 1961.

———. *The Political Offender and the Warren Court.* Boston, 1958.

Reel, Adolf F. *The Case of General Yamashita.* Chicago, 1949.

Riddle, Donald H. *The Truman Committee: A Study in Congressional Responsibility.* New Brunswick, N.J., 1964.

Rodel, Fred. *Nine Men: A Political History of the Supreme Court from 1900-1950.* New York, 1955.

Rose, William. *Cleveland: The Making of a City.* Cleveland, 1950.

Salomon, Leon H., ed. *The Supreme Court.* New York, 1961.

Schubert, Glendon A. *Constitutional Politics: The Political Behavior of Supreme Court Justices and the Constitutional Policies That They Make.* New York, 1960.

――――. *The Judicial Mind: The Attitudes and Ideologies of Supreme Court Justices, 1946-1963.* Evanston, 1965.

Seidman, Joel. *American Labor from Defense to Reconversion.* Chicago, 1953.

Thomas, Helen S. *Felix Frankfurter: Scholar on the Bench.* Baltimore, 1969.

Truman, Harry S. *Memories: Years of Trial and Hope.* Garden City, N.Y., 1955.

Ulmer, S. Sidney. *Courts as Small and Not So Small Groups.* New York, 1971.

――――, ed. *Political Decision-Making.* New York, 1970.

Vose, Clement. *For Caucasians Only: The Supreme Court, the NAACP and the Restrictive Covenant Cases.* Berkeley, 1959.

Weaver, John D. *Warren: The Man, the Court, the Era.* Boston, 1967.

Westin, Alan F. *The Anatomy of a Constitutional Law Case: Youngstown Sheet and Tube Co. v. Sawyer; The Steel Seizure Decision.* New York, 1958.

Young, Roland. *Congressional Politics in the Second World War.* New York, 1956.


B. ARTICLES

Arval, Morris. "Academic Freedom and Loyalty Oaths." *Law and Contemporary Problems,* vol. 28 (1963), 487-524.

Atkinson, David N., and Newman, Dale A. "Toward a Cost Theory of Judicial Alignments: The Case of the Truman Bloc." *Midwest Journal of Political Science,* vol. 13 (1969), 271-83.

Atkinson, David N. "American Constitutionalism Under Stress: Mr. Justice Burton's Response to National Security Issues." *Houston Law Review,* vol. 9 (1971), 271-85.

Barber, Henry W. "Religious Liberty v. Police Power—Jehovah's Witnesses." *American Political Science Review,* vol. 41 (1947), 226-47.

Berman, Daniel M. "Mr. Justice Stewart: A Preliminary Appraisal." *University of Cincinnati Law Review,* vol. 28 (1959), 401-20.

————. "Mr. Justice Whittaker: A Preliminary Appraisal." *Missouri Law Review,* vol. 24 (1959), 1-15.

Beth, Loren P. "Group Libel and Free Speech." *Minnesota Law Review,* vol. 39 (1955), 167-84.

Bioff, Alan L. "Watkins v. United States as a Limitation on the Powers of Congressional Investigating Committees." *Michigan Law Review,* vol. 56 (1957), 272-84.

Blaustein, Albert P., and Field, Andrew H. "Overruling Opinions in the Supreme Court." *Michigan Law Review,* vol. 57 (1958), 151-94.

Bozell, L. Brent. "Blueprint for Judicial Chaos." *National Review,* vol. 4 (July 20, 1957), 80-85.

Brandwen, Maxwell. "Punitive-Exemplary Damages in Labor Relations Litigation." *University of Chicago Law Review,* vol. 29 (1963), 460-82.

Bromley, Bruce. "Business's Views of the DuPont-General Motors Decision." *Georgetown Law Journal,* vol. 46 (1958), 646-54.

Brown, Ernest J. "The Supreme Court, 1957 Term, Foreword: Process of Law." *Harvard Law Review,* vol. 72 (1958-59), 77.

Corwin, Edward S. "The Steel Seizure Case—A Judicial Brick Without Straw." *Columbia Law Review,* vol. 53 (1953), 53-66.

Cox, Archibald. "The Legal Nature of Collective Bargaining Agreements." *Michigan Law Review,* vol. 57 (1958), 1-36.

Cramton, Roger C. "The Supreme Court and State Power to Deal with Subversion and Loyalty." *Minnesota Law Review,* vol. 43 (1959), 1052-82.

Currie, David. "Suitcase Divorce in the Conflict of Laws." *University of Chicago Law Review,* vol. 34 (1966), 26-77.

Danielski, David. "A Supreme Court Justice Steps Down." *Yale Review,* vol. 54 (1965), 411-25.

Dillard, Irving. "Truman Reshapes the Supreme Court." *Atlantic Monthly,* vol. 184 (1949), 30-33.

Dodd, E. Merrick. "The Supreme Court and Fair Labor Standards, 1941-1945." *Harvard Law Review,* vol. 59 (1946), 321-73.

Dutton, C. B. "Mr. Justice Tom C. Clark." *Indiana Law Journal,* vol. 26 (1951), 169-84.

Fairman, Charles. "The Supreme Court, 1955 Term, Foreword: The Attack on the Segregation Cases." *Harvard Law Review,* vol. 70 (1956), 83-94.

Frank, John P. "Court and Constitution: The Passive Period." *Vanderbilt Law Review,* vol. 4 (1951), 400-26.

————. "Fred Vinson and the Chief Justiceship." *University of Chicago Law Review,* vol. 21 (1954), 212-46.

————. "The United States Supreme Court: 1946-47." *University of Chicago Law Review,* vol. 15 (1947-48), 1-50.

————. "The United States Supreme Court: 1948-49." *University of Chicago Law Review,* vol. 17 (1950), 1-55.

————. "The United States Supreme Court: 1949-50." *University of Chicago Law Review,* vol. 18 (1950-51), 1-54.

Freund, Paul A. "The Supreme Court, 1951 Foreword: The Year of the Steel Case." *Harvard Law Review,* vol. 66 (1952), 89-97.

Friedman, Edward L., Jr. "Mr. Justice Harlan." *Notre Dame Lawyer,* vol. 30 (1955), 349-59.

Gibbons, Gerald R. "Price Fixing in Patent Licenses and the Antitrust Laws." *Virginia Law Review,* vol. 5 (1965), 273-304.

Glass, Carter, III. "Intergovernmental Immunities from Taxation." *Washington and Lee Law Review,* vol. 4 (1946), 48-68.

Gorfinkel, John A., and Mack, Julian W., II. "Dennis v. United States and the Clear and Present Danger Rule." *California Law Review,* vol. 39 (1951), 475-501.

Harlan, John M. "What Role Does Oral Argument Play in the Conduct of an Appeal?" *Cornell Law Quarterly,* vol. 41 (1955), 6-11.

Harper, Fowler V., and Etherington, Edwin D. "What the Supreme Court Did Not Do in the 1950 Term." *University of Pennsylvania Law Review,* vol. 100 (1951-52), 354-409.

Harper, Fowler V., and Rosenthal, Alan S. "What the Supreme Court Did Not Do in the 1949 Term—An Appraisal of Certiorari." *University of Pennsylvania Law Review,* vol. 99 (1950-51), 292-325.

Haugh, Richard Lee. "The Jehovah's Witnesses Cases in Retrospect." *Western Political Quarterly,* vol. 6 (1953), 78-92.

Hays, Paul R. "State Courts and Federal Preemption." *Missouri Law Review,* vol. 23 (1958), 373-400.

Howard, J. Woodford. "Judicial Biography and the Behavioral Persuasion." *American Political Science Review,* vol. 65 (1971), 704-15.

————. "On the Fluidity of Judicial Choice." *American Political Science Review,* vol. 62 (1968), 43-56.

Jacobs, Clyde E. "The Warren Court After Three Terms." *Western Political Quarterly,* vol. 9 (1956), 938-45.

Kauper, Paul G. "Church and State: Cooperative Separation." *Michigan Law Review,* vol. 60 (1961), 1-40.

Kelley, E. W., and Leiserson, M. "The Use of Power in the Supreme Court: The Opinion Assignments of Earl Warren, 1953-1960." *Journal of Public Law,* vol. 19 (1970), 49-68.

McGovern, William L. "The Power and the Glory: The DuPont-GM Decision." *Georgetown Law Journal,* vol. 46 (1958), 655-71.

McKay, Robert. "With All Deliberate Speed: Legislative Reaction and Judicial Development, 1956-1957." *Virginia Law Review,* vol. 44 (1958), 1205-45.

McLaren, William G. "Constitutional Law: Military Trials of Civilians." *American Bar Association Journal,* vol. 45 (1959), 255-58, 308-09.

McQuade, Francis P., and Kardon, Alexander T. "Mr. Justice Brennan and His Legal Philosophy." *Notre Dame Lawyer,* vol. 32 (1958), 321-49.

Malick, Clay P. "Terry *v.* Adams: Governmental Responsibility for the Protection of Civil Rights." *Western Political Quarterly,* vol. 7 (1954), 51-64.

Mollan, Robert. "Smith Act Prosecutions: The Effect of the Dennis and Yates Decisions." *University of Pittsburgh Law Review,* vol. 26 (1965), 705-48.

Murphy, Walter F. "Courts as Small Groups." *Harvard Law Review,* vol. 79 (1966), 1565-72.

Nagel, Stuart. "Characteristics of Supreme Court Greatness." *American Bar Association Journal,* vol. 56 (1970), 957-59.

Nathanson, Nathaniel L. "The Communist Trial and the Clear-and-Present-Danger Test." *Harvard Law Review,* vol. 63 (1950), 1167-75.

Note. "Developments in the Law—Immigration and Nationalism."*Harvard Law Review,* vol. 66 (1954), 643-745.

———. "The Jencks Legislation: Problems and Prospects." *Yale Law Journal,* vol. 67 (1958), 674-99.

———. "The Released Time Cases Revisited: A Study of Group Decision-making by the Supreme Court." *Yale Law Journal,* vol. 83 (1974), 1202-36.

Parrish, Michael. "Cold War Justice: The Supreme Court and the Rosenbergs." *American Historical Review,* vol. 82 (1977), 805-42.

Powell, Thomas Reed. "And Repent at Leisure: An Inquiry Into the Unhappy Lot of Those Whom Nevada Hath Joined Together and North Carolina Hath Rent Asunder." *Harvard Law Review,* vol. 58 (1945), 930-1017.

Ratner, Leonard G. "Child Custody in a Federal System." *Michigan Law Review,* vol. 62 (1964), 795-848.

Rehnquist, William H. "The Bar Admission Cases: A Strange Judicial Aberration." *American Bar Association Journal,* vol. 44 (1958), 229-32.

———. "Who Writes Decisions of the Supreme Court?" *U.S. News and World Report* (December 13, 1957), 74-75.

Richardson, Richard J., and Vines, Kenneth N. "Review, Dissent, and the Appellate Process: A Political Interpretation." *Journal of Politics,* vol. 29 (1967), 597-616.

Richardson, Seth. "The Federal Employee Loyalty Program." *Columbia Law Review,* vol. 51 (1951), 546-63.

Reisman, David. "Democracy and Defamation: Control of Group Libel." *Columbia Law Review,* vol. 42 (1942), 727-80.

Robinson, James A., ed. *Political Science Annual and International Review,* vol. 3 (1972), 73-280.

Rodell, Fred. "An Open Letter to Mr. Justice Burton." *Progressive* (October 1, 1945), 50.

———. "Our Not So Supreme Court." *Look* (July 31, 1951).

———. "The Supreme Court is Standing Pat." *New Republic* (December 10, 1949).

Schmidhauser, John R. "The Justices of the Supreme Court: A Collective Portrait." *Midwest Journal of Political Science,* vol. 1 (1959), 1-57.

———, Berg, Larry L., and Melone, Albert. "Dimensions in Supreme Court-Congressional Relations, 1945-1968." *Washington University Law Quarterly* (1971), 209-51.

Shapiro, Martin, "Judicial Modesty: Down with the Old!—Up with New." *University of California at Los Angeles Law Review,* vol. 10 (1963), 533-60.

———. "Toward a Theory of Stare Decisis." *Journal of Legal Studies,* vol. 1 (1972), 125-34.

Snyder, Eloise. "The Supreme Court As A Small Group." *Social Forces,* vol. 36 (1958), 236-38.

Sorauf, Frank J. *"Zorach v. Clauson:* The Impact of a Supreme Court Decision." *American Political Science Review,* vol. 53 (1959), 777-91.

Spaeth, Harold J. "An Analysis of Judicial Attitudes in the Labor Relatins Decisions of the Warren Court." *Journal of Politics,* vol. 25 (1963), 290-311.

———. "The Judicial Restraint of Mr. Justice Frankfurter: Myth or Reality." *Midwest Journal of Politics,* vol. 8 (1964), 22-38.

———. "Race Relations and the Warren Court." *University of Detroit Law Journal,* vol. 43 (1965), 255-72.

Tanenhaus, Joseph. "Picketing as Free Speech: The Growth of the New Law of Picketing from 1940 to 1952." *Cornell Law Quarterly,* vol. 38 (1952), 1-50.

Ulmer, S. Sidney. "An Analysis of Behavior Patterns on the United States Supreme Court." *Journal of Politics,* vol. 22 (1960), 629-53.

———. "Bricolage and Assorted Thoughts on Working in the Papers of Supreme Court Justices." *Journal of Politics,* vol. 35 (1973), 286.

———. "Dissent Behavior and the Social Background of Supreme Court Justices." *Journal of Politics,* vol. 32 (1970), 580-98.

———. "Earl Warren and the Brown Decision." *Journal of Politics,* vol. 33 (1971), 691-97.

———. "Supreme Court Behavior and Civil Rights." *Western Political Quarterly,* vol. 13 (1960), 288-311.

Wallace, Henry L. "Mr. Justice Minton: Hoosier Justice on the Supreme Court." *Indiana Law Journal,* vol. 34 (1959), 145-205.

Wiener, Frederick B. "Court Martial and the Bill of Rights: The Original Practice." *Harvard Law Review,* vol. 72 (1958), 1-49.

## III. Mr. Justice Burton's Writings in Legal History

"The Cornerstone of Constitutional Law: The Extraordinary Case of Marbury *v.* Madison." *American Bar Association Journal,* vol. 36 (1950), 805-08, 881-83.

"The Darthmouth College Case: A Dramatization." *American Bar Association Journal,* vol. 38 (1952), 991-94, 1055-57.

Hudon, Edward G. *The Occasional Papers of Mr. Justice Burton.* Brunswick, Maine (1969).

"An Independent Judiciary: The Keystone of Our Freedom." *American Bar Association Journal,* vol. 39 (1953), 1067-73.

"John Marshall, The Man." *University of Pennsylvania Law Review,* vol. 104 (1955), 3-8.

"Justice the Guardian of Liberty: John Marshall at the Trial of Aaron Burr." *American Bar Association Journal,* vol. 37 (1951), 735-38, 785-88.

"The Legal Tender Cases: A Celebrated Supreme Court Reversal." *American Bar Association Journal,* vol. 42 (1956), 231-34.

"The Supreme Court: Mr. Justice Burton Gives Interesting Comparisons." *American Bar Association Journal,* vol. 33 (1947), 645.

"Two Significant Decisions: *Ex Parte Milligan* and *Ex Parte McCardle.*" *American Bar Association Journal,* vol. 41 (1955), 121-24, 176-77.

With Waggaman, T. E. "The Story of a Place: Where First and A Streets Formerly Met at What Is Now the Site of the Supreme Court Building." *George Washington Law Review,* vol. 21 (1953), 253-64.

# Index

## ABOUT THE AUTHOR

Mary Frances Berry, Professor of History and Law at the University of Colorado, Boulder, and a specialist in American Constitutional and Legal History, is presently serving as Assistant Secretary for Education in the Department of Health, Education, and Welfare. Among her publications are *Black Resistance and White Law* and *Military Necessity and Civil Rights Policy*.